Contesting Christendom

Contesting Christendom

Readings in Medieval Religion and Culture

Edited by
James L. Halverson

ROWMAN & LITTLEFIELD PUBLISHERS, INC.
Lanham • Boulder • New York • Toronto • Plymouth, UK

ROWMAN & LITTLEFIELD PUBLISHERS, INC.

Published in the United States of America
by Rowman & Littlefield Publishers, Inc.
A wholly owned subsidiary of The Rowman & Littlefield Publishing Group, Inc.
4501 Forbes Boulevard, Suite 200, Lanham, Maryland 20706
www.rowmanlittlefield.com

Estover Road, Plymouth PL6 7PY, United Kingdom

British Library Cataloguing in Publication Information Available

Library of Congress Cataloging-in-Publication Data

Contesting Christendom : readings in medieval religion and culture / edited by
    James L. Halverson.
    p. cm.
    Includes bibliographical references and index.
    ISBN-13: 978-0-7425-5471-9 (cloth : alk. paper)
    ISBN-10: 0-7425-5471-6 (cloth : alk. paper)
    ISBN-13: 978-0-7425-5472-6 (pbk. : alk. paper)
    ISBN-10: 0-7425-5472-4 (pbk. : alk. paper)
    1. Church history—Middle Ages, 600-1500. 2. Civilization, Medieval.
3. Christianity and culture. I. Halverson, James L.
BR162.3.C66 2008
270.3—dc22
                                                                    2007008398

Printed in the United States of America

∞™ The paper used in this publication meets the minimum requirements of
American National Standard for Information Sciences—Permanence of Paper
for Printed Library Materials, ANSI/NISO Z39.48-1992.

Contents

CHAPTER ONE

~

Introduction

Since the term "Middle Ages" was first used in the fourteenth and fifteenth centuries, the pervasiveness of the Christian religion has been treated as one of the key features of medieval society. Indeed, the Middle Ages are often described simply as a "Christian culture." Such a description begs at least two questions: (a) What do we mean when we say that medieval Europe was a Christian culture, and (b) what did it mean to be a Christian in the Middle Ages? While these questions are fundamental to any understanding of the medieval European society, the variety of theoretical approaches and conclusions represented in this volume reveal the complexity inherent in achieving that understanding. The intellectual and institutional aspects of medieval Christianity are readily accessible in textbooks and primary source readers. This volume will emphasize the ongoing attempt to understand the social and cultural aspects of medieval Christianity.

Before surveying the current state of the scholarship on medieval religion, it is important to note that the field itself has a long and contentious history. From the sixteenth century until the creation of the historical profession in the nineteenth century, the history of medieval Christianity usually served polemical purposes. Protestant writers portrayed the Middle Ages as a time of horrendous abuse by the institutional church and rampant paganism and superstition among laypeople. According to this view, Christianity declined throughout the medieval period from a pristine golden age. Roman Catholic scholars responded with one of two alternate stories. For some, the Middle Ages *were* the golden age of Christian unity, community, and piety. Others took the view that medieval Christianity may not have been perfect, but the problems and abuses of the medieval church could have been reformed without shattering the unity of Western Christendom.

While confessional approaches to medieval Christianity still exist, the use of history for overtly polemical purposes is strongly discouraged in the academy today. However, that does not mean that historians of medieval religion are objective or indifferent to their subject matter. The history of Christianity still attracts Christian scholars who are unapologetic about their religious commitments, but equally committed to the standards of the historical profession. Two examples are Kenneth Scott Latourette and Christopher Dawson. Latourette[1] was a pioneer in expanding the scope of the history of Christianity to include non-Western traditions. He also took seriously the reciprocal relationship between Christianity and the cultures into which Christianity spread. These emphases, which are normative in the field now, came out of Latourette's close association with the ecumenical and evangelistic currents in early twentieth-century American Christianity. A committed and theologically active Protestant (Baptist), Latourette was both sympathetic to and critical of the forms of Christianity that arose in medieval Europe. Christopher Dawson was the first occupant of a Chair for Roman Catholic Studies at Harvard University. Like earlier Roman Catholic scholars, Dawson defended the achievements of medieval Christianity.[2] His point, however, was not polemical. Dawson did not want to show that the Reformation was bad, but that medieval Christianity, often dismissed in Protestant American culture as "too Catholic," has had an immense and positive impact on all Western culture.

More recent scholarship explains medieval Christianity without reference to confessional or denominational frameworks. The late 1960s and early 1970s saw the publication of two classic textbooks on medieval Christianity that sought to create narrative frameworks independent of confessional concerns. R. W. Southern's *Western Society and the Church in the Middle Ages* is one installment in his larger project of expanding the study of the Middle Ages beyond institutional and political topics.[3] Freed from the necessity of critiquing medieval Christian theology and practice, Southern set the agenda for much later work by focusing on the relationship between the medieval church as an institution and medieval society in general. For Southern, medieval Christianity is worthy of study for its own sake, and not merely as context for later conflicts. In *A History of Medieval Christianity: Prophecy and Order*, Jeffrey Burton Russell argued that the key to understanding medieval Christianity was the dynamic tension between the forces of "order" (traditional institutions) and "prophecy" (dissenting or subversive individuals or movements).[4] While Russell's approach has not been as influential on the scholarship of medieval Christianity as has Southern's, it has had a lasting effect on the teaching of it, especially in North America. Along with his late University of California, Santa Barbara colleague, C. Warren Hollister, Russell has trained numerous scholars who now hold posts in North American colleges and universities. Published in 1968, his book was revised in 2000 and reprinted in 2003. One of the few primary source readers on medieval Christianity published for undergraduates is edited by a Russell protégé; the book explicitly uses his "prophecy and order" approach.[5] Nevertheless, in terms of research on medieval Christianity, the most important and influential approach in the last several decades has revolved around the idea of *christianization*. In his now classic article, "The Christian Middle Ages as an Historiographical Problem," John Van Engen outlined six important features to this approach:[6]

1. What did Christianity mean to people at the time? Medieval people used the term *Christianitas* (Christianity/Christendom) to refer to their entire religious culture.
2. Conversion of leaders is only a part of christianization. Formal institutions must exist throughout the society that regulates and facilitates the expression of Christian thought and practice.
3. Studying christianization means taking religion seriously. Medieval Christians saw themselves as primarily religious beings. By reducing religious belief and behavior to underlying social or economic factors, we dismiss as irrelevant the presuppositions of the culture that we are attempting to understand.
4. While Christendom encompassed all European society after 1000, medieval religious culture was not uniform. Careful scholars need to pay attention to both the broad commonalities throughout medieval Christianity and the social, regional, and cultural distinctions within it.
5. Medieval Christianity was essentially performative. Historians must often "look through" the written and material sources to study a largely illiterate religious culture.
6. There is no sharp distinction between literate clerical and illiterate popular religious culture in the Middle Ages. The clerical elite came from the mostly illiterate laity and often spent their lives in close contact with the laypeople in their roles as parish priests and urban and courtly bureaucrats.

Overview of the Book

This volume represents a brief introduction to research into medieval Christianity that incorporates the six features mentioned above. Organized chronologically, the readings are grouped according to the standard divisions of the Middle Ages into three phases: early, central (high), and late. Because of the velocity and intensity of religious change in the central Middle Ages (roughly 1000–1300), two sections are devoted to it.

Section One

For scholars of the early Middle Ages, employing the concept of christianization has produced a much more detailed picture of the religious culture of the period. For example, because early medieval Europe consisted of various distinct societies, it is no longer acceptable to speak of a monolithic pagan or barbarian culture into which Christianity spread. Even works with broad topics and even broader titles betray an emphasis on particular regions and societies. While the title of his book refers to Western Christendom, Peter Brown describes early medieval Christianity as a group of diverse "micro-Christendoms." Richard Fletcher takes equal care to highlight regional and temporal diversity in his account of the christianization of Europe.

Contemporary accounts of mass conversions emphasized dramatic moments when rulers and their peoples broke with their pagan past; the evidence now suggests that christianization was a long process that involved a great deal of accommodation to local conditions, as Karen Louise Jolly shows in her study of elf charms in late Saxon England. Nor was it always the case that the pagans had no prior experience with Christianity. While disagreeing on the exact nature of sixth-century Anglo-Saxon religious culture, Ian Wood and Rob Meens both agree that Christian influences were already present before the missionary activities of Augustine of Canterbury.

Section Two

Christianization of newly converted groups, particularly in Eastern Europe, continued throughout the Middle Ages. The emergence of a recognizable European culture, at least among intellectual and political elites, and the important role of Christianity in shaping the identity of that culture between the ninth and the twelfth centuries, create a new set of issues for historians. The focus now changes to the quality and penetration of Christianity throughout European society during this period. In the Middle Ages, education and literacy were a monopoly of the professional clergy or those who studied in church-sponsored institutions. Because of this, priests and monks produced most of the literary output of the Middle Ages. Moreover, texts produced by the professional religious were more likely to be copied and preserved. Thus, we have a very good picture of the religious culture of the clerical and intellectual elite. In order to broaden our perspective on medieval religious culture, historians have begun studying these sources to find out about the rest of society. For instance, Joan M. Ferrante reads these traditional sources for what they can tell us about the role of women in forming an elite Christian culture. According to Ferrante, women were often the patrons of religious literature. Furthermore, she points out that these women were not merely passive recipients of the commissioned work, but active participants in their production.

Although scholars no longer draw a sharp distinction between popular and elite religion in the Middle Ages, by rereading traditional sources and expanding the range of sources, some scholars have argued that medieval Christendom included a plurality of Christian cultures. Georges Duby argues for two competing elite Christianities with a clerical elite of bishops, priests, and monks attempting to tame and control a secular, political elite whose Christianity has been compromised by the demands of dynastic competition and the feudal warrior ethos. Important studies of the nobility in various regions have questioned this assertion and have revealed that many in the military elite were close allies with the clerical elite. Constance Brittain Bouchard explains that the nobility of Burgundy were not only strong supporters of the clerical elite, but were often in the vanguard of religious reform. Marcus Bull argues that crusaders were motivated primarily by piety, and only secondarily, when at all, by the material and dynastic benefits of conquest.

The foundational role of Christianity in the emerging European society considerably altered the status of non-Christian Europeans. Using the anthropological concepts of hierarchy and marginality, Mark Cohen describes how the creation of a European Christendom left European Jews in a fragile and peripheral situation.

Section Three

New sets of issues arise yet again for scholars studying the religious culture of Europe between the eleventh and thirteenth centuries. During this time, Europe underwent a series of massive changes: The population doubled; a commercial economy arose, bringing with it the rise of towns and a merchant class; and sophisticated governments developed, staffed by graduates of the newly formed universities. Christian institutions were shaped first by the papal reforms of the eleventh and twelfth centuries and then by the creation of new religious orders of wandering preachers in the thirteenth century. For these new religious orders and lay movements, the focus of a Christian life became the imitation of the life of Jesus and the Apostles, exemplified by voluntary poverty and itinerant preaching.

The starting point for all scholarship in this field in the last half century has been the groundbreaking work of German scholar Herbert Grundmann. Challenging the assumption that the popular religious movements were symptoms of lower-class rebellion against political and religious elites, Grundmann described the tension between traditional Christian institutions and the new movements as a conflict between two groups of cultural leaders. Grundmann believed that the movements were a reaction to the less popular aspects of the papal reforms of the eleventh century. He also suggested that new social and economic conditions created the necessary context for the new religious movements. Grundmann's explanations of the rise of the new religious movements have received a great deal of scholarly attention. Taking voluntary poverty as the defining feature of the new spirituality, Lester Little sees the new religious orders and lay movements as spiritual responses to the shift from an economy based on gift giving and the control of land, to a money economy based on making a profit. Because of the new economic conditions, earlier forms of religious thought and expression became unintelligible to the new urban class.

Grundmann's work on the religious culture of this period also emphasized the importance of gender as a significant category of analysis. Ultimately, medieval women were denied the opportunity to adopt a mendicant lifestyle of poverty and preaching. The question then is how did women experience and express the changes in religious culture during this period? Because of the nature of the sources, the study of religion and medieval women has often focused on extraordinary women who have left traces in the documentary record. Even so, elite women, or at least affluent women, experienced and expressed their religious beliefs differently than men of the same class. For instance, while male saints tended to be honored for the rejection of power, money, or sex, female saints were more often associated with fasting. Two important studies attempt to explain this phenomenon, using theoretical models derived from other disciplines. Rudolf Bell uses modern psychoanalytical theories developed from the study and treatment of anorexia nervosa to make sense of the fasting behaviors exhibited by these women. Caroline Walker Bynum, taking her cues from cultural anthropology, urges us to enter the symbolic world of these women in order to understand the importance of food in their spirituality.

Not all of the religious trends of this period were incorporated into the dominant Christian culture. During this period, we begin to see the first recorded movements that dissented from the official religious institutions. The most obvious examples are groups that explicitly rejected orthodox Christianity. Andrew P. Roach is only the most recent scholar to study the Cathars of southern France and northern Italy. According to Roach, Cathars competed with orthodox mendicant preachers in a sophisticated religious economy. Cathar success in southern France derived from their ability to provide a wide range of religious services to the people.

Section Four

Most historians of medieval Christianity treat the fourteenth and fifteenth centuries as yet another distinct period. Many of the developments of the previous period accelerated, including increasing literacy, more sophisticated political and religious institutions, and the continued growth of an urban middle class. Conversely, famine, plague, and new military techniques reversed the demographic gains of the twelfth and thirteenth centuries. Because of the more widespread use of written records and the ability of more kinds of people to read and write, the breadth and depth of evidence allows historians to reconstruct a much fuller picture of religion in the late Middle Ages than is possible for earlier eras. In addition, because of the importance of the period for scholars of the Reformation, late medieval religion, particularly in Germany and England, has received more sustained scholarly attention than previous periods. Unfortunately, this scholarly attention was often concerned with explaining the Reformation by figuring out what was "wrong" with late medieval religion, with historians focusing on ecclesiastical abuses and theological controversies.

While intellectual and ecclesiastical history are still important components of the scholarship of the period, in recent decades, social and cultural history have shed light on crucial but neglected aspects of late medieval religion. An important starting point in this direction is Bernd Moeller's emphasis on the "churchliness" of the period. Focusing on Germany, Moeller describes a religious culture expressed almost exclusively through the ritual and symbols of the institutional church. In the three decades since Moeller's work, it has become commonplace to study late medieval religious culture by analyzing how European Christians appropriated and expressed themselves through the generally sanctioned rituals of organized religion. The goal of this approach is to understand the meaning of these symbols and rituals to the participants. The literature on this subject is vast, but a few works are generally acknowledged as classics. Keith Thomas' "Religion and the Decline of Magic" was one of the first major works to analyze the meaning of late medieval religious symbols and rituals to the common Christian. Thomas contends that the typical late medieval person saw Christian ritual as a form of magic and was primarily interested in how objects and words associated with Christian worship could be manipulated to improve one's material situation. In "The Stripping of the Altars," Eamon Duffy allows that ritual objects were often assumed to possess magical powers, but painstakingly details how rituals, particularly the Mass, both reinforced social harmony and provided the context for a rich and nuanced variety of individual and corporate devotion among participants.

The late Middle Ages also saw the first successful rejection in medieval Europe of the dominant religious culture. During the fifteenth century, the Bohemian (Czech) nobility rejected the religious authority of the papacy by force in favor of the religious ideas of their own Jan Hus. Ironically, the Hussite rebellion only served to emphasize the importance of Christianity in late medieval European society. Using popular songs as sources, Thomas Fudge argues that the German Catholics and Bohemian Hussites accused each other of being bad Christians.

Having surveyed recent scholarship on religion and culture in medieval society, we can now return to our two basic questions: (a) What do we mean when we say that medieval Europe was a Christian culture, and (b) what did it mean to be a Christian in the Middle Ages? The selections do not arrive at consensus answers to the questions, but they do point to certain lessons learned in the process of asking them. First, the diversity of medieval society over time and space defies the simple answers given in textbooks. Second, students of medieval religion must be sensitive to issues such as class, gender, and literacy. Finally, any serious investigation of medieval religious culture must both expand its range of sources and be more creative in its methods of interpreting those sources.

Primary Sources, Secondary Sources, and Historians' Biases

Historians commonly distinguish between primary and secondary sources. Primary sources are artifacts from the period under study. Primary sources for studying medieval religious culture include theological or devotional treatises, sermon collections, parish records, liturgical books, paintings of religious subjects, religious architecture, and eyewitness accounts of religious activities. Secondary sources are scholarly interpretations of primary sources after the fact. This book is a collection of secondary sources. One of the first things that you will notice is that the scholars whose works are excerpted here do not always agree on how to interpret the primary sources. In fact, I have intentionally included some works that disagree over particular issues. Historians are often portrayed as detectives. To a certain extent, this is true. The most basic task of a historian is to discover the relevant facts. But that is only the first part of the process. Those familiar with the television show "Law and Order" know that around the middle of the show, the detectives hand off the facts to the prosecutors who organize the facts into a compelling story for the jury. Using the same facts, the defense attorney tries to offer an equally compelling alternate story exonerating his client. Historians act as both detectives and prosecutors. They gather evidence and shape it into a story that they hope will be compelling enough to persuade their peers. Like prosecutors, they must present their evidence to prove that they are not making things up. But that does not mean that historians are neutral or objective.

Like all people, historians have biases. Historians' biases often arise from the presuppositions that they bring to their research. We have already encountered some of the common presuppositions that affect the study of medieval religious culture. Some historians wish to critique or defend the doctrine and/or practice of medieval Christianity. At a more basic level, some historians believe that religious belief and experience is a function of other social and economic factors, while others believe that religion is a fundamental aspect of human nature in its own right. Not too long ago, historians denied the idea that they brought biases and suppositions to their research that might affect their conclusions. These days, the best historians admit to biases and presuppositions, share them with their readers, and are careful to deal with evidence or arguments that might contradict their own conclusions. Because of the biases and presuppositions of historians, you need to read the selections in this book critically. As you read each selection, ask yourself these questions: What is the author trying to prove? What evidence does he or she use? How does he or she interpret the evidence? What biases or presuppositions does the author bring to the evidence?

Where Are the Endnotes?

No doubt, your professors (and high school teachers before them) have impressed upon you the importance of citing your sources. With the exception of this introduction, you will find no endnotes in this book. The purpose of this book is to introduce you to the field of medieval Christianity. My introductory remarks for each section and selection are commonly held opinions among those working in the field or are derived from the books and articles listed in the bibliography for each section. If the purpose of this book was to contribute to the scholarship in this field, I would have cited primary and secondary sources in order to distinguish my arguments from those of other scholars. Rest assured that the authors included in this book were meticulous in citing both primary and secondary sources. But I eliminated the notes in each selection in order to include more of the main text of the work while remaining within certain space limitations. Because of this, you should not cite the selections as they appear in this book for any research paper that you write. You should locate the original work using the references I have supplied.

Notes

1. Kenneth Scott Latourette, *The Thousand Years of Uncertainty: 500 A.D. to 1500 A.D.*, *A History of the Expansion of Christianity*, vol. 2, New York: Harper & Row, 1938.

2. Christopher Dawson, *Formation of Christendom*, New York: Sheed and Ward, 1967.

3. R.W. Southern, *Western Society and the Church in the Middle Ages*, New York: Penguin Books, 1970.

4. Jeffrey Burton Russell, *A History of Medieval Christianity: Prophecy and Order*, Arlington Heights, IL: Harlan Davidson, Inc, 1968.

5. Karen Louise Jolly, *Tradition and Diversity: Christianity in a World Context to 1500*, M.E. Sharpe, 1997.

6. John Van Engen, "The Christian Middle Ages as an Historiographical Problem," *American Historical Review*, 1986, pp. 537–552.

Further Reading

Dawson, Christopher, *Formation of Christendom*, New York: Sheed and Ward, 1967.

Latourette, Kenneth Scott, *The Thousand Years of Uncertainty: 500 A.D. to 1500 A.D.*; *A History of the Expansion of Christianity*, vol. 2, New York: Harper & Row, 1938.

Lynch, Joseph H., *The Medieval Church: A Brief History*, London: Longman, 1992.

Russell, Jeffrey Burton, *A History of Medieval Christianity: Prophecy and Order*, Arlington Heights, IL: Harlan Davidson, Inc., 1968.

Southern, R. W., *Western Society and the Church in the Middle Ages*, New York: Penguin Books, 1970.

Thomson, John A. F., *The Western Church in the Middle Ages*, London: Arnold, 1998.

Van Engen, John, "The Christian Middle Ages as an Historiographical Problem," *American Historical Review*, 1986, pp. 537–552.

THE EXTENT OF CHRISTIANIZATION IN THE EARLY MIDDLE AGES

THE EXTENT OF CHRISTIANIZATION IN THE EARLY MIDDLE AGES

Most surveys of medieval Christianity (and even more so histories of medieval Europe in general), give only a cursory treatment to the religious culture of the early Middle Ages. A typical account usually goes something like this: As Roman power evaporates in Europe, Germanic tribes attempt to construct viable political units in the former provinces. Many of these tribes had previously converted to Arian Christianity. Eventually, however, they convert again to the Trinitarian Christianity of the local Roman elite. Pagan conquerors such as the Franks and Anglo-Saxons are converted en masse through missionary activity directed at the royal household. In any case, the conversion of the Germanic kings and aristocracy is not described for its own sake, but rather as the first step toward the later development of Latin Christendom (see section two). While this is occurring in the former imperial provinces, Irish monks to the north develop a rigorous new form of penitential piety that will forever change Christian spirituality. The cultural context of Irish monasticism is sometimes described in detail. These details, however, are not given in order to understand early medieval religious culture, but because they provide essential background knowledge for understanding later medieval piety.

To be fair, there are some good reasons for this situation. There is little evidence, written or material, upon which to construct a detailed picture of early medieval Christianity. Compared with later periods, few texts revealing religious life from the sixth through the eighth centuries survive. Ironically, the success of Christianity in Western Europe has also eradicated much archeological evidence. While churches from the period exist in North Africa and the Middle East, many early medieval churches in Europe were destroyed in order to build larger Romanesque and Gothic cathedrals. Others have succumbed to modern urban sprawl. In a further irony, recent successes in uncovering the details of early medieval religious culture have not made the picture any clearer. Historians now describe an early medieval Europe composed of several interconnected but distinct cultural zones. Thus, conclusions that can be drawn for Anglo-Saxon England cannot be drawn for Visigothic Spain, Lombard Italy, or even neighboring west Francia. We know little of the vast majority of people, regardless of the cultural zone, who were illiterate peasants. Even among the elite, there is little uniformity. Ethnic and cultural differences between the Germanic ruling class and the indigenous Romanized elites remained for some time after conversion.

Nevertheless, in the past decade, scholars have made significant progress toward rectifying this gap in the history of Christianity. Scholarship has been most fruitful concerning the context of the conversions of the Franks and Anglo-Saxons in the sixth and seventh centuries. While these two "events" are standard fare in textbooks because of their long-term consequences, recent work has shed light on the cultural context in which they took place. This new knowledge is not the result of new evidence. Rather, it is the result of creative new ways of interpreting the existing evidence. Historians and archeologists can wring new information from old sources by asking new questions of them. For instance, in the first selection below, one can see how the few surviving texts concerning the conversion of the Frankish king Clovis can be read to yield a more detailed picture of the cultural, political, and social factors surrounding it. In the next three selections, you will see how innovative approaches to the evidence have resulted in new theories about the christianization of Anglo-Saxon England. Then our attention turns to the efforts by the Frankish aristocracy and British churchmen to spread Christianity farther east and north into what is now Germany. By shifting the focus away from the conversions themselves and onto the context in which the conversions took place and the short-term implications of conversion, historians are able to see previously overlooked details and nuances in the evidence.

Any description of early medieval religious culture must begin with the Roman Empire's abandonment of its western provinces. The later Roman Empire was officially Christian. Formal pagan worship had been successfully banned in Roman cities and prominent pagans were often persecuted in the fifth century. The urban elite of the later Roman Empire produced enduring works of Christian scholarship. The extent to which Roman Christianity penetrated the countryside is less certain. That the Latin word *paganus*, from which the term "pagan" is derived, literally means "from the countryside" suggests that Christianity was not as widespread or deeply rooted outside the cities as in them. This is especially true for the western provinces. Recent scholarship suggests that, with the exception of Italy, Roman culture, including Roman Christianity, had little impact in the western provinces outside of towns. Because Roman Christianity depended on the support of the state and had become identified with Roman culture, the abandonment of the western provinces by the Roman government forces us to carefully assess the level of Christian survival in the early Middle Ages. An elite Roman Christian culture survived in places like Spain, Italy, and southern France. We have already mentioned the phenomena of Germanic Arian kings converting to Trinitarian Christianity. These conversions suggest that the minority Germanic ruling class found it expedient to convert to the religion of the indigenous elite. Second, these regions continued to produce eloquent and learned Christian scholars after Roman government collapsed. Finally, bishops in these regions often filled the administrative vacuum left behind by the Romans. We have little direct evidence of popular belief in these regions but know that Christianity survived, at least in those areas easily influenced by urban bishops. These bishops gave regular sermons. It would be presumptuous to think that rank and file Christians mirrored the beliefs and piety of their erudite and cultured leaders, but we can at least assume that some people showed up to listen. The encouragement of the cult of the saints by these same bishops points to a certain level of responsiveness among the common people.

The situation is more complicated farther to the north. The most vibrant Christian culture of the early Middle Ages centered on monasteries in Ireland and southern Scotland. It is no surprise that a Christian culture that did not depend on Roman state power and Romanized urban clergy was able to thrive in the absence of the empire. Former provinces such as Britain and northern Gaul are more difficult to describe. These areas were the least "Romanized" and became subject to pagan overlords. Our sources treat the conversions as miracles resulting from direct divine intervention. Thus, they tend to treat the pagan Franks and Anglo-Saxons as openly hostile to Christianity. They also depict Anglo-Saxon Britain and Merovingian Gaul as mission fields with little or no prior Christian presence. We should not take these depictions at face value. Much the same phenomena occurs today when evangelistic groups depict Muslim or former Marxist nations as devoid of indigenous Christians in order to inspire American and European missionaries to work there. In fact, the conversion of the Franks and Anglo-Saxons occurred within a matrix of political complexities, ethnic tensions, and diverse religious options.

The conversion of royal dynasties, though significant, was only the first step in christianizing a particular society. Germanic kings were not autocrats, but warlords. Their word was not law and their military companions might abandon them if they showed weakness or made decisions without seeking their approval. The monarchs themselves did not immediately become models of Christian piety upon their baptism. Finally, Germanic kings lacked the resources of Roman emperors to enforce an official religion on the populace. Over time, the Germanic warrior aristocracy blended in with local elites and created a religious culture that would mature in the eleventh and twelfth centuries. This will be the subject of section two, although the selection by Richard Fletcher sketches out the initial stages of this process among the Franks.

Besides the paucity of sources, gauging the depth and breadth of Christianity in a particular society presents other difficulties. What evidence we have is indirect, produced by those who could write. Moreover, those who could write were invariably Christian scholars who often held a very dim view of popular forms of religion. We have a clear idea of what religious leaders wanted their flock to believe and how they wanted them to act. Descriptions of popular religion, however, are typically caricatures. Defining popular religion is another problem. There was also no bright line separating elite from popular belief. From our scientific point of view, even the most learned scholars of the early Middle Ages seem credulous and superstitious, rarely drawing a distinction between the natural and the supernatural. We must keep in mind that ideas that seem naïve to us were the accepted science of the day. Warrior aristocrats may have been the political elite, but they were scarcely more sophisticated than their peasant subjects. Finally, trying to assess the success of Christianity is controversial. Judging the genuineness of a particular belief or practice is the responsibility of the theologian, not the historian. What one observer deems a creative way of articulating the Christian message in a particular culture will be judged unforgivable compromise by another. Early medieval people, from bishops to noblemen to peasants, believed that certain people, places, and objects held supernatural power. Does trusting in the power of a saint mean a lack of faith in the direct providence and protection of Jesus Christ? Can someone simultaneously believe in the power of the God of the Bible and fear the power of elves? Social scientists circumvent (but do not solve) this dilemma by discerning what their subjects believe about their beliefs. For instance, a Protestant or Roman Catholic theologian may deny that Mormonism is a form of Christianity on doctrinal grounds. Social scientists usually treat Mormons as Christian because Mormons consider themselves Christian. Unfortunately, historians of early medieval Europe cannot administer questionnaires to their subjects. They must infer beliefs from other sources. Each of the following selections is an example of scholars attempting to overcome these obstacles.

Further Reading

Armstrong, Guyta and Ian Wood, eds. *Christianizing Peoples and Converting Individuals*, Turnhout, Belgium: Brepols Publishers, 2000.

Brown, Peter. *The Rise of Western Christendom*, London: Blackwell, 2003.

Fletcher, Richard. *The Barbarian Conversion from Paganism to Christianity*, Berkeley: University of California, 1997.

Flint, Valerie I. J. *The Rise of Magic in Early Medieval Europe*, Princeton, NJ: Princeton University Press, 1991.

Mayr-Harting, Henry. *The Coming of Christianity to Anglo-Saxon England*, 2nd ed., University Park: Pennsylvania State University Press, 1991.

Herrin, Judith. *The Formation of Christendom*, Princeton, NJ: Princeton University Press, 1987.

Hillgarth, J. N. *Christianity and Paganism: The Conversion of Western Europe, 350–750*, Philadelphia: University of Pennsylvania Press, 1987.

Jolly, Karen Louise. *Popular Religion in Late Saxon England: Elf Charms in Context*, Chapel Hill: The University of North Carolina Press, 1996.

McLaughlin, Megan. *Consorting with Saints: Prayer for the Dead in Early Medieval France*, Ithaca: Cornell University Press, 1994.

Schulenburg, Jane Tibbets. *Forgetful of Their Sex: Female Sanctity and Society, ca. 500–1100*, Chicago: University of Chicago Press, 1998.

Wemple, Suzanne Fonay. *Women in Frankish Society: Marriage and the Cloister, 500–900*, Philadelphia: University of Pennsylvania Press, 1985.

CHAPTER TWO

~

Background to Augustine's Mission to Anglo-Saxon England*

Rob Meens

The most important source for the conversion of the Anglo-Saxons in the early seventh century is Bede's History of the English Church and People, *written a century later. Bede was a gifted, thorough, but biased historian. According to Bede, Anglo-Saxon England was devoid of Christianity when the missionary Augustine of Canterbury arrived to bring the Gospel to its pagan rulers. Using Bede's own work in comparison to other circumstantial evidence Rob Meens constructs a different version of the story. According to Meens, the Anglo-Saxons were familiar with Christianity before Augustine arrived. A variety of evidence, as well as geopolitical reality, indicate that the Anglo-Saxons had close contact with both Irish and Frankish Christianity. Moreover, Meens also claims that there was a significant British Christian presence at the time of Augustine's mission, which survived the transfer from Roman to Anglo-Saxon hegemony. Not only did British Christianity endure the upheavals of the fifth and sixth centuries, but British clergy were actively proselytizing among their Anglo-Saxon overlords. What evidence does Meens use to support his claims? How does he use Bede's writings to prove the opposite of what Bede intended to show? How does Meens distinguish among British, Irish, Frankish, and Roman Christianity?*

As is well known, Bede gives a biased account of the conversion of Anglo-Saxon England. He highlights the role of the Roman mission, initiated by

* © 1994 Cambridge University Press. Reprinted with the permission of Cambridge University Press. Rob Meens, "Background to Augustine's Mission to Anglo-Saxon England," *Anglo-Saxon England* (1994): 5–6, 11–17.

Pope Gregory the Great and led by Augustine, the first bishop of Canterbury. Almost as important in the *Historia ecclesiastica gentis Anglorum* is the effort made by the Irish to christianize Northumbria. The Frankish contribution to the missionary process, however, is not mentioned at all, though Frankish clerics certainly played an important role in the conversion of England. This role is attested by later contacts between England and the Frankish church. The letters of Gregory the Great relating to the mission of Augustine, moreover, make it clear that this mission also benefited greatly from help supplied by the Frankish church. The continuity of the British church seems to have been stronger than Bede suggests and his statement that the Britons did nothing to convert the Angles and the Saxons should be regarded as an overstatement. It has been argued recently that Bede left out an account of the conversion of the Anglo-Saxons living west and south-west of the Mercians, the Hwicce, the Magonsæte and the Wreocensæte, not because of a lack of information, but because of the part the Britons played in it. Biased though Bede's account may be, his work remains the cornerstone of every history of the conversion of Anglo-Saxon England. Fortunately he also provides us with opportunities to detect other missionary activities in England, though this has not been fully appreciated yet. Out of reverence for Gregory the Great, Bede includes several letters written by this pope in his *Historia*. These are amply used in historical works treating the conversion of Anglo-Saxon England. I would like to draw attention to some implications of one of these letters, the so-called *Libellus responsionum*, that have gone unnoticed. This "booklet" contains a number of questions from Augustine of Canterbury to the pope concerning problems in the newly converted regions together with the answers provided by Gregory. The questions asked by Augustine show that some of the missionary activity in southern England was not Roman in character.

Until now attention has focused mainly on the question of the authenticity of the *Libellus*. Who or what provoked Augustine to ask questions concerning ritual purity has never been satisfactorily considered. Henry Mayr-Harting assumes that ideas about the uncleanness of women, which led to their exclusion from communion after giving birth and during their menstrual periods, were alien to Anglo-Saxon society and were introduced by the Christian missionaries. Stephanie Hollis correctly stresses the importance of discovering what prompted Augustine to raise these questions. She assumes, contrary to Mayr-Harting, that it was, at least partly, "the cultural constructs of pre-literate Anglo-Saxons" that formed the basis of Augustine's questions. She supposes, however, that more such questions were asked. It was Augustine's "own prior cultural construct," trained as he was by reading the early Fathers and the Bible (including, of course, *Leviticus*), that made him choose questions about ritual purity among others, to refer to the pope. His supposed lack of experience in pastoral care, due to his monastic upbringing, would have been another factor. Though Hollis thus gives credit to Augustine's own upbringing and the ecclesiastical traditions behind it, she strongly suggests that it was Anglo-Saxon attitudes which, like similar Judeo-Christian beliefs, conspired to prevent "carnal profanation of the sacred."

It is possible that similar ideas existed amongst the Anglo-Saxons, aimed at protecting the sacred from pollution caused by childbirth, menstruation and sexual activity. Nevertheless it seems highly unlikely that someone expounding a new faith, and who was, we should therefore suppose, well versed in its tenets, would have to consult the pope for answers. Although there existed a tendency in Christianity to view sexual activity, menstruation and childbirth with suspicion, the answers as given by Gregory do not convey the impression that these views prevailed at the time. Gregory did not want to endorse the concepts of ritual purity embodied in Augustine's questions. In a very humane way he avoided any legalistic approach to the subject, and opted, in characteristic manner, for a spiritual interpretation of the Old Testament precepts. His answer to the question when can a woman enter church aft childbirth provides a good example:

> When a woman has been delivered, after how many days ought she to enter the church? You know by the teaching of the Old Testament that she should keep away for thirty-three days if the child is a boy and sixty-six days if it is a girl (Lev. X11.4-5). This, however, must be understood figuratively. For if she enters the church even at the very hour of her delivery, for the purpose of giving thanks, she is not guilty of any sin; it is the pleasure of the flesh, not its pain, which is at fault. But it is in the intercourse of the flesh, that the pleasure lies; for in bringing forth the infant there is pain. That is why it was said to the first mother of all: 'In sorrow thou shalt bring forth children' (Gen. 111.16). So if we forbid a woman who has been delivered to enter the church, we reckon her punishment as a sin.

How very different this is from the attitude implicit in the British and Irish texts! And these words were spoken by a former monk who was well versed in the early Fathers and the Bible, a man who became "one of the greatest popes in History." Would Augustine's attitude in these matters be so different from Gregory's, who picked him for the important task of bringing Christianity to the Anglo-Saxons? And would Gregory choose someone without experience in the pastoral field to accomplish this task? To the contrary, a recent study stresses the influence of Gregory on Augustine's ideas and missionary activities.

Gregory's answers rule out the possibility that Augustine, so impressed by the similarity between taboos existing among the Anglo-Saxons and contemporary Christian thinking, felt obliged to refer these matters to the pope. Augustine, charged with bringing his faith to a pagan country, must have felt authorized to dispose of native taboos which did not correspond to the teachings of Christianity. Boniface, in his missionary work amongst the Germans, only turned to the pope for advice when he met opposition from other Christians. In his letter to Pope Gregory II he raised several questions concerning proper Christian conduct, which are, though they address different topics, comparable to Augustine's questions. They concern mainly Christian subjects: marriage and affinity, baptism, mass, liturgical practices. It is clear whose practices prompted Boniface's questions, for he referred to "adulterous and unworthy priests" and to "priests and bishops entangled in many vices, whose life stains the priestly office." Boniface, then, during his missionary work, came across other Christian priests and bishops with whose views he did not agree. These experiences prompted his letter seeking advice from the pope, not the attitudes of pagan Germans. As in Boniface's letters to the pope, Augustine of Canterbury in his correspondence with Gregory the Great addressed explicitly Christian questions. His problems concerned baptism, holy communion and entering the church. It therefore seems improbable that these taboos arose from a pagan context.

Yet another analogue is found in the *Responsa ad consulta Bulgarorum* of the year 866, in which Pope Nicholas I addressed several problems concerning the conversion of the Bulgarians. He touched on issues similar to those which Gregory the Great had considered, and made use of arguments advanced by his predecessor in the *Libellus responsionum*. This papal guideline for a newly converted people was also provoked by rival missionary activities, mainly by the Greeks, but apparently also by Armenians and others. Gregory's answers therefore rule out the possibility that the notions of ritual impurity were alien to Anglo-Saxon society and only introduced by the Roman missionaries. Rather, it is clear from his answers that beliefs about ritual purity were alien to Gregory the Great and thus, we may assume, to Roman Christianity at the time. If we can attribute these ideas neither to Anglo-Saxon attitudes nor to Roman conventions, then the question arises as to who raised the concerns which provoked Augustine to appeal to the pope. It seems reasonable to assume that Augustine would have referred these matters to the pope only if his authority had been questioned, that is, if the questions were posed not by pagans, but by Christians, in particular by priests or bishops.

We have already seen that in Irish texts a similar attitude towards questions of ritual purity existed, based on the Old Testament. This would make the Irish plausible candidates to have challenged Augustine. There are some signs of Irish Christians visiting England before or at about the same time as Augustine. According to a late tradition, St Columba of Terryglass may have visited an unnamed English kingdom as early as the middle of the sixth century. From an *ogham* inscription at Silchester it can be inferred that two Irish Christians visited the place around the year 600. Bede himself tells us that in the first or second decade of the seventh century an Irish bishop called Dagan visited Kent. These Irishmen may have been engaged in missionary activity, though there is no positive evidence. Though it cannot be ruled out that Augustine came in contact with Irish missionaries, this does not seem very probable. We should, therefore, look elsewhere for the source of Augustine's concerns about ritual purity.

Kent was at this time also influenced by Merovingian political power and by Frankish Christianity. Bede tells us that King Æthelberht was married to a Frankish princess named Berta, who was a Christian. She was accompanied by a bishop named Liuthard, who may have had missionary intentions. In the Frankish church, as is clear from the writing of Caesarius of Arles, sexual activities were considered to imply pollution. Hence there was a ban on sexual activity during certain periods of the liturgical year. The bishop of Arles also admonished men to abstain from intercourse with their wives during menstruation, because from such unions deformed children would be born: lepers, epileptics and those possessed by demons. This suggests that menstruation implied pollution, though in Caesarius's writings there are no traces of a ban on women entering the church during menstruation. While Caesarius's attitude corresponds in a way with ideas we encountered in the *Libellus responsionum*, we find no evidence of childbirth being regarded as pollution in sixth-century Gaul. Furthermore, menstruation does not seem to have prevented women from entering the church or from receiving communion.

This makes the Frankish church an implausible candidate for spreading ideas on impurity connected with sexuality, childbirth and menstruation in Anglo-Saxon England. At the time of Augustine's mission to the Anglo-Saxons, Frankish Christianity had not yet been influenced by Insular conceptions of ritual purity. Columbanus had just left for the Continent and his writings show no signs of the pre-occupations evident in Augustine's questions. The earliest evidence for the use of the penitentials of Cummean and Finnian and of the *Collectio Hibernensis* in the Frankish realms dates from the beginning of the eighth century. Is this in itself a reason to question the assumption of Frankish influence on late sixth-century Anglo-Saxon Christianity? It should be noted, in addition, that the major missionary effort of the Frankish church came at a later date, when it had been influenced by "Iro-Frankish" monasticism.

Only the British Church remains as a plausible source for the concerns about ritual purity expressed by Augustine. We have seen that the *Excerpta de libro Davidis*, a text from the British church, prescribes a penance for seminal emission. This attitude towards ritual purity is similar to those that prompted Augustine's questions. Moreover, we know that regular contacts existed between Irish and British churchmen. Finnian, the author of one of the penitentials evincing similar concerns about ritual purity, may, as has been argued recently, have been a Briton who migrated to Ireland later in life. The Irish penitentials developed out of earlier British texts such as the *Excerpta de libro Davidis*. Augustine's successor Laurence wrote about the similarities between the Irish and the British churches, of which he had gained knowledge through acquaintance with the Irish bishop Dagan and (though one wonders in what way) with Columban. From all this it is clear that the Irish and British churches shared some common views, which were alien to the Roman church. Attitudes toward ritual purity may well have formed part of these views.

Could it be, then, that Augustine is referring to beliefs held by the British bishops he encountered in that famous meeting on the borders of Hwicce and the West Saxons, at a place known in Bede's time as "Augustine's Oak"? Bede recalls that the dispute was not only about the Easter controversy, but also about other British practices that were not in keeping with the unity of the church. This meeting took place after Augustine received the *Libellus* from the pope. If this rules out the possibility that Augustine first became acquainted with British ideas on ritual purity at this meeting, it strengthens the case for the view that Augustine's questions referred to British customs. For Augustine probably had an agenda for this meeting and these points of difference in ecclesiastical mores may well have been part of it. In that case it seems only natural that he sought backing from the pope and that the *Libellus* might have been designed and used in preparation for this meeting. Augustine's questions in the *Libellus*, concerning his attitude towards the British bishops, fit well into this picture. Gregory's answer on this, moreover, implies that British ecclesiastical customs were experienced as alien by the Roman missionaries.

Augustine, however, does not say that he asks these questions because of a dispute with the British, but because of the ignorance of the "ignorant English people." There seems to be no reason to doubt Augustine's statement. As has been argued above, it is hardly conceivable that Augustine would have seen any necessity to ask the pope for advice if these questions were asked by pagans. If they were asked by *Angli*, they were probably Christian *Angli* who had received Christianity from the British. For that is the only plausible way they could have come into contact with such ideas.

The questions raised by British missionary activity among the *Angli* could very well have been treated in meetings with British bishops. Accordingly the *Libellus* may well have been conceived as a preparatory work for those meetings. In that case it is significant that Augustine met the British bishops at the borders of the Hwicce and the West Saxons, for it was in this region particularly that the British seem to have played a part in the christianization of the Anglo-Saxons. The *Libellus responsionum* can thus be seen as another piece of evidence of missionary effort by the British church. Though Bede explicitly denies any missionary activity by the British, his inclusion of the *Libellus* in his *Historia ecclesiastica* nonetheless offers us the opportunity to detect it. Furthermore, it shows some points of difference between the British and the Roman churches on matters of ritual purity, differences which Gregory's answers could not settle.

CHAPTER THREE

~

Some Historical
Re-identification and the
Christianization of Kent*

Ian Wood

In this selection by Ian Wood, we can see how the ideas of one scholar can inspire another. Wood reinforces Meens's description of the complex religious context, which Augustine encountered in Anglo-Saxon England, but he approaches the topic from a different direction. While Meens challenged Bede's inaccurate depiction of British Christianity, Wood challenges Bede's description of the Anglo-Saxons. According to Wood, the distinction between pagan and Christian should not be drawn too sharply when dealing with Anglo-Saxon England. He points out that Anglo-Saxon kings did not immediately abandon their gods when they acknowledged the Christian God. More provocatively, Wood contends that Christianity had significantly influenced Anglo-Saxon paganism. If Meens and Wood are correct, Augustine's successful missionary journey was the culmination of centuries of Christian influence on the Anglo-Saxons. What evidence does Wood use to prove his thesis? In what ways does he disagree with Meens and why? According to Wood, why did the Anglo-Saxons convert to Augustine's Roman Christianity and not to British or Frankish Christianity?

My purpose in this paper is to raise certain questions about religion in Kent and in the rest of England in the years on either side of Augustine's arrival in 597. For Kent itself several questions seem to me to follow logically from Rob Meens's 1994 article *A Background to Augustine's Mission to Anglo-Saxon*

* © 2000 Brepols Publishers. Reprinted with the permission of Brepols Publishers. Ian Wood, "Some Historical Re-identification and the Christianization of Kent," *Christianizing Peoples and Converting Individuals*, eds., Guyda Armstrong and Ian Wood, Turnhout: Brepols, 2000.

England: an article of crucial importance, which provides the chief "re-identification" of my title, but which, I think, has not yet been fully brought into discussion of religion in England at the end of the sixth century. More generally, several years of grappling with continental paganism has led me to the conclusion that far too much has been assumed about our knowledge of its counterpart in England. It is with one aspect of this problem that I shall start, before coming back to Rob Meens's argument.

In a famous letter written to Mellitus in 601, Gregory explained that the *fana idolorum* of the English should not be destroyed, but that the idols in them should be, and that altars with relics should be placed in the purified buildings. Similarly, the sacrifices of cattle which used to be offered on pagan festivals should instead be made on Christian holy days, when the people would set up wattle huts round the churches (*ecclesias*) constructed out of idolatrous *fana*. In this letter Gregory was responding to an eye-witness account of Kentish paganism, and its information must, therefore, be taken seriously as evidence for religion in Kent between 597 and 601. It reveals that the pagans had *fana* and made sacrifices, which appear to have involved the setting-up of booths. This much must be accepted. But Gregory also pushes us to a particular understanding of the word *fana*, which I have carefully not translated. These *fana* are clearly of some size, at least in Gregory's imagination: they can serve as churches, and they have altars in them. They could be similar to the *fanum* of King Rædwald, who, according to Bede, had an altar for Christian sacrifice and an altar for sacrifices to demons in the same building. Although one might question whether Rædwald's religious position became quite as straightforwardly pagan as the *Ecclesiastical History* implies, the type of syncretism envisaged, with old gods being thought still to have some power, is not uncommon among first-generation Christians elsewhere in the Early Middle Ages. And there is also the *fanum* at Goodmanham destroyed by the priest Coifi: though it should be noted that Bede makes Coifi speak not of *fana*, but of *templa* in his rejection of Christianity.

Colgrave clearly saw no problem in swithering between translating *fanum* as "temple" or as "shrine." In doing so he may be accurately reflecting a vagueness in Gregory and Bede: yet to the modern ear at least there may be a difficulty. The word "temple" tends to carry with it a greater impression of size than does the word "shrine." Did the Anglo-Saxons have sizeable temples? John Blair thinks they did, and he may have identified some. Brian Hope-Taylor thinks there is one at Yeavering—though I personally have my doubts about his interpretation of many of the individual buildings on the site. Nevertheless, Gregory the Great and Bede thought that there were *fana* in England in the sixth century, and that *fanum* could be big enough to house at least two altars. On the whole, I suspect that we are not just dealing with Gregory's imagination: there are enough indications in Gregory and Bede to show that there were *fana* big enough to hold one or more altars in England, though there may have been very few of them outside Kent, and there they may not have been found because we may not know what to look for.

In thinking about the whole issue of temples in England, we should re-member that Germanic temples have not been found on the continent, and here, for once, archaeological evidence is in tune with what Tacitus tells us about the *Germani*. Of course, there may have been considerable differences between the religions of Tacitus's *Germani* and those of the Germanic peo-ples of the sixth century: indeed there is some reason to believe that this was the case. One need only look at the linguistic evidence for the spread in pop-ularity of certain Germanic gods in the course of Roman and post-Roman pe-riods. Nevertheless, there is an absence of references to temples not only in Tacitus's *Germania*, but also in most texts referring to the Germanic peoples of the *Völkerwanderungzeit*: and this taken together with the absence of tem-ples in the archaeological record should be significant. Further, the negative point seems all the stronger in that Slav temples are very much in evidence in both literature and archaeology.

The one area on the continent where sources make regular reference to *fana* is Frisia. They are referred to, for instance, in accounts of the desecra-tion, first by Willibrord and then by Liudger, of the cult site of Fosite, prob-ably on Helgoland. Although Altfrid in his *Vita Liudgeri* borrowed from Al-cuin's *Life of Willibrord*, it should be remembered that he was the nephew of Liudger, and may have heard an eyewitness account of the *fana* with their holy spring. Thus, while Alcuin's references to shrines in the *Vita Willibrordi* might be attributed to literary license, it is possible that he and Altfrid were presenting a recognisable image of the realities of Frisian religion. The one other temple which is frequently cited by modern historians is that at the Irminsul in Saxony, but only the *Annales Regni Francorum* mention such a building: other sources are silent. A temple at the Irminsul may well be the fantasy of one Carolingian—and most modern historians.

It seems, therefore, that *fana* had some significance for pagan religion among the Frisians and Anglo-Saxons, but rather less elsewhere in the Ger-manic world, and that one has to move east to the Slav lands to find un-questionably temple-based religions. One possible explanation for the signif-icance of temples in England and Frisia is that both areas had either been under direct Roman rule, or, in the case of parts of Frisia, were Roman fron-tier territory. If this explanation is right, while temples are unlikely to have been traditional aspects of Germanic paganism, they could well have been borrowings from the Roman world.

That pagan cult sites in England and Frisia had a Roman past might have an echo in Alcuin's account of Willibrord's actions at a shrine in the villa at Walcheren, which may well have been associated with the trading site of Domburg. One might guess further and postulate that this Frisian villa, which was run by a *custos*, was in some way connected to the Roman temple of the goddess Nehalennia. Roman temples, dilapidated though they might have been, might well have provided the pagan *Germani* with a model for their own shrines on the lower Rhine and in England. On the other hand, if pagan Germanic *fana* in England and in Frisia did take over previously existing sacred places, one should consider the possibility that the sites taken over were actually Christian: put simply, Christian churches of the Late Roman period could have provided the model for Germanic temples within what had been the Roman Empire, and on occasion may even have constituted the physical building itself.

In other words, since Frisians and Anglo-Saxons seem to have been unusual among the Germanic peoples in the religious significance that they accorded to buildings, it may well be that this stemmed from the fact that they settled in areas where the religion of the indigenous population was associated with buildings (which must usually have been churches, although some pagan survival is not impossible, since sites associated with pagan cults continued to be religious centres). In short, I would like to suggest that Anglo-Saxon paganism was already modelled in part on Christianity, even before Augustine arrived. Further, if there are Germanic shrines or temples to be found, some are likely to be reused Roman temples or churches.

It may not only have been holy buildings, or at least the notion of sacredness being found in buildings, which the Anglo-Saxons borrowed from the Romano-British: there is an absence of a priestly caste in our sources for traditional Germanic religion of the Migration period and the centuries on either side. There is the *custos* at Walcheren, if he may be called a priest, and, more obviously, Coifi in Northumbria: otherwise, kings fulfill a priestly function, at least in officiating over such rites as the casting of lots. It is not impossible that Coifi's role—assuming that he existed—was itself a borrowing from Christianity.

Anglo-Saxon paganism, then, was made in England, however much certain gods, rituals, and aspects of cosmology may have been traditional to the Germanic peoples. It was, thus, syncretist, before Augustine's arrival, because it had already borrowed from Christianity. This, of course, instantly raises the problem of British survival, but in a rather different way from, say, the question of Eccles place-names. It is not my intention to enmesh myself in this question here. Instead, I wish to turn to the second aspect of my enquiry, which is to ask whether there are any traces of British Christian practices in what can be deduced about Anglo-Saxon religion prior to Augustine's arrival. Once again it is necessary to turn to Gregory the Great, this time to the *Responsiones*: for the most part I follow Meens's reading of them, although I wish to reconsider the transmission of ideas of ritual purity, which, Meens argued, resulted from British influence on the *Angli*.

What Meens's article of 1994 did, beyond any doubt, was to show that the questions relating to ritual purity, that is sections 8 and 9 of Gregory's *Libellus Responsionum* to Augustine, could well have been written by the pope, and that they relate not to questions which originated with pagans, but rather to questions raised by Christians influenced by Irish and British ideas of purity of the type expressed in the penitentials, even if Augustine heard them from Anglo-Saxons. Further, Meens dealt with the relationship of the *Libellus* to Augustine's meetings with the British bishops. According to Bede, there was a showdown in those encounters, over the dating of Easter and also over Augustine's authority. Meens argued that, since Bede places these meetings after the *Libellus Responsionum*, which itself is dated to 601 in Gregory's *Register*, the questions of ritual purity must have come up separately, asked by *Angli* who had already experienced British missionary activity.

Before accepting the whole of Meens's argument, it is necessary just to remember the problems of the *Libellus Responsionum*. It exists in more than one version, and it has yet to be properly edited, though Meens himself is currently doing that. That edition will no doubt solve many of the problems associated with the work. What can be said is that, despite a considerable amount of argument to the contrary, the majority of the answers are now known to be Gregorian. Further, since the text of the *Libellus* in Gregory's *Register* has a date of 601, it is reasonable to infer that Gregory answered questions put to him in that year over and above the famous question concerning *fana* and sacrifice. Certainly, the seventh question on relations between Augustine and the bishops of Gaul and Britain seems particularly appropriate for the year 601, since it can be juxtaposed with points made in the letters of commendation which Gregory sent to the Frankish bishops on behalf of Mellitus and Laurentius in that year.

Whether all the *Responsiones* came from the same original document of 601 is, however, not quite so clear—and what that original document looked like is distinctly problematic. Most obviously, Augustine cannot have asked one of the questions ascribed to him at any moment after he arrived in Gaul in 596. In Colgrave's translation of Bede's *Historia Ecclesiastica*, Augustine is made to ask, "Even though the faith is one are there varying customs in the churches? and is there one form of mass in the Holy Roman Church and another in the Gaulish churches?" As Gregory points out, Augustine has already found (*invenisti*) that there are varying customs, so the first part of the question is otiose, and must be an editorial invention. Since there are three known versions of the *Libellus Responsionum*, and only one of them has the form of a set of questions and answers, there is no difficulty in seeing "Augustine's questions" as having been added to the Gregorian statements.

Working from the standpoint that the *Responsiones* are Gregorian, even though they have been subject to early medieval editorial intervention, it is worth returning to Meens's argument, in particular, to his view that the *Responsiones* predate the meeting with the British bishops, and that they are evidence of the attitudes of *Angli* who had already been converted to Christianity by British clergy before Augustine's arrival. Quite apart from the date of the *Responsiones* in Gregory's *Register*, the reference to the British bishops in the context of the seventh question, about Augustine's relations with the bishops of Gaul and Britain, does give us a date of 601, by which time Augustine was clearly thinking about the British Church. It may well suggest that Augustine was already looking forward to the meeting at Augustine's Oak, which Meens would place sometime in the future. Yet although Bede places the meeting later than the *Responsiones*, he gives it no date, and there is no reason to think that he had any knowledge of the chronology of Augustine's dealings with the British Church—indeed there are signs that his account of the mission is schematically arranged: the episode may have been misplaced. In other words, Augustine might have asked Gregory questions about ritual purity before his meeting with the British bishops, but he might also have asked it after meeting them for the first time.

This, however, need not invalidate Meens's point that it was the English who had raised the question of ritual purity with Augustine, whose question in Bede's version concludes with the statement: "All these things the ignorant English need to know." The problem here is that Gregory makes no reference to the English in his answer: and given the fact that the question concerning variety of ecclesiastical ritual cannot have been posed by Augustine in the way presented in Bede's text of the *Responsiones*, we cannot rely on the questions on ritual purity as preserved in the *Historia Ecclesiastica* as the sole proof that it was the English rather than the British who raised the issue in Augustine's mind, even if the issue originated with the latter.

Here it is worth considering the extent to which Gregory's *Responsiones*— as opposed to Augustine's questions—concern the English, as opposed to other groups. Although the first of "Augustine's questions" is set out as a general enquiry about the life of bishops, Gregory's response is explicitly couched in terms of the nascent English Church, the *Ecclesia Anglorum*, as is the sixth response, dealing with episcopal consecration. So too the second question which concerns variety of custom is answered specifically with regard to the *Ecclesia Anglorum*. The response to the fifth question on incest deals directly with the *gens Anglorum*. Gregory must, therefore, have been answering questions about practices among the *Angli*. Less directly concerned with the English Church is the seventh response, which explicitly deals with Augustine's relations with Gallic and British bishops. The other answers are unspecific in their regional application, although number four, on incest, may be treated as a subsection of five, and thus can be seen as being relevant to the English. The third response deals with the very general issue of theft from churches. This leaves the eighth and ninth responses on ritual purity, where the answers once again lack any geographical specificity, although, as Meens has shown, they relate to British practices.

Given the uncertain authenticity of "Augustine's questions," as opposed to Gregory's answers, we do not have to conclude that *Responsiones* eight and nine concern the English rather than the British—though it is possible that a full survey of the manuscripts of all three versions of the *Responsiones*, which after all survive outside Bede's *Ecclesiastical History*, will clarify the status of those questions. What we can say is that Augustine was having to deal with traditions of the British Church over a much wider range of issues than is suggested by Bede's account of the meeting at Augustine's Oak: a point which itself suggests close association with that Church, something which in turn can be inferred from Gregory's seventh response.

That Augustine's dealings with the British Church were much more complex than Bede implied is shown above all by an additional response of Gregory, the so-called *Obsecratio Augustini*, not contained in Bede's selection, which deals with the problem raised by the cult of a martyr called Sixtus, whom Augustine could not identify. Gregory simply tells him to equate the cult with that of the martyred pope of the same name. The cult may have been based at Church in Essex, and in any case shows Augustine having to deal with British Christians on his own doorstep. It is not impossible that Bede himself was responsible for excluding it from his version of the *Libellus*.

If we do accept that the responses on purity relate to problems raised by the English, as opposed to the British—and this is called into question, but is not ruled out, by my caveats—then like Meens we have to accept that British clergy had started to evangelize the English before Augustine's arrival. We might, moreover, think that questions of ritual purity had arisen through direct contact between the *Angli* and surviving pockets of British Christians in eastern England. On the other hand, whereas the English might have taken their notions of temples from the conquered British, notions of purity are perhaps more likely to have been transmitted from the free British Churches of the West, since the surviving evidence tends to suggest that the religious traditions to which the notions of purity belonged were developed by the British and Irish Churches after the beginning of the English settlement in the East.

There is one further point which, I think, ought to be fitted into this model. Before news reached Gregory that the English wished to be converted, they had turned to *sacerdotes e vicino*, who had refused to provide them with missionary help. Most historians have assumed that the reference is to British clergy. It is, however, clear from Gregory's recurrent use of the phrase that the *sacerdotes e vicino* were Frankish, not British. In other words, Gregory's letters do not prove that the British remained aloof from evangelizing the Anglo-Saxons. Despite the fact that some British did not wish to work among the English, as can be seen in the canons of the Synod of the Grove of Victory, there is no reason to think that all British clergy had refused to do so in the years before 596. That the people of Kent turned first to the Franks and then to Rome for missionary help, and not to the Britons, might be explained by the fact that the Britons could be seen as a conquered people, and that victors rarely take a new God from their victims: though it is interesting to note that in this case they did take the God of their victims, even if they preferred to do so from a third party.

What all this suggests is that early Anglo-Saxon religion was a much less fixed entity than is often supposed. However much Germanic tradition they brought with them, the Anglo-Saxons seem to have borrowed from religious practices within Britain in developing their own religion. Even as they did so, it seems possible that the British Church of the West, with its developing ideas, made some attempt to keep an eye on Christians who remained in the conquered territory, but perhaps also to spread Christianity to the invaders. The latter, however, turned not to the British, but to the Franks and ultimately to Rome for the last stage in their conversion, and this in time prompted Gregory the Great's policy of assimilation of tradition, rather than a hard-line break, in order to facilitate the process of mission. Instead of a static model of pagan versus Christian, in early Anglo-Saxon England we seem to be faced with non-stop religious development and fluctuation in which paganism and Christianity were never hermetically separate.

CHAPTER FOUR

~

The Barbarian Conversion from Paganism to Christianity*

Richard Fletcher

While missionaries and other church leaders intentionally focused on converting kings, they knew that the complicated process of creating a Christian culture had just begun. The next step was to convert the powerful warrior aristocrats. At first, Frankish aristocrats tolerated the conversion of their kings. Soon, most became at least nominally Christian. Eventually, they seem to have embraced Christianity. In the following selection, Richard Fletcher gives a detailed account of how this process took place. Fletcher points out three different factors that contributed to the eventual creation of a Christian Frankish aristocracy: political pressure from the king, Gallo-Roman bishops from southern Gaul reestablishing Roman Christianity in urban centers, and Irish missionaries creating monasteries in the countryside. He contends that Irish missionaries, such as Columbanus, were the decisive factor in transforming the Frankish aristocracy from nominal to committed Christians. As you read the selection, keep these questions in mind. According to Fletcher, what was the appeal of Irish monastic culture to the Frankish nobility? What was unappealing to them about traditional, Roman Christianity? What are the limits of royal pressure in creating a religious culture? Finally, what are some of the difficulties in ascertaining the religious beliefs of the Frankish aristocracy?

Barbarian kings like Edwin might make judicious use of "gifts and threats" to bring pressure to bear upon their leading subjects. But we should not suppose that these persons became Christians only "through fear of the king or to win

* © Richard Fletcher, *The Barbarian Conversion from Paganism to Christianity*, Berkeley: University of California, 1997, pp. 133–142. Reprinted with the permission of Rachel Fletcher.

his favour." The acceptance of Christianity by the men and women of the barbarian aristocracies was critical in the making of Christendom because these were the people who had the local influence necessary to diffuse the faith among their dependants. John Chrysostom, Maximus of Turin and Augustine of Hippo had been correct in perceiving the pivotal role of local elites, and in this respect (if not in others) the seventh and eighth centuries were no different from the fourth and fifth. This chapter and the next will examine some aspects of the conversion of the barbarian aristocracies, first in Gaul and Spain in the seventh century, then in the British Isles in the seventh and eighth, and attempt to point up significant common features. One word of warning. Surviving sources tend to be more concerned with kings than with their nobilities. It is accordingly more difficult—even more difficult—to get to grips with aristocratic than with royal conversion.

Germanic settlement in what had been imperial Roman territory wrought changes in Europe's linguistic boundaries. The eastern frontier of the empire on the continental mainland had been marked, roughly speaking, by the course of the rivers Rhine and Danube. Within that line the language of everyday speech for many, and of authority for all, had been Latin, the ancestor of the Romance languages of today. The influx of Germanic peoples in the fourth and fifth centuries pushed Latin westwards and southwards and substituted Germanic speech in a swathe of territory within what had once been the imperial frontiers. That is why Austrians and many Swiss speak varieties of German to this day. It need hardly be stressed that the pattern of linguistic change is neither neat nor simple. It therefore affords plentiful opportunity for lively academic debate. Philologists are a combative lot, and scholarly wrangling has been made the fiercer by the nationalistic dementia of the nineteenth and twentieth centuries. Particularly has this been so in relation to the area upon which we must first concentrate attention in this chapter, the valleys of the Rhine and its western tributary the Mosel (or Moselle—which neatly encapsulates the debate). The linguistic frontier was never static. . . . Germanic speech was current as far west as Boulogne and as far southwest as Metz and Strasbourg, with outposts farther to the west, for example among the Saxon settlers in the Bayeux region and near the mouth of the Loire. And there were enclaves of Latin/Romance farther to the east, for example at the city of Trier.

There is every reason to suppose that the fortunes of Christianity had run in tandem with those of its Roman language. We can detect a flourishing urban or suburban Christianity in the late fourth century. Trier, as befitted a city which was then the imperial capital in Gaul, was emphatically Christian. We might recall the community which had so impressed Augustine's friend Ponticianus. The sense of burgeoning vitality imparted by that story is confirmed by the archaeological evidence of Christian building activity in Trier—and elsewhere. At Bonn, for example, a Christian church was rebuilt at the end of the fourth century, replacing on a more generous scale an earlier chapel. Matters were different, of course, in the rural hinterland. But there were grounds for optimism. Martin had visited Trier and made an impression upon members of the local elite such as Tetradius. His friend Bishop Victricius of Rouen was making sorties into the pagan countryside of Artois.

Quite suddenly the light was snuffed out. The seat of government was removed from Trier to Arles—with all that this implied for influential concern and wealthy patronage. The Rhine frontier was pierced by the barbarian invasion of the winter of 406–7. Trier was attacked by the Franks four times in thirty-four years. Roman order collapsed, and with it the apparatus of organized Christianity. This is not to say that the faith itself entirely disappeared. It withdrew into little enclaves here and there, where best it could survive under the protection of town walls or powerful men. We know little of its fortunes, for the written sources give out almost as completely as they do in fifth-century Britain: a silence which is itself eloquent. There are gaps in the episcopal lists. At Cologne, for example, no bishop is known between Severinus in about 400 and Carentius, attested in 566. We catch glimpses of Christianity in the occasional Rhineland tombstones. The sorrowing parents of the eight-year old Desideratus could commission a gravestone, at Kobern near Koblenz, inscribed with Latin hexameters and Christian symbols, at some point in the fifth century. Sometimes we can spot the new arrivals embracing the faith of Rome. The parents of Rignetrudis—presumably Frankish, from her name (though this argument is not without its difficulties, as we shall see presently)—erected an elegant Christian tombstone with a Latin inscription to mark the grave of their beloved sixteen-year-old daughter at Bruhl-Vochem, a little to the south of Cologne, sometime in the sixth century. But frequently the signals are ambiguous. Consider the Frankish nobleman buried at Morken, between Aachen and Cologne, a likely contemporary and a near neighbour of Rignetrudis. His relatives buried him in a wooden chamber with weapons and whetstone and shield, with jewellery and coin, with vessels of glass and bronze, bit and bridle and bucket, hefty joints of pork and beef. Was he a pagan or a Christian? There is no conclusive evidence either way. And what of the warrior commemorated in the famously enigmatic stone at Niederdollendorf, a bit farther up the Rhine, at some point in the seventh century? What did he believe in? It may be that these are the wrong sort of questions: well, less appropriate than some others. The antithesis pagan/Christian may be too neat and simple. Reality tends to be fuzzy. (It will be a part of the argument of this and the following chapter that fuzziness is an essential and important part of the process of barbarian conversion. But this is to anticipate.) For the moment let us simply observe that grave-goods and uninscribed tombstones are at best ambiguous witnesses to belief.

Gregory of Tours, however, is not. He tells a story of his uncle Gallus (not to be confused with Columbanus' disciple of the same name), set in Cologne in about the year 530. Gallus had gone there in the company of King Theuderic I, son of Clovis.

> There was a temple there filled with various adornments, where the barbarians of the area used to make offerings and gorge themselves with meat and wine until they vomited: they adored idols there as if they were gods, and placed there wooden models of parts of the human body whenever some part of their body was touched by pain. As soon as Gallus learned this he hastened to the place with one other cleric, and having lit a fire he brought it to the temple and set it alight, while none of the foolish pagans was present. They saw the smoke of the temple going up into the sky, and looked for the one who had lit the blaze; they found him and ran after him, their swords in their hands. Gallus took to his heels and hid in the royal palace. The king learned from the threats of the pagans what had happened, and he pacified them with sweet words, calming their impudent anger. The blessed man used to tell this often, adding with tears, "Woe is me for not having stood my ground, so that I might have ended my life in this cause."

The evidence, such as it is, leaves us with a sense that in north-eastern Gaul the Frankish invasions and settlement had obliterated much, though not all, of the Christian culture of the region. An effort of "re-Christianization" was called for. In about 500 or shortly afterwards Bishop Remigius of Rheims sent a man named Vedastus (Vedast, Vaast), a native of Aquitaine who had been living as a hermit near Toul, to become bishop of Arras. His biographer, writing in about 640, tells of how he found his cathedral church overgrown with brambles and defiled by animals, the city deserted since its sack by Attila the Hun: Vedastus had to expel a bear from the town, commanding it never to return. These are hagiographical commonplaces, not to be taken literally. (Attila never went anywhere near Arras but he was a convenient hate-figure to whom acts of destruction could unhesitatingly be attributed.) However, they convey vividly a sense of what the seventh century thought had been going on in the sixth. We know little if anything for certain of what Vedastus might have achieved in the course of his long episcopate at Arras—he died in about 540. It was probably not much. But it was a start.

The most famous churchman to concern himself with re-Christianization was Nicetius (Nizier), bishop of Trier from c. 525 to c. 565. We had a sight-ing of him in the previous chapter, sending a letter of advice to the Frankish princess Chlodoswintha upon the occasion of her marriage. Like Vedastus, he was a native of Aquitaine. It was a time when King Theuderic I was encouraging clerics from Aquitaine to go to work in the languishing churches of the Rhineland: an interesting sidelight on the shortage of suitable clergy in the north-east. It was under Theuderic's patronage that Nicetius became bishop of Trier. As long-lived as Vedastus, he devoted his episcopate to the restoration of church life there. We hear, for example, of how he imported Italian craftsmen to build churches in the city. (A further indication of his *mission civilisatrice* was his planting of vineyards on the hillsides above the Mosel. This was another act of restoration: the region's wine had been celebrated two centuries before by Ausonius in his poem *Mosella*; but viticulture as well as Christianity had been a casualty of the fifth century.)

All the tales told of Nicetius by Gregory of Tours (on the authority of his friend Aredius, Nicetius' pupil) have an urban setting. The point is not without significance. An episcopal city with a distinguished and very visible Roman past; its churches; its wine supply: these were at the heart of his concerns, at any rate as celebrated by the poet Venantius Fortunatus, Italian born but domiciled in Gaul. These were the characteristic concerns of the Aquitanian contingent of the sixth century. Men like Vedastus and Nicetius—and, we might add, Aredius and Gallus and Gregory of Tours—came from a part of Gaul which had suffered less disruption than the north-east. Beyond the Loire in Aquitaine city life had maintained an unbroken continuity, there had been little Germanic settlement, much of the administrative and legal routine of daily life was still recognizably Roman, and the church had experienced few of the tremors which had caused it to crack and crumble farther north. We must not undervalue the contribution of the Aquitanian clergy in restoring church life in the north-east. They brought determined personnel—Nicetius was clearly a very formidable personality; they brought endowments, books, cults. With royal help they breathed new spiritual life into cities such as Trier. But, an important reservation, they failed to fling out any very attractive spiritual lifeline to the new masters of the region, the local Frankish aristocracy. The re-establishment of a Roman, city-based ecclesiastical pattern was not of itself going to win over the hearts and minds of a rural, tribal warrior aristocracy. The man buried at Morken may have been a Christian—indeed, it is almost inconceivable that a Frankish nobleman of the late sixth century could not have been formally a Christian, serving as he did kings who had been conspicuously Christian for nearly 100 years. He and Nicetius might even (who knows?) have met one another. But one cannot help feeling that their worlds scarcely overlapped or interpenetrated at all.

In the age of Nicetius it is likely that kings were more influential than Gallo-Roman bishops in bringing the aristocracy to adhere to Christianity. As we saw in the last chapter, kings set an example which their aristocracies were likely to follow, if only because it was useful to be in good standing with your king. Frankish kings were becoming more assertively Christian in the course of the sixth century. Childebert I (511–58) issued an edict ordering the destruction of idols: it was more than his father Clovis had done. He brought back relics of St Vincent of Saragossa from a military campaign in Spain and built a church in the saint's honour in Paris, in which he was later buried. (It is now Saint-Germain-des-Pres.) Other leading members of the Merovingian dynasty were buried in Christian churches in the course of the century. The grave of one of them, Childebert's sister-in-law Arnegund, was excavated from beneath the church of Saint-Denis in 1959. (The identification has been doubted: whatever the truth of the matter, the woman buried there was clearly of very high social rank.)

A Frankish church many of whose bishoprics were generously endowed, their incumbents therefore rich and powerful, must have been attractive to a predatory aristocracy. The prevalence of simony in sixth-century Gaul—that is, the practice of buying church office—shows this: people will pay for something worth having. Gregory of Tours was worried about simony and Pope Gregory I wrote several letters to Gallic kings and bishops condemning it in severe terms. Yet these simoniacs were Gallo-Roman, not Frankish aristocrats. When did bishops start to be drawn from Frankish, as opposed to Gallo-Roman families? It is a difficult question to answer because the enquirer is dependent almost entirely on the evidence of personal names, and a "Roman" name need not indicate Gallo-Roman blood any more than a "Germanic" name need indicate Frankish blood. Even so impeccable a Gallo-Roman nobleman as Gregory of Tours—and one who was very proud of it too—had an uncle who bore the Frankish name Gundulf. Frankish names among the bench of bishops are rare before the latter years of the sixth century, when we start to encounter such bishops as Magneric of Trier or Ebergisel of Cologne. They become common in the seventh century. After the dynasty's acceptance of Christianity Frankish rulers came rapidly to exert a large measure of control over episcopal appointments. Kings used this power of patronage to reward loyal servants. Service to the crown became the standard route to episcopal office. We shall see plentiful examples of this in the seventh and later centuries.

In the complicated tissue of relationships between Frankish kings and their aristocratic warrior elite there were all sorts of pressures which might bring these men and their families into the Christian fold. But these pressures of themselves were insufficient to bring about full-hearted commitment to the new faith. Additional stimulus was needed from outside; we may call it, if we wish, a missionary stimulus. This was provided by one man above all others, the Irish exile and pilgrim for Christ, St Columbanus. Under the influence of his evangelizing mission the character of the northern Frankish church was transformed.

Columbanus was introduced briefly towards the end of Chapter 3. Here it is necessary only to remind the reader that he was active as a monastic founder in the eastern parts of Francia from about 590 for some twenty years. His most influential foundation was the monastery of Luxeuil, in Burgundy. We can know a fair amount about Columbanus, partly through his own writings, partly by means of the spirited if partisan biography composed within thirty years of his death by his disciple Jonas of Bobbio. Much of the appeal of Columbanus must have lain in his commanding, his tremendous personality. If he strikes the reader of his biography as in many ways reminiscent of Martin of Tours, this is not just because Jonas, like every good hagiographer, had read his Sulpicius Severus and knew how a charismatic holy man should be presented. We have the word of Columbanus himself to attest his veneration of Martin, and Martinian qualities of character repeatedly shine forth from his own works—the awesome spiritual concentration of the man, his courage, his self-denial, his asperity, his unexpected tenderness. A meeting with Columbanus could change the course of a life. We shall see examples of this presently.

Columbanian monasticism appealed to the Frankish aristocracy because it, like them, was rural. Pre-Columbanian monasticism in Gaul had been largely urban or suburban. There were a few exceptions to this rule, such as the Jura communities of the fifth century, but generally the monastic locale was in or close to a town. One might think of Queen Brunhilde's foundation at Autun or Queen Radegunde's at Poitiers (for the latter of which Venantius Fortunatus composed two of the most magnificent hymns ever written, *Vexilla Regis* and *Pange Lingua*). Even Martin's Ligugé and Marmoutier were close respectively to Poitiers and Tours. Columbanus came from townless Ireland, where the rural monastery was the norm because there could be no other. Luxeuil was nowhere near a city (though it may not have been quite the wilderness that Jonas claimed). Columbanus showed a rural aristocracy that it was acceptable, indeed desirable to found monastic houses far from the madding crowd.

There were other qualities of Columbanian monasticism deriving from the Irish model which made it attractive to Frankish aristocrats. It allowed room for the solidarity of kinship. Frankish, like Irish, founders could be confident that family interests would not be neglected in the monasteries they established. Its emphasis on the supervisory role of the abbot (perhaps a kinsman) of a monastic network—rather than, as previously, the local bishop—was reassuring to families who might be apprehensive, sometimes with justice, of the covetous designs of the nearby bishop upon its endowments. (Columbanus did not get on well with the Frankish episcopal hierarchy. It is characteristic of both his resource and his lack of tact that he brought a tame Irish bishop with him to carry out episcopal functions at his behest.) Its adaptability appealed to founders who might have special needs to accommodate or special forms of piety to indulge.

At the kernel of Columbanus' spiritual nourishment lay his teachings on penance. He was prominent among those churchmen who were slowly bringing about a change from "public" to "private" penance. This requires a few words of explanation. The penitential discipline of the early church as administered by, let us say, Gregory of Pontus was of an exceptional harshness. Its characteristics were as follows. It could be administered only by a bishop, and it could be undergone by the penitent only once in a lifetime. It was public and it was shaming. The penitent sinner formally entered an "order of penitents" in a ceremony which took place before the entire congregation of his or her Christian community. Penitents were thereafter segregated into a special part of the church building for future services, where they had to listen to the communal intercessions for them of their neighbours. The penitent had to observe lifelong chastity thereafter and was debarred from ever holding any public office: a seventh-century king of Spain who underwent penance had to abdicate. Penance thereby aimed mortal blows at family and civil life. The penitent became in effect a nonperson. Cleansed of sin, penitents were assured that all that human effort could do had been done to purchase their salvation from the everlasting torments of hell. But the price was terribly high.

Because of the savage nature of the demands of the penitential process it became customary to defer the experience of it until the deathbed. This was all very well, but it left a spiritual void during life. "Private" penance filled this void. It could be administered by any priest, as confessor, not just by a bishop. It could be repeated any number of times. Its central principles were the unburdening of the conscience in a private act of contrition witnessed only by the confessor, followed by the doing of an act of penance, usually fasting, commensurate with the gravity of the sin. Confessors were guided in their recommendations by the tariffs of sins and appropriate penances to be found in the texts known as "penitentials" or "penitential books" drawn up by revered spiritual guides. Columbanus was the author of one such guide. These are its introductory words: "True penance is not to commit things deserving of penance but to lament such things as have been committed . . . Diversity of offences causes diversity of penances. Doctors of the body compound their medicines in diverse kinds . . . So also should spiritual doctors treat with diverse kinds of cures the wounds of souls, their sicknesses, pains, ailments, and infirmities." Columbanus thus conceived of penance as a form of spiritual medicine. The encounter between confessor and penitent became the opportunity for spiritual teaching. In this fashion private penance was the ideal vehicle for furthering and deepening the Christianization of the recently converted. For their part the men and women of the barbarian aristocracies took to it with gusto. It has often been observed that the notion of a tariff of penances for sins was instantly intelligible to a society which regulated wrongdoing by the norms of law codes which were essentially tariffs of compensations for crimes. True, if superficial. The new penitential system was not an easy option, as a glance at the penitential of Columbanus will show. Its attraction was that it held out—humanely, intimately, personally—a lifeline to the individual members of an aristocratic society that was violent, guilty, and fearful. The violence and the guilt we can read about in the pages of Gregory of Tours or in the self-abasing preambles to deeds of gift to God and His saints. So let us especially remember the fear, which could not be admitted publicly: fear of treachery, fear of revenge, fear of shame, fear of pain, and above all fear of death and what might lie beyond it. Penance healed guilt and drove out fear. Its disciplines helped to make sense of misfortune and deflected divine anger provoked by human depravity. And if sin could be wiped out by the discipline of penance, could not the offering to God—in a society where every cog of social intercourse was oiled by the giving of gifts—of a monastery, richly endowed, splendidly furnished, peopled by the founder's own kin turned monks expert in prayer, buy His favour?

It should by now be a little easier to understand why the Frankish aristocracy adopted Columbanian monasticism with such reckless abandon. It called to their hearts. One last and more mundane point needs to be made. There was a coincidence in time between the arrival of Columbanus and a change in the nature of the aristocracy of the Frankish north-east. In the half-century or so between, roughly, 575 and 625 this aristocracy became more cohesive and self-conscious. For the first time it acquired legal privileges which underpinned its distinctness from other social groups. It became less exclusively dependent for status on royal patronage. It became more solidly landed and probably, taken by and large, wealthier. Columbanian monasticism, it has been suggested, "was eagerly seized upon by the northern Frankish aristocracy as a means of expressing a newly acquired power and prestige." As often, social change and religious innovation dovetailed neatly together.

CHAPTER FIVE

~

Forgetful of Their Sex: Female Sanctity and Society, ca. 500–1100*

Jane Tibbets Schulenburg

One of the most important developments in the study of history over the last several decades has been an increased attention to gender as a category of historical analysis. Not only have women been significant actors in history, but also historical events shape women's experiences differently than they do men's. Almost all written sources from the early Middle Ages were produced by men and focus on men as their subjects. This presents a problem for historians who wish to study women in that period. Narrative accounts of the conversion of a brutal warlord written by celibate ecclesiastics might seem like strange sources from which to cull information about women's roles in medieval society, but Jane Tibbets Schulenburg has discovered a wealth of information in them. In fact, she argues that the problem is not so much the masculine bias of the sources, but the masculine bias of the modern scholars who study them. According to Schulenburg, Christian queens played significant roles in the conversion of their pagan husbands. Moreover, the important role of queens in this process was obvious and acknowledged at the time. Schulenburg uses only standard, well-known sources to make her argument. How does she read them differently from previous scholars?

While a few modern historians have noted the integral part played by women in the conversion of the Germanic Kingdoms and Western Europe to Christianity, for the most part this rather important phenomenon has been frequently overlooked or treated merely in passing. Women's influence has been

* © 1998 The University of Chicago. Jane Tibbets Schulenburg, *Forgetful of their Sex: Female Sanctity and Society ca. 500–1100*, Chicago: University of Chicago Press, 1998, pp. 177–190, 208–209.

viewed as "unofficial," informal, or "secondary," and therefore of only marginal significance. Although a neglected field of inquiry, it is of critical importance to an understanding of the complexity of the total movement of
conversion and the various impulses and influences involved. This chapter
will explore in some detail a few of the more prominent cases of conversion
and the active participation of these *mulieres sanctae* in the ecclesiastical
strategies of "domestic proselytization." The cumulative effect of these early
women's activities, which encompassed the areas of France, Italy, Spain, and
Britain, as well as a number of countries in Eastern Europe and Russia, is extremely powerful.

The word "conversion" has two rather distinct meanings. It can refer to a
personal religious experience or "inner conversion," or to a "conscious moving from one organized religion to another," which is called an "ecclesiastical
conversion." This chapter is concerned essentially with "ecclesiastical conversion" and the basic shift in allegiance from paganism to a new and different religion, i.e., Christianity. In contrast to "inner conversions," "ecclesiastical conversions" are usually not sudden or precipitous acts; rather, they are
frequently the result of a gradual, deliberate process. Also the new converts do
not necessarily undergo the heightened emotional or spiritual experiences
which are essential to inner conversions, nor does religion necessarily become
a central focus of their lives. Their reasons for conversion are complex and diverse: they are often the consequence of socio-political strategies, power, eco-
nomics, intellectual or psychological issues, and other motives or expediencies
that have, in fact, very little to do with religious feelings.

Although the medieval sources frequently depict the conversions as occurring in a relatively short period of time, Edward James has argued with regard to the conversion of Germanic kings that "there may be at least three
stages in the process: first of all, intellectual acceptance of Christ's message,
the 'conversion' proper; secondly, the decision to announce this publicly, to
followers who may be hostile to the change; thirdly, the ceremony of baptism
and membership of the community of Christians." Thus the strategy of the
missionaries was initially directed toward the "conversion," or its outward
manifestation in baptism, of the king or ruler of each tribe or region, along
with that of his family and household. It was, then, after winning over the
king and this "inner circle" that the missionaries could convert en masse the
entire social group which owed the king their allegiance. The end result of
these conversions of expediency was usually a formalistic, superficial adherence to the new faith with frequent lapses into paganism. Full conversion,
with the adoption of the new Christian lifestyle and values, was usually
achieved only after many years of indoctrination.

In light of this strategy, the missionaries were clearly aware of the influence that the wife of a pagan ruler might exercise in winning her husband over to the new faith and in ultimately bringing about the conversion or baptism of their household and followers. While the kings seemed to be frequently away from the court, involved in battle and other activities, queens and aristocratic women were perhaps more accessible to the priests and missionaries. And in general, it seems that from the beginning they were more receptive to learning about the new faith. This in part may have been simply a function of the fact that the activities of these women were centered in the great hall. And although they were occupied with administrative and economic duties of the kingdom as well as their household, part of their responsibility as queen or noblewoman included welcoming guests to the court and overseeing their stay. This in itself would entail a certain amount of contact with their visitors during meals and at other times. In addition, it was their duty to organize and oversee the household: they supervised the distribution of food, clothing, charity, salaries, and gifts. These queens or noblewomen also maintained valuable networks of clientage, friendships, and extended family. As guardians of their own culture, responsible for the welfare of their *familia*, they seemed to be perhaps more open to new religious ideas and beliefs. The missionaries therefore actively cultivated the friendships of these well-connected aristocratic and royal women and clearly recognized the importance of winning over their support for the success of their mission. It was, thus, into this sphere of the royal or noble family, the household controlled by the queen or noblewoman, that the missionaries were usually welcomed; and from this center or outpost they began their local operations. In an environment which might otherwise be unwelcoming and hostile, the queen and her household could be called upon to provide the missionaries with the necessary foothold, protection, and, very importantly, moral and material support for conversion activities.

The Church also realized that the queen could become a particularly invaluable ally in conversion if she espoused the new faith first, even though her husband and his followers "lagged behind" and continued in their "pagan errors." Occupying a position of great power and influence, the queen through her own example could provide the stimulus for the conversion of her household and people. And of special importance to the missionaries and churchmen was the exceptional influence which they believed the queen could exercise over her husband in his crucial decision to espouse the new faith. As wife, *consocia*, or partner of the king, it was believed that she would be able to gain his attention—"get his ear"—in a way that churchmen would never be able to do. Apparently, it was also assumed that whatever the outcome of her attempts at converting her husband might be, the queen would be allowed to have her children, the future kings and queens, baptized according to her own faith. And this would then forge the first link in the process and prepare the way for the future success of the movement.

The prototype of domestic proselytization can be traced back to the early Christian world where a number of prominent women are portrayed as espousing the new faith and then dedicating themselves to the conversion of their husbands and children. One of the most famous *exampla* in this tradition is that of the empress-saint Helena (d. ca. 330) and her alleged conversion of her son, the emperor Constantine. There has been a great deal written about Constantine's conversion as well as the role assumed by Helena in these events. While a number of ancient authors did not ascribe this important religious shift to the influence of the empress, Paulinus of Nola noted that Constantine "deserved to be prince of the princes of Christ as much through the faith of his mother Helena as through his own," and in the Middle Ages popular tradition credited the empress-saint Helena for her primary role in the conversion of Constantine. With the spread of Christianity to the north of Europe, Helena would become an important exemplum or role model of domestic proselytization for other queens and noblewomen and was cited as a prototype for a number of these early medieval women saints.

Among the Germanic peoples, the royal missionary tradition began with Saint Clotilda/Clotild (d. 544), queen of the Franks and wife of Clovis. Portrayed as an extremely effective domestic proselytizer, Clotilda was to become a "second Helena," the model of pious behavior for successive Catholic queens and noblewomen. Her name would be mentioned by later chroniclers and hagiographers as the prototype of their saintly protagonists, as well as a standard against which to measure their achievements. Moreover, in addition to spiritual ties and affinities, the line of female leadership involved in the conversion of many of the Germanic nations would trace its ancestry, for the most part, directly back to Clotilda.

Clotilda's activities as an emissary for the Church and domestic broker are described in some detail by Gregory of Tours in his *History of the Franks* and also in the anonymous *Liber Historiae Francorum*, written in the late seventh or early eighth century. Information from these early sources was then utilized by Clotilda's hagiographer, who compiled her formal vita sometime between the year 814 and the end of the ninth century.

Clotilda was the daughter of Chilperic, son of the king of Burgundy and his Gallo-Roman Catholic wife, Caretena. It was, then, apparently Caretena, who, in the capital at Lyons, raised her two daughters in the Catholic faith. According to the *Liber Historiae Francorum*, Chilperic and his wife were killed by Gundobad, one of Chilperic's brothers. Their eldest daughter was exiled and became a nun; the younger daughter, Clotilda, was kept at home by Gundobad. "Since Clovis frequently sent legations into Burgundy, it happened that the girl, Clotild, was noticed by the legates. These legates noticed Clotild's beauty, grace, and intelligence, and told Clovis." After Clovis learned of these things, he sent his legate, Aurelianus, who was on another mission to Gundobad, to ask for the hand of his niece. The author then carefully adds the important detail that "Clotild was a Christian." Disguised as a poor pilgrim, the legate Aurelianus arranged to meet secretly with Clotilda and to present her with a ring inscribed with the name and image of Clovis and other betrothal gifts which she hid in King Gundobad's treasury. After this, Clotilda sent greetings to Clovis: she acknowledged his proposal, but because of her commitment to Christianity and the prohibition of "mixed marriages" (and perhaps foreseeing potential problems in gaining Gundobad's approval), she requested that it remain secret. According to the *Liber Historiae Francorum*, she said, "It is not permitted for a Christian woman to marry a pagan, therefore do not let our betrothal be known. Whatever my Lord God orders, I confess that I will do."

The following year Clovis sent his legate to Gundobad to bring Clotilda back to his court for marriage. Gundobad, apparently unaware of the earlier "secret" betrothal, was taken aback. Prepared to go to war against Clovis and the Franks to avenge this affront, he was advised to ask his officers and chamberlain whether a legate of Clovis had previously brought gifts to the court in "an ingenious manner." And in checking his treasury, they indeed found the ring. Gundobad confronted Clotilda, who admitted that over the years "'small gifts of gold were brought to you by Clovis's messengers. It so happened that a little ring was placed in my hand, your little servant. I then hid it in your treasury.' He said: 'This was done innocently and without advice.' Then he grasped her angrily and handed her over to Aurelianus." Clotilda was taken by Aurelianus and his followers to King Clovis and they were married in 493 in Soissons.

In this description we can note first of all the active, rather surreptitious role that Clotilda apparently assumed in arranging her own marriage and determining her future. Despite Gundobad's statement that this was done "innocently and without advice," the secrecy which Clotilda exacted in these negotiations would seem to tell us something quite different. Using this strategy, she was able to contract an advantageous marriage without obtaining her uncle's permission. Considering that Gundobad had killed her parents and exiled her sister, and continued to espouse Arianism, Clotilda was no doubt anxious to escape from his court and to start a new life. (The *Liber Historiae*

Francorum and Gregory of Tours' *History*, for example, note Clotilda's un-remitting hatred for her uncle, as manifested in her later attempts to have her husband and sons avenge her family's honor in a vendetta directed against Gundobad.)

The sources stress the young bride's classic attributes, such as her beauty, grace, intelligence, and royal blood, as well as the fact that she was a Christian; but modern scholars have suggested that Clotilda's Catholic faith was in fact a prime consideration in Clovis' selecting her as his wife. In his classic study *The Invasion of Europe by the Barbarians*, J. B. Bury, for example, writes: "If we remember that the Burgundians were largely Arian, that King Gundobad was an Arian, and Clotilda was exceptionally a Catholic, it is certainly remarkable, if it were mere chance, that Clovis' choice should have fallen on one of the Catholic exceptions." Bury believed that he was "not rash in suggesting that it was just because she was a Catholic that Clovis chose her out." Although he was hesitant to personally embrace the new religion, the king appreciated the power of the Gallo-Roman Church; he no doubt realized what an enormous help Clotilda would be in winning over its confidence, as well as in negotiations with the ecclesiastics. His marriage to Clotilda, as noted by Bury, "was deliberately intended as a substitute for becoming a Christian himself, and it made clear what form of Christianity he would embrace, if he ever embraced any." Moreover, from the perspective of the Church, this "mixed marriage" was clearly perceived as politically advantageous: it provided them with a proven ally who could assist them "informally" from the "inside"; one who could perhaps bring about the desired conversion of the Frankish king, his children, and his followers.

It was, then, Clotilda's commitment to Catholicism and her single-minded domestic missionary activity which would attract more public attention and praise on the part of the Church than any other aspect of her life. According to the *Liber Historiae Francorum*, the saintly queen's work began in earnest on their wedding night. At this rather propitious moment she attempted to use her conjugal influence over Clovis. In a wedding-night/ honeymoon sermon, the bride is described as enumerating her special conditions of marriage. "When it was late that day, at the time when by custom the marriage was to be consummated, Clotild, moved by her accustomed prudence, confessed to God and said: 'now is the time my lord king that you hear your servant so that you may deem to concede what I pray for before I become part of your family and pass under your lordship.' The king answered: 'Ask what you wish and I will grant it.'" She asked the king first of all to believe in God the Father, in Christ, and in the Holy Spirit. He was to give up and burn his "meaningless idols which are not gods but worthless carvings" and also to restore the Christian churches that he had destroyed. He was finally asked to avenge her honor. "And remember also that I ask that you should demand the estate of my father and of my mother whom my uncle Gundobad evilly killed. Thus the Lord may avenge their blood." Clovis responded saying: "Only one thing that you have asked remains difficult and that is your request that I give up my gods and follow your God. Anything else that you ask, I will do as the opportunity arises." She answered: "I ask this above all else, that you worship the omnipotent Lord God who is in heaven." According to the sources, Clotilda continued to persevere in her attempts to convert Clovis to Christianity. With the birth of their first child, another opportunity presented itself which the queen could use to win over the king and his followers to the new religion. She was able to convince Clovis to allow her to have their son baptized in the Catholic faith. In this way the Church would be assured that the next generation of Frankish rulers would be Catholic. Clotilda no doubt also hoped that this event would have a special appeal for Clovis and would consequently influence him to adopt the new faith. Thus, according to Gregory of Tours, after the birth of their first son, Clotilda "wanted to have the baby baptized, and she kept on urging her husband to agree to this." In her arguments with the king, Clotilda again stressed the worthless aspects of his gods compared to the omnipotence of her God: "'The gods whom you worship are no good,' she would say. 'They haven't even been able to help themselves, let alone others.'" But "However often the queen said this, the king came no nearer to belief." Still Clotilda persisted and prepared to baptize the infant in her own faith. The king did not attempt to stop her. "She ordered the church to be decorated with hangings and curtains, in the hope that the King, who remained stubborn in the face of argument, might be brought to the faith by ceremony." The child received baptism and was given the name Ingomer. But tragically, no sooner had he been baptized than he died while still in his white baptismal robes. With marvelous understatement Gregory of Tours describes this sad event: "Clovis was extremely angry," and he reproached Clotilda for having had the child baptized as a Christian rather than dedicating him to his pagan gods. However, according to Gregory, Clotilda, with Christian resignation, gave thanks to God for welcoming a child who was conceived in her womb into His kingdom.

Clotilda's remarkable perseverance and continuing influence over Clovis are again underscored by the fact that she had their second son baptized in the Christian faith. When this child too began to ail and seemed to be following the same pattern that his older brother had, Clovis again reproached Clotilda for having him baptized in the name of Christ. According to Gregory of Tours,

"Clotilda prayed to the Lord and at His command the baby recovered." Thus with the baptism of this son, the first step of her conversion strategy was accomplished.

However, Clovis still remained unconvinced of the new religion. Gregory relates, "Queen Clotild continued to pray that her husband might recognize the true God and give up his idol-worship. Nothing could persuade him to accept Christianity." Then during the course of a difficult war against the Alamanni, Clovis "was forced by necessity to accept what he had refused of his own free will." Witnessing the annihilation of his own troops in battle, and faced with a desperate situation, the king called on his own gods for assistance. Realizing that they were powerless and had no intention of helping him, he then turned to call on Christ's assistance. According to Gregory of Tours, he raised his eyes to heaven and prayed, "'Jesus Christ,' he said, 'you who Clotild maintains to be the Son of the living God, you who deign to give help to those in travail and victory to those who trust in you, in faith I beg the glory of your help.'" The *Liber Historiae Francorum* notes that "Aurelianus [Clovis' legate], seeing the turn of events, said to the king, . . . believe only in the lord of heaven whom your queen proclaims." Thus compelled by this extremely desperate plight in battle, Clovis called upon Clotilda's God for assistance. He then promised in return for evidence of Christ's strength and miraculous powers—specifically, victory over his enemies—that he would accept Christian baptism. According to the sources, even as he prayed, the Alamanni turned and fled. And on his return home, Clovis "told the Queen how he had won a victory by calling on the name of Christ."

After this pivotal event, Gregory of Tours notes: "the Queen then ordered Saint Remi, Bishop of the town of Rheims, to be summoned in secret. She begged him to impart the word of salvation to the King."(Here again Clotilda took the initiative and assumed a major role in realizing her husband's conversion.) The bishop met privately with Clovis, and soon after, the king was baptized in great ceremony. He was described by Gregory of Tours as a "new Constantine" stepping into the baptismal pool. At this same time, we are told, more than three thousand of the king's army, along with two of his sisters (Albofled and Lanthechild), were baptized.

In discussing Clovis' shift of allegiance from paganism to Christianity, scholars have traditionally focused on the king's "miraculous" victory in the war against the Alamanni and Suevians, which closely echoed the events surrounding the impressive, historical prototype of imperial conversion, namely, that of Constantine. Clovis' baptism, as we have noted, was also seen in larger-than-life terms: this first Christian king of the Franks was portrayed as a "new Constantine." Yet, despite the emphasis by chroniclers and scholars on the unexpected, "miraculous" element of Clovis' conversion, as well as the official institutional involvement of St. Remi, Clotilda had in fact assumed the primary role in "conditioning" her husband for this event—in making him susceptible to a Christian "solution," namely, by calling on Clotilda's God for assistance when his own gods were failing him on the battlefield. As Clovis' wife and *consocia*, or partner in ruling, as well as trusted religious adviser, Clotilda had worked unremittingly toward this goal. Through her position within the family and household, she was able to provide consistent reinforcement of Christian precepts as well as incentive for Clovis to lose faith or become disillusioned with his pagan religion. She was therefore able to provide the crucial groundwork for Clovis' official conversion. Despite her inability over the years to fully persuade him on her own to get rid of his pagan gods and accept Christianity, it was then in this "public" moment of desperation, when he was on the verge of defeat, that the king clearly acknowledged his debt to Clotilda's persistence in "domestic proselytization." It appears that he had after all been "passively" attentive to her case for Christianity over the years, but had apparently not felt the need to take a chance in making this momentous and perhaps ill-advised shift while his pagan gods continued to support him and bring him "luck." More a pragmatic than theoretical decision, the time had not been right to deny his pagan heritage. Thus in his desperate hour, when he witnessed his own gods failing him, he resorted to Clotilda's arguments which had directly attacked the impotency of his pagan gods while promoting the miraculous power of the Christian faith. In the official description of the "miracle" of conversion, the name of Clotilda appears alone as a model of faith, as perhaps a sort of interceder with Christ. It is, after all, the "Christ of Clotilda" whom Clovis invokes. It should be emphasized that at this critical moment in the history of the Church, neither St. Remi nor other members of the official church hierarchy were similarly awarded this type of prominence.

Moreover, in the ninth-century redaction of the *Life of St. Clotilda* (based on Gregory of Tours' *History of the Franks* and the *Liber Historiae Francorum*), the author also describes the important ceremonial role that the queen assumed in Clovis' baptism. According to this vita, "The new Constantine came to baptism with the blessed Remigius leading the way and blessed Chrothild [Clotilda] following, the Holy Spirit governing these procedures in characteristic fashion. For it was fitting, that when the pagan king came to his baptism, holy Remigius should precede in the place of Christ Jesus and holy Chrothild [Clotilda] should follow in the place of the Church interceding with God." Her hagiographer continues: "Happy Gaul, rejoice and be glad, give thanks in the Lord, take joy in the true God, for your first king chosen by the King of heaven, was drawn away from the veneration of the demons by the prayers of holy Chrothild [Clotilda] acting in the character of the Church, was converted to God by the preaching of blessed Remigius and baptized by him." Clotilda's vita also notes that the queen continued to exercise religious influence over the king and worked toward the general conversion of her country. "At the advice of blessed Chrothild [Clotilda], the king undertook the destruction of pagan shrines and the erection of churches, and he enriched them abundantly with lands and privileges: he undertook generously to confer alms on the poor, to support widows and orphans in the spirit of mercy and to attend with zealous devotion to every good work."

Other sources of the Middle Ages continue to acknowledge Clotilda's influential role in the conversion of Clovis and the Franks. The vita of the queen-saint Balthild, for example, notes the impressive legacy found among its female Frankish saints. Balthild's hagiographer compares her favorably with these royal predecessors: "Let us recall that there were in the kingdom of the Franks some noble queens, true servants of God: Clotild, first of all, wife of the first Clovis, niece of Gundobad, who through holy exhortation converted to Christianity and the catholic faith her most powerful and pagan husband and with him many of the Franks."

In the thirteenth-century *Speculum Historiale*, compiled by Vincent of Beauvais, Clotilda still retains a primary role in the conversion of Clovis and the Franks. This work devotes three chapters to the events leading up to and culminating in the baptism of Clovis.

Christine de Pizan, in *The Book of the City of Ladies* (1405), a collection of biographies of "women worthies," dedicates a chapter to Clotilda. She writes: "As for the great benefits brought about by women regarding spiritual matters, just as I told you before, was it not Clotilda, daughter of the king of Burgundy and wife of the strong Clovis, king of France, who first brought and spread the faith of Jesus Christ to the kings and princes of France? What greater good could have been accomplished than what she did?"

Even the notorious *Malleus Maleficarum* (*The Hammer of Witches*), written in 1486 by the Dominican inquisitors Heinrich Kramer and Jacob Sprenger and used to identify and condemn women as witches, includes Clotilda as one of the few positive female figures in history. In the chapter on "Why Superstition is chiefly found in Women," Kramer and Sprenger cite I Corinthians 7:14: "If a woman hath a husband that believeth not, and he be pleased to dwell with her, let her not leave him. For the unbelieving husband is sanctified by the believing wife. . . ." And all this is made clear in the New Testament concerning women and virgins and other holy women who have by faith led nations and kingdoms away from the worship of idols to the Christian religion." They then cite as a source Vincent of Beauvais: "Anyone who looks at Vincent of Beauvais will find marvellous things of the conversion of Hungary by the most Christian Gilia, and of the Franks by Clotilda, the wife of Clovis."

It appears then to be only in the more recent retelling and synthesizing of these events that the miraculous and the official or institutional aspects of this conversion have frequently worked to overshadow and marginalize Clotilda's primary contribution to this significant episode in history. In contrast, for the medieval world, the success of Clotilda in persuading Clovis and the Franks to accept baptism seems to have been clearly recognized and appreciated.

CHAPTER SIX

~

Popular Religion in
Late Saxon England:
Elf Charms in Context*

Karen Louise Jolly

For many scholars the presence of pre-Christian folk lore in post-conversion Germanic culture is seen as a failure of christianization. They depict early medieval Christianity as a thin patina covering deep, persistent paganism. The sources reveal a society in which the common person believed in elves and healing potions. Indeed, this patina may be thinner than the sources suggest, since surviving documents were written by Christian clergy with a stake in making popular religion look more Christian than it was. Karen Louise Jolly encourages us to look at the evidence differently. Where most scholars see failure, she sees success. If we employ what she calls a "popular religion model," we will see that the sources reveal a successful accommodation between Christianity and pre-Christian Germanic culture that preserved the essential identity of both. What is the "popular religion model" and how does it support her thesis? According to Jolly, what is the difference between formal and popular religion? Do you find her arguments convincing?

Consider the following ceremony for blessing the fields, found on a few folios from the late tenth or early eleventh century, and ponder the contexts in which it was developed, performed, and written.

ÆCERBOT [FIELD REMEDY] RITUAL:

> Here is the remedy, how you may better your land, if it will not grow well or if some harmful thing has been done to it by a sorcerer [*dry*] or by a poisoner [*lyblace*].

* © 1996 The University of North Carolina Press. Used by permission of the publisher. Karen Louise Jolly, *Popular Religion in Late Saxon England: Elf Charms in Context*, Chapel Hill: The University of North Carolina Press, 1996, pp. 6–11, 27–32.

Take then at night, before dawn, four sods from four sides of the land, and mark where they were before.

Then take oil and honey and yeast, and milk of each animal that is on the lands and a piece of each type of tree that grows on the land, except hard beams, and a piece of each herb known by name, except burdock [*glappan*] only, and put then holy water thereon, and drip it three times on the base of the sods, and say then these words:

Crescite, grow, *et multiplicamini*, and multiply, *et replete*, and fill, *terre*, the earth. *In nomine patris et filii et spiritus sancti sit benedicti.* [In the name of the father and the son and the holy spirit be blessed.] And the *Pater noster* [Our Father] as often as the other.

And then bear the sods into church, and let a masspriest sing four masses over the sods, and let someone turn the green [sides] to the altar, and after that let someone bring the sods to where they were before, before the sun sets.

And have made for them four signs of Christ [crosses] of quickbeam and write on each end: Matthew and Mark, Luke, and John. Lay that sign of Christ in the bottom of the pit [where each sod had been cut out], saying then: *crux Matheus, crux Marcus, crux Lucas, crux sanctus Iohannes.*

Take then the sods and set them down there on [the crosses], and say then nine times these words, *Crescite* [grow], and as often the *Pater noster*, and turn then to the east, and bow nine times humbly, and speak then these words:

> Eastwards I stand,   for mercies I pray,
> I pray the great *domine* [lord],   I pray the powerful lord,
> I pray the holy guardian of heaven-kingdom,
> earth I pray   and sky
> and the true   *sancta* [holy] Mary
> and heaven's might   and high hall,
> that I may this charm [*galdor*]   by the gift of the lord
> open with [my] teeth   through firm thought,
> to call forth these plants   for our worldly use,
> to fill this land with firm belief,
> to beautify this grassy turf,   as the wiseman said
> that he would have riches on earth   who alms
> gave with justice   by the grace of the lord.

Then turn thrice with the sun's course, stretch then out lengthwise and enumerate there the litanies and say then: *Sanctus, sanctus, sanctus* to the end. Sing then *Benedicite* with outstretched arms and *Magnificat* and *Pater noster* thrice, and commend it [the land] to Christ and saint Mary and the holy cross for praise and for worship and for the benefit of the one who owns that land and all those who are serving under him. When all that is done, then let a man take unknown seed from beggars and give them twice as much as he took from them, and let him gather all his plough tools together; then let him bore a hole in the beam [of the plough, putting in] incense and fennel and hallowed soap and hallowed salt. Take then that seed, set it on the plough's body, say then:

Erce, Erce, Erce, earth's mother,
May the all-ruler grant you, the eternal lord,
fields growing and flourishing,
propagating and strengthening,
tall shafts, bright crops,
and broad barley crops,
and white wheat crops,
and all earth's crops.
May the eternal lord grant him,
and his holy ones, who are in heaven,
that his produce be guarded against any enemies whatsoever,
and that it be safe against any harm at all,
from poisons [*lyblaca*] sown around the land.
Now I bid the Master, who shaped this world,
that there be no speaking-woman [*cwidol wif*] nor artful man [*craftig man*]
that can overturn these words thus spoken.
Then let a man drive forth the plough and the first furrow cut, say then:
Whole may you be [Be well] earth, mother of men!
May you be growing in God's embrace,
with food filled for the needs of men.

Take then each kind of flour and have someone bake a loaf [the size of] a hand's palm and knead it with milk and with holy water and lay it under the first furrow. Say then:

Field full of food for mankind,
bright-blooming, you are blessed
in the holy name of the one who shaped heaven
and the earth on which we live;
the God, the one who made the ground, grant us the gift of growing,
that for us each grain might come to use.

Say then thrice *Crescite in nomine patris, sit benedicti* [Grow in the name of the father, be blessed]. Amen and Pater poster three times.

How should we read this ceremony for blessing the fields? As pagan or Christian? Demonic or Godly? Manipulative magic or supplicative prayer? By the standards of a later age, this remedy is problematic because it defies the neat categories used to judge what is Christian or rational. The text was the product of the literate clergy who represented the formal church in late Saxon England. Yet it has enough identifiably pre-Christian elements to cause consternation among many later theologians and modern scholars, who see it as evidence of the retention of paganism in the practice of magic and as a failure of the Christianizing effort in the late Saxon church. My argument in this work is that the Christian charms, such as the formulas in the remedy above and the elf charms analyzed in Chapter 5, are not some kind of "Christian magic" demonstrating the weakness of early medieval Christianity but constitute evidence of the religion's success in conversion by accommodating Anglo-Saxon culture. This book proposes a different model for understanding Christian conversion, one that allows us to consider these folk rituals within their own context. This model is popular religion, a modern construct that examines the broader religious experience of a society.

Popular religion, as one facet of a larger, complex culture, consists of those beliefs and practices common to the majority of the believers. This popular religion encompasses the whole of Christianity, including the formal aspects of the religion as well as the general religious experience of daily life. These popular practices include rituals marking the cycles of life (birth, marriage, and death) or combating the mysterious (illness and danger) or assuring spiritual security (the afterlife). Popular belief was reflected in those rituals and in other symbols exhibited in the society, such as paintings, shrines, and relics.

The cultural history approach employed here departs from traditional church history studies that focus on the well-defined area of formal Christianity—the institution of the church with its hierarchy of clergy and its canons, councils, and theological constructs. Representatives of this formal religion, the missionaries, reformers, and church historians, present conversion as a dramatic shift in religious orientation, a radical transformation in belief—a definition that is still common today. Writers such as Gregory of Tours, Bede, Ælfric, and Wulfstan follow a long tradition dating back to Eusebius and Augustine that tends to portray the world in a dualistic fashion, pagan versus Christian, magic versus miracle, Devil versus God. Conversion for them is therefore a dramatic event switching from one side to the other.

This formal religion, however, is only a subset of a larger whole; popular religion encompasses all practicing Christians and all everyday practices and beliefs. Expanding our view to this larger Christian community allows us to see the gradual nature of conversion. Under the influence of recent cultural history, the study of popular religion has begun to elucidate the slower processes of accommodation between culture and religion in everyday life that show how Christianity became an integral part of culture and, vice versa, how emerging European cultures changed Christianity.

In the context of popular religion, then, conversion is both an event and a process whereby an individual or a group changes religious orientation, in both belief and practice. Even though early Christian and medieval narratives frequently emphasize conversion as a dramatic event for a prominent individual and his or her society, these narratives also suggest that it was a dynamic process stretched over time involving a great deal of cultural assimilation between the imported Romano-Christian religion and the native folklife of the various "Germanic" peoples settling in Europe. This acculturation process creates many gray areas, containing practices that do not fit into tidy categories and are subject to differing interpretations, such as the Christian charms against the attack of elves examined at length in Chapter 5.

Late Saxon England, circa 900-1050, was a dynamic period of growth for popular religion, as seen in expanding local churches and in more documents recording folk religious remedies. In order to understand popular religious practices in this period, we need to place them in the context of this gradual process of cultural conversion, in which Germanic folklore and Christian belief bled into each other as much or more than they sought to destroy each other. Instead of focusing, as many histories do, on the traditional dualistic view of oppositions in conversion (magic versus religion, for example), this study examines the middle ground, the gray area of encounter and accommodation between Germanic cultures and the incoming Christian traditions.

The Field Remedy quoted at the outset is an excellent example of a ritual that needs to be seen in the context of a developing popular Christianity. In its invocation of both Father God and Mother Earth (subordinated here to the Allruler) and in its appeal to the combined forces of earth, sky, Mary, and Heaven, it draws on both the Germanic and Christian traditions in an unself-conscious way. The multiple spiritual agencies, mostly chthonic in nature, referenced in this remedy show continuity from Germanic animistic belief, and yet the use of masses and prayers and the ultimate appeal to a supreme divinity demonstrate the overlordship of Christianity. It is more appropriate, then, to see these practices as the retention of Germanic folklore in a popular Christianity rather than as the continuance of paganism as a religious system.

Folk medical remedies, merging across the boundaries into the spiritual cures found in liturgy, are one clear type of evidence illustrating the conversion of Germanic folkways to Christianity or, to put it the other way, the adaptation of Christianity to Germanic ways. Anglo-Saxon charms against the attack of invisible elves, and their demonization in late Saxon remedies, exist in sufficient numbers in the medical manuscripts to show a variety of accommodation techniques that reveal this conversion process. These middle practices, as I term them, symbolize a unique creation, an Anglo-Saxon

Christianity. This model of popular religion thus highlights the flash points between the formal religion and the popular, the areas where some kind of negotiation between the two took place. Folklore as an areligious concept is therefore a more appropriate term than paganism or magic to describe the transmission of Germanic practices and beliefs that ultimately lost their pagan context as they were integrated into popular Christianity.

I am arguing here for a more favorable view than that reflected in previous scholarship of this mixture of Germanic folklore and Christian belief: not as evidence of the lowest, degenerate fringe of a dominant Christian orthodoxy (the older view prominent in nineteenth- and early twentieth-century treatment of charms) or even as evidence of the failure of Christianization in the face of a recalcitrant pagan population (the more recent view promulgated especially by Jacques Le Goff), but as evidence of the dynamic interaction that takes place between a native culture and an introduced religion. This is Christianity succeeding by way of acculturation and Germanic culture triumphing in transformation. Neither is the passive victim of the other. Likewise, most ordinary Anglo-Saxon Christians were not suffering from a split personality; rather, they created a wholeness out of their mixed heritages. Whether to refer to this hybridization process as Christianizing the Anglo-Saxons or as Germanicizing Christianity is problematic. The biblical analogy of new wine in old skins shows the dilemma of trying to understand this transformation: Is Christianity the new wine put into old skins? Or is it the new skin into which old wine is poured? These questions about form and substance defy precise answers because they are a matter of perspective.

The cult of the saints, as established and fostered by church leaders, consciously or unconsciously made accommodations to the animistic beliefs of Germanic peoples. This accommodation is seen, for example, in the desire for local sites of worship focused on a specific and immediately accessible being such as a saint, and the need for sources of spiritual power to solve life's problems. The concept of saints' relics as a doorway between this world and the next developed in the late antique Roman-Christian synthesis but easily made itself at home in the worldviews of Germanic peoples in the early Middle Ages.

In general the Germanic peoples monastic missionaries contacted were polytheistic with a strong animistic element in their practice. To them, all of nature was alive with spiritual entities, a very holistic view of the world that focused on nature as a source of food and healing, without much distinction between natural and supernatural forces. While the major deities, the *Æksir* and the *Vanir*, were honored by the male priests at the temples, they were also memorialized in stories and were part of the fabric of society. For example, their names were, and are, retained in the days of the week (Tyr or Tiw/Tuesday, Woden/Wednesday, Thor/Thursday, and Friga/Friday). Besides these major deities, lesser spiritual entities in trees, wells, and stones, who were propitiated with offerings by local people, inhabited the landscape. Elves, dwarves, and the *Norns* caused illness or other misfortune, for which cures were handed down in the folk memory. Some of the elements of the belief in these entities were retained in the Field Remedy in the sense of an animate nature addressed as mother, in the use of symbolic elements of trees and other produce, and in the "offerings" planted in the pits in the four corners of the field.

The cult of the saints Christianized this animistic landscape, populating it with loci of Christian power by supplanting the holy trees, wells, and stones of pagan religion and setting up a revised calendar based on saints' festivals. In so doing, Christianity began penetrating everyday life and belief. Church leaders promoted saints by telling their stories as part of a conscious educational effort to spread Christian ideas among the populace and to encourage the laity to patronize saints' holy places. The miracles accomplished by saints at these sites served as validation for the truth of Christianity and a sign of the sanctity of God's chosen messenger, the saint, and by extension the church or monastery for whom the saint was a patron.

This conflation of pagan and Christian holy sites seen in the cult of the saints is increasingly evident in tenth-century textual and archaeological remains. By this time Anglo-Saxon Christianity was emerging as a distinctive entity, different in its local flavor from the Roman Christianity initially imported from the continent. This Germanic-Christian synthesis can be found in the adaptation of the Anglo-Saxon language to Christian concepts, in the writing of texts reflecting a Germanic-Christian worldview, and in changing burial habits.

One example of the effects of this synthesis in the language is in the concept of lordship. The personal and reciprocal relationship between a lord and his vassal in Germanic society became a model for the personal relationship between God and a believer, who was frequently portrayed as a warrior for God. The Anglo-Saxon *hlaford*, modern lord, literally means "bread-source." This Germanic concept of lord as a giver of life and sustenance to his faithful retainers and the one to whom allegiance was owed was easily transmuted into the Christian concept of Christ as Lord, the source of life, the giver of bread (his body), in whom faith was placed. Likewise, Jesus' disciples were portrayed as *thegns*, the Anglo-Saxon knightly aristocracy.

This Christian warrior ideal is evident throughout Anglo-Saxon art and literature in the merger or overlap of Germanic heroic and Christian images.

The entire modern debate over Beowulf as Christian or pagan, both or nei-ther, is evidence of this Anglo-Saxon duality and the difficulty of recapturing what these traditions meant to late Saxon culture. Likewise, the Franks Cas-ket, with its marvelous mixture of Roman, Germanic, and Christian myths, demonstrates a unique and compelling synthesis of traditions. The Franks Casket is a useful corrective to modern explanations of early medieval con-version in two respects. It first reminds us that the origins of a tradition, its earliest formulation, should not obscure or take precedence over the ways that the tradition is adapted. Romulus and Remus, the Adoration of the Magi, and Weland the Smith can coexist. Second, the ivory carvings on the casket demonstrate that assimilation is a creative effort central to conver-sion. Conversion does not necessarily entail the obliteration of pre-Christian traditions but opens the possibility of cultural transformation.

This two-way transformation is evident in such Christian heroic literature as *Guthlac* and *The Dream of the Rood*. The Anglo-Saxon saint Guthlac (circa 700) was a young warrior who, upon seeing the death and destruction inher-ent in the warrior lifestyle, converted to a monastic existence, withdrawing into the fens of Lincolnshire. His biography, and the poem of his life in par-ticular, not only followed the pattern of earlier saints' lives but incorporated secular warrior imagery, transforming the pacific monk into a "belligerent *miles Christi*" (soldier of Christ). Guthlac's contests with spiritual forces in the wilderness resound with images of battles and hillforts.

> Good was Guthlac!   He bore in his spirit
> heavenly hope,   reached the salvation
> of eternal life.   An angel was close to him,
> faithful peace-guardian,   to him, who, as one of a few
> settled the borderland.   There he became to many
> an example in Britain,   when he ascended the mountain,
> blessed warrior,   hardy of battle.
> Geared himself eagerly   with spiritual
> weapons . . .   he blessed the land,
> as a station for himself   he first raised up
> Christ's rood,   where the champion overcame many dangers.

The imagery here is typical of the monastic sense of the wilderness as a place to conquer the Devil and convert the pagan. Guthlac's first act is to Christianize the landscape by setting up a cross, just as a hero might stake a spear or banner on conquered territory.

This mixture of the Germanic warrior ideology and Christian beliefs con-tained in Anglo-Saxon poetry strikes some modern readers as odd, but to the

Anglo-Saxon Christian poet it made sense to idealize and imitate Christ as a heroic figure taking on the cross as a kind of battle. Perhaps the best example of this ideology is in the Anglo-Saxon poem *The Dream of the Rood*. This tenth-century poem personifies the cross, who presents himself to the dreamer as a noble warrior who faithfully stood by his lord (Christ) at his final battle ("There I dared not bow or break against my Lord's command"). The cross-narrator describes Christ not as passively submitting to the humiliation of crucifixion as the soldiers nail him to the cross but as actively mounting the cross himself. "Then the young warrior—who was God Almighty—stripped Himself, strong and resolute. He climbed upon the high gallows, brave in the sight of many, when he wished to redeem mankind." This is a radical departure from the usual Christian emphasis on Christ's humility and submission to death. Heroic death in particular was a strong component of the Germanic *comitatus* (warband), and this warrior ethic was part of the pagan cosmology as represented in the *Æsir*. Thus the poem portrays Christ as aggressively taking on the cross as a battle in which his victory through death heroically saves his people. *Guthlac* and *The Dream of the Rood* contain powerful symbolism for Anglo-Saxon Christians, evidence of a successful acculturation process.

Death and its treatment are among the most revealing aspects of religious beliefs. The establishment of Christian cemeteries and the Christian symbolism used in burial are symptomatic of the Christianization of Germanic culture. Many of these cemeteries, in continuous use from pre-Christian time until long after, show layers of burial practices. Churches were sometimes founded at cemetery sites predating conversion; either the remains were exhumed and the land cleansed or the new place of worship overlaid the old. Pagan burial customs included grave goods such as coins, medallions, and other memorabilia that are subsequently found in Christian burials at churches. For example, a grave could be marked with a cross or be clearly placed in a churchyard yet contain within it a person buried with grave goods. The inclusion of such grave goods in a Christian-marked grave indicates not necessarily the survival of the pagan religion or its structure of beliefs, but the retention through folklore of an important ritual now being subsumed into the Christian framework. These archaeological layers reveal a gradual transition in burial practice, with the Christian progressively overlaying the pagan. This evidence displays graphically how religious practices were gradually converted and how ideas about life and death were transformed.

Churchmen such as Aelfric and Wulfstan greeted this popular synthesis between Christian and Germanic with ambivalence. Confronted with a practice that was a mixture of Christianity and folklore, a Christian leader might have responded to it in one of two ways, depending on which direction he thought the transmission was going. If he perceived a successful Christianization of the Germanic folk practice, then he viewed such an amalgamation as a praiseworthy attempt at getting people into church (as in the case of the pagan temples being renovated as churches). If, however, it appeared to him that "paganism" obscured (lowered, degenerated) Christian belief, then such a leader might call for reform and issue laws against practices such as observing special days for certain actions or leaving offerings at trees, stones, or wells. In either case the churchman was reacting to a synthesis already going on, initiated at a grassroots level.

The existence of a reformer's complaint about such syncretic activities has too often been taken at face value by modern scholars who conclude that Christianity was failing to penetrate popular culture. On the contrary, reformer reactions indicate that Christianization was taking place among a laity actively seeking to incorporate Christianity into their everyday lives. Reform movements such as those found in the tenth and eleventh centuries were not just a sign of degeneracy in Christian culture, but of an awareness of how this new synthesis was functioning. The issue for these reformers was one of control over the rapid diversification of Christian practice and belief. Unlike conversion aimed at making pagans into Christians, reform was an effort by churchmen to improve a society already Christian in some general sense. In the tenth and eleventh centuries, simultaneous calls for the exclusion of paganism and for Christian reform indicate the transitional nature of this period, in part due to the influx of pagan Scandinavians in eastern England. By the tenth century a number of different, sometimes competing processes were at work in the development of Anglo-Saxon Christianity, initiated from both the popular and formal spheres; taken as a whole they indicate a vibrancy in the religious experience of late Anglo-Saxon England.

CHAPTER SEVEN

~

The Rise of Western Christendom*
Peter Brown

Few modern scholars have done as much to shed light on Christianity in the late Roman and early medieval worlds as Peter Brown. In fact, his most significant work has caused historians to rethink the traditional distinction between the ancient and medieval periods. He contends that even though Roman political power evaporated throughout most of Europe by the end of the fifth century, Roman culture, including religious culture, persisted for many centuries after. Spanning the third through the eighth centuries, the breadth of the book from which this selection is taken displays Brown's point of view. While the book encompasses all of western Christendom, Brown is also sensitive to regional differences, referring to various religious cultures as "microchristendoms."

As he explains in the following selection, the spread of Christianity beyond the old Roman cultural borders into northern and central Europe was not a natural progression. Instead, it came about through an odd combination of Frankish political ambition and peculiarities in British Christianity. The Frankish aristocracy, particularly the new Carolingian dynasty, wished to expand to the north and east. Since the Frankish elite worshipped the Christian God, their subject people were expected to as well. At the same time, some Irish and British monks in self-imposed, penitential exile wanted to spread Christianity to the peoples that they met in their wanderings. Under the protection and patronage of the Frankish king Pepin, British missionaries Willibrord and Boniface went to Frisia and western Germany, respectively. How did

* © 2003 Peter Brown, *The Rise of Western Christendom*, London: Blackwell, 2003, pp. 414–428. Reprinted with the permission of Peter Brown.

Willibrord and Boniface go about their missionary work? These men saw themselves as missionaries to pagans. Does Brown think that they were portraying themselves accurately?

The decision made in the course of the eighth century to convert such peoples to Christianity, by force if needs be, was by no means an inevitable development. Christianity had always thought of itself as a "universal" religion, in that Christians believed that all peoples could be Christians, or, at least, that there could be Christians among all peoples. But in Continental Europe, Christians had been slow to draw the conclusion that Christianity should be the religion of all peoples, even if this involved having to send "missionaries" to the heathen in distant regions. The idea of the "missionary" seems so normal to us that we have to remember that it was only in this period that anything like a concept of "missions" developed in Western Europe. Up to then a more old-fashioned, more "Roman" view of the world had prevailed. The Franks assumed, much as the Romans had assumed, that beyond the *limes* a barbarian "back-country" would always exist. It was important that the inhabitants of this "back-country" should be held in check and, if possible, cowed into submission. Those pagans who found themselves on the Frankish side of the old frontier had to be absorbed. In the seventh century, a series of efforts were made by Frankish bishops, many of whom had been disciples of Columbanus, to convert the "un-churched" populations of the Channel coast and the southern side of the estuary of the Rhine (modern Flanders in Belgium). But this was seen as a "firming up" of an untidy frontier. It was not a missionary drive directed to faraway pagans. The populations of the back-country of Frisia and inner Germany were left free to continue their "barbarous" lives. By and large, western Christians on the Continent had not felt the need to reach out to gather in the unruly peoples who lived along the fringes of Christianity.

Things looked different when viewed from the British Isles. In Ireland and Saxon Britain, the imaginative barrier of the *limes* did not exist. What mattered was *peregrinatio*, the act of becoming a stranger to one's country for the sake of God. After that, one could go anywhere. Compared with the elemental wrench of self-imposed exile, by which a man breached the barrier of his own kin and his own small tribe, the ancient frontiers of Europe meant nothing. For a religious exile, everywhere was equally strange. To find oneself among "heathens" was not unusual. Furthermore, if one had become an exile to save one's own soul, the sense of urgency which drove one to that desperate remedy might also lead to a sense of the urgent need to save the souls of others.

As we have seen, the idea of "exile of God" had developed in Ireland. But Ireland was not alone in this. By the year 700, the structures of the newly established Anglo-Saxon churches in Britain were calculated to produce a supply of highly motivated wanderers. The urge to become an exile often coincided with a "middle age crisis." Indeed, the call of exile occurred at the same time of life as the great converts of the late fourth century (such as Augustine and Paulinus of Nola) had experienced the call to a higher life.

But the reasons for their conversion were different. The exiles of the eighth century wanted to get out of ecclesiastical structures in which they felt themselves to be held too tightly. Given to a local monastery at an early age, between five and seven, able men found themselves entering middle age only to confront a dangerous emotional and social situation. Between the ages of thirty and forty, they faced the prospect of becoming abbots or bishops. They would be compelled to settle down as figures of authority among their own kin and region. This meant that they found themselves inextricably implicated in the compromises that had produced, in Britain as in Ireland, an established Christianity that was shot through with deeply profane elements. For a devout person, it was better to leave home, so as to seek elsewhere the clarity of a true Christian order. Among such persons, religious exile and the sharp sense of a Christian order as it should be went hand in hand.

The first of this new generation of strangers, Willibrord (658–739), was a product both of Wilfrid's micro-Christendom in Northumbria and of Ireland. He received his vocation when studying, already as an exile, at Cluain Melsige (Clonmelsh, County Carlow). In 690, he arrived, with a small party of monks, to offer his services to Pippin of Herstal, the father of Charles Martel. Unlike an earlier stranger from Ireland, Columbanus, Willibrord did not offer "medicine" for the souls of Pippin and his entourage. His burning wish was, rather, to save the souls of real pagans. He was encouraged to preach to the Frisians of the Rhine estuary, who had recently fallen under Frankish domination. But he also wished to reach out to pagan peoples as far away as the Danes and the Old Saxons.

We have Willibrord's own Calendar, written in a clear Irish script, with entries in his own hand. It is a glimpse of the new Europe of an exile. It was a wide, northern world held together by the ritual commemoration of saints and dead persons from the distant British Isles: Patrick, Brigid, and Columba, the three great saints of Ireland, appear together with three kings of Northumbria. Furthermore, when writing the date of his seventieth birthday, Willibrord adopted a new dating system: he wrote of it, much as we do, as "A.D. 728"—"in the 728th year from the Lord's Incarnation."

The system of A.D. dating had been elaborated earlier; but it suddenly became important for a small group of men whose sense of time was as majestically universal as was their sense of space. (In this, of course, they had been preceded by the Muslims, who regularly dated the year, throughout their vast empire, from the *hijra*, the fateful journey from Mecca to Medina of the Prophet and his Companions in 622.) Up to then, time in Europe had been regional time. Often, it was time which still looked straight back to Rome. Many regions still used the old Roman "provincial era." This was a time-scale where the years were counted from the year in which the region had been incorporated, as a province, into the Roman empire. Local rulers used their regnal years. And the popes, ever intent on proving that they were good "Romans" and loyal subjects of the Byzantine emperors, placed the regnal years, even the honorary consulships and the tax-cycles (the Indictions) of the East Roman emperors, on every document that they wrote. These old-fashioned dating systems were maintained in much of Europe. But in Willibrord's world (as in the dating system used by Bede in his *Ecclesiastical History*) there was only one time because there was only one world-ruler—the Lord Christ, whose reign over all humankind began with the year of his birth. It was a time-frame that all Christians could share. The choice of the "Anno Domini," A.D., dating communicated a sense of time that was as universal, as independent of local traditions, as Willibrord's vision of the world was independent of local frontiers. All time began with the beginning of Christianity and, by implication, all time was about the time it took for Christianity to reach its fulfillment, through the conversion of ever more pagan regions.

Seen across the sea from Willibrord's Northumbria, Frisia was the gateway to Europe. Frisian merchants linked the fast-spending Saxon kings of Britain to the goods of the Rhineland. Precious glasswork, minted silver, even heavy mortars of German stone were exchanged for slaves. Throughout northwestern Europe, Frisian commercial activity brought about the end of a very ancient world. After 670, Merovingian gold coins, greatly reduced but still recognizable echoes of Roman imperial coinage, gave way to silver *sceattas*. These were minted for the use of merchants in a thriving economy now tilted toward the North Sea. Franks and Frisians fought for the control of Dorestad (Duurstede, Holland), an emporium on the Rhine south of Utrecht. Dorestad became one of the great ports of Europe. In 800, its wooden wharves and merchants' houses covered 250 hectares, while a Roman Rhineland city such as Mainz covered no more than 100. Farther north, among the *terpen*—the artificially raised mounds—of modern Gröningen and Friesland, a society of free farmers and merchants enjoyed rare affluence. Well fed, they had livestock to spare. They produced large quantities of valuable, tweed-like cloth. Frisia was a standing rebuttal of the growing Christian conviction that paganism was synonymous with underdevelopment.

Pagan Frisia represented a still undecided "might have been" for the entire North Sea. The Frisian chieftain, Radbod (685–719), established a sub-Frankish state on the borders of Francia. He was a strong ruler with the power to command his chieftains and to hurt his enemies. And he was a pagan. Just because he and his aristocracy had, in many ways, come so close to their Frankish neighbors, it was all the more important for him to assert an essential point of difference. Radbod was careful to maintain the pagan rites which gave so much prosperity to his people and which separated them from the Franks.

The Franks, in turn, were prepared to believe the worst of Radbod. It was rumored in Francia that he had upheld the grim practice of the sacrifice of victims, who were chosen by lot and left to drown in the tide as the great North Sea rose to take them to itself. It was later remembered about Radbod that, when once persuaded to accept baptism by a Frankish bishop, he asked whether the majority of the nobles and kings of Frisia were in Heaven or in Hell. The Frankish bishop's answer was unambiguous: all were in Hell. Wherewith the old king stepped back out of the font. He would rather be in Hell with the great men of his lineage than share Heaven with Christians such as the bishop.

Willibrord was not expected to win over men such as Radbod. Rather, Willibrord acted as a consolidator. When the tide turned in favor of the Franks, Willibrord and his monks set to work, in the re-established city of Utrecht, to "weed out" paganism in zones that had fallen under Frankish rule. "Consolidation," however, meant many things on such a frontier. In 698, Willibrord received from Pippin of Herstal a former Roman fort at Echternach, near Trier, in which to found a monastery. Echternach was not a place set in the wilds. It lay near the site of what had once been a magnificent Roman villa. An ancient Roman road, which ran through the lands of Pippin's family, connected Echternach to Utrecht, some 250 miles away.

Echternach throve. It was, in its way, as much a center of Christianization as was Willibrord's frontier bishopric at Utrecht. The local nobility rallied round. They defined themselves through public acts of giving to Willibrord, recorded in charters that were witnessed by their peers. Willibrord was a holy person, a *vir stremius*, "an active, Apostle-like worshipper of God." He was the favored holy man of Pippin, their own lord. To give to Willibrord was to touch a source of salvation and, at the same time, to join a group of fellow-givers who stood out in their region as loyal to Christianity and to a lordly, Frankish way of life.

The circle revealed by the charters of Echternach is a microcosm of the changes that were affecting the entire region to the north and east of the Frankish heartlands. These men were landowners whose families had, comparatively recently, established themselves in what had once been an inhospitable frontier zone between the Waal and the Maas/Meuse in modern Belgium and Holland. Their ancestors had been quite content to be buried, as chieftains, among their own dependents, in isolated settlements on the land that they themselves had won. They may or may not have been Christians. Those who gave to Willibrord, by contrast, were a new generation. They formed a tight, distinctive group. They were "nobles" in the up-to-date Frankish manner. They were no longer buried with their retainers, but elsewhere, near Christian churches. They had broken with the pre-Christian code that had linked them, as chieftains, to their followers, in death as in life. They were great landowners, and their followers had become mere peasants. They had been greatly enriched by their own lord, Pippin, so they were ostentatiously faithful to Pippin's invisible Lord, the God whom Willibrord served with such Apostolic zeal. It is in these small ways that an open frontier came to be closed, region by region, through the establishment of a new, more tightly organized social system along the edges of the Frankish kingdom.

In 716, Willibrord was joined by an impressive but troubled compatriot from a monastery in southern Britain—a six-foot tall man of forty called Wynfrith. Wynfrith came to be known as Saint Boniface (675–734), the "Apostle of Germany." He had come to the Continent as a man already gripped by passionate loyalty to principles of order. He was a gifted schoolmaster. He had even written a handbook of Latin grammar. This handbook was utterly up-to-date because totally Christian. In grammar, as in all else, so he declared, "the customs of past ages" must he measured by "the correct taste of modern times." For him, the classical past was irrelevant. All the examples of good style that were cited in his handbook were taken from the writings of the Christian Fathers alone. Wynfrith drew on its opening pages a square enclosing a Cross with the name of Jesus Christ. His own heart remained filled with a similar sense of four-square solidity. He stood for a new form of Christianity, unburdened by the past. He was prepared to shed much of his own past and that of others in favor of a well-organized Christian present. On his first visit to Rome, for instance, in 719, he followed the Saxon custom of taking a Roman name, Boniface. But, unlike Benedict Biscop, he abandoned forever his Saxon name. From henceforth, Wynfrith was Boniface and only Boniface.

Yet, although he saw himself as an exile, the churches of southern Britain remained close to Boniface. His extensive correspondence with his supporters in Britain reveals a particularly poignant aspect of his life. He felt bound to his Christian correspondents "through golden chains of friendship made for heaven." Looked at from Anglo-Saxon Britain, Boniface summed up the hopes of an entire generation, frustrated by the very success of their own, less heroic Christianity. For Anglo-Saxon bishops, monks, and nuns in Britain, it was good to think of Boniface. His letters to noble nuns are moving to read. Less free to follow a man's stern road to exile, they looked to him as a distant, comforting *abbas*, even as a surrogate brother.

Boniface reminded the Saxons of Britain, on one occasion, that the Old Saxons claimed to be kin to them: "we are of the same blood and bone." Indeed, his view of his own mission was deeply influenced by ideas which many Anglo-Saxon clergymen had come to share with the Venerable Bede. As we have seen, as Bede presented it in his memorable *Ecclesiastical History* (which appeared in 731), conversion to Christianity had made the Anglo-Saxons special and had turned Britain into their Promised Land. As an Anglo-Saxon, Boniface intended to re-enact among the Germans the triumphal coming of Christianity to the Anglo-Saxons of Britain. Not everyone agreed with such claims. But, at least, it was agreed in Britain that Boniface lived a heroic, "apostolic" life in a heroic environment. Even a king of Kent wrote to him for a gift of falcons: for he had heard that falcons were "much swifter and more aggressive" in Saxony!

Boniface's lifelong friend, bishop Daniel of Winchester, soon plied him with advice as to how to argue with pagans. He must not do so "in an offensive and irritating manner, but calmly and with great moderation." Among other arguments, he should point out that

whilst the Christians are allowed to possess the countries that are rich in oil and wine and other commodities [the gods] have left to the heathens only the frozen lands of the North . . . [They were] frequently to be reminded of the supremacy of the Christian world.

Boniface was protected by Charles Martel. Later, in the 740s, he was called upon by Charles' son, Pippin, the future king of the Franks, to act as a "troubleshooter" and reformer in the Frankish church. But he also went out of his way to receive from the popes (between 722 and 739) a series of ever-widening commissions to act as a missionary bishop and supervisor of new churches throughout Germany. In presenting himself as a special servant of the popes, Boniface, once again, was influenced by his own distinctively Anglo-Saxon view of history. He was convinced that the Church in England had been founded through the mission sent from Rome to Canterbury by Gregory the Great. Had this not happened, the English, he believed, might still have been heathen. It was only proper, therefore, that he should turn to the successors of Gregory in order to validate his own mission to the heathen.

In the course of thirty years, Boniface came to leave his mark throughout western Germany, from Bavaria to the watershed of the Lahn and the Weser, beyond which stretched the territories of the unconverted Old Saxons. He always presented himself as having brought light and order to a wild country. But Boniface's letters are so fascinating because they reveal the opposite. They show how little Germany, in fact, resembled the virgin heathen lands which the Anglo-Saxon myth of the missionary had led him to expect. Christianity already had a long and complicated history in central Europe. But that was not how Boniface and those who supported him saw the matter. Thus, when he founded his monastery at Fulda, in 744, he reported to the pope that the monastery lay "in a wooded place, in the midst of a vast wilderness." That was what Romans expected to be told. Fulda, in fact, lay on the main prehistoric trackway that crossed central Germany from east to west. It had been a Merovingian fort. A deserted church was already present on the site. It was far from being lost in the woods in a land untouched by Christianity.

Altogether, nothing in Germany was quite what it seemed. Boniface had been sent, in the words of the pope, "for the enlightenment of the German people who live in the shadow of death, steeped in error." What he found, instead, was much Christianity, and almost all of it the wrong sort. Cultic practitioners exchanged rituals. Pagans baptized Christians. Christian priests sacrificed to Thunor, ate sacrificial meats, and presided at the sacral funerary banquets of their Christian parishioners. Theirs was an oral Christianity, which mangled essential Latin formulae. A Bavarian priest performed his baptisms In nomine Patria et Filia. He had confused both case and gender. Boniface doubted that such a baptism was valid. In Hesse and Thuringia, local chieftains were anxious to please the Franks. But they knew the limits of their powers over their followers. They could not bully them to accept Christianity. They had learned to coexist with pagans. It was not to convert a totally pagan population but, rather, to end an age of symbiosis between pagans and Christians that Boniface decided, in 723/4, to cut down the mighty Oak of Thunor at Geismar. This oak had stood at a joining point between half-Christian Hesse and the pagan Saxons. It may well have been visited by Christians as well as by pagans. He was careful to use its holy timbers to build an oratory of Saint Peter, which would serve as a Christian place of pilgrimage on the same spot.

More disturbing yet, for Boniface, were Christian rivals—clerical entrepreneurs who had moved into the new territories from Ireland and Francia. He met these particularly in Bavaria, between 735 and 737 and again in

739–740. Despite Boniface's coldness toward them, many such clergymen were far from being mere adventurers. In Bavaria, they represented a previous missionary establishment, set up largely by Irish "exiles of God," whose methods had proved quite as effective, in southern Germany, as they had been in northern Britain at an earlier time. Vergil, abbot and later bishop of Salzburg (745–784) had once been Ferghil, abbot of Aghaboe (County Laois, Ireland). He was as much a zealous "Roman" stranger as was Boniface. A man of combative esoteric learning, Vergil shocked Boniface by preaching that "there is below the earth another world and other men." The bishop's opinion blended classical speculation on the Antipodes with Irish belief in the world of "the Other Side," a fairy counter-kingdom which flanked the human race. It was a notion calculated to frustrate the efforts of a man such as Boniface. He had striven hard enough to bring Christianity to all the nations already known to him. It was dispiriting to be told that there were yet others, as yet unbaptized, on the far side of the earth. Yet bishop Vergil also had the ear of the pope. He was able to intervene successfully with the pope to protect the poor priest who had muddled the Latin of his baptismal formula. The pope told Boniface, sharply, that mere lack of grammatical precision did not invalidate a Christian sacrament.

Far more dangerous than rival bishops were those who, in Francia and Germany, threatened to create their own idiosyncratic version of a Christian mission. They did so from elements long associated with a dramatic style of "frontier" Christianity. In 745, at a Roman synod, Boniface secured the condemnation as heretics of Clement, an Irishman, and Aldebert, a Frank. Clement and Aldebert stood for very different Christian options from those upheld by Boniface. They offered very different solutions from his own to contemporary problems.

Take, for example, the views of Clement on the prohibited degrees of marriage. The nature of restrictions on marriage partners was a particularly charged topic at the time among the Franks and in Germany. It was a concern driven by a strong sense of the need to avoid incest in a society based on family solidarity and on complicated family alliances. Clement had his own solution. He supported the marriage of the widow to the dead man's brother (a practice abhorrent to Boniface) precisely because it was a practice that was found in the Old Testament. As an Irishman, he did this in the same spirit as that shown by the lawyers of the Senchas Mar. As we saw in chapter 14, Irish lawyers had appealed to the Old Testament to justify pre-Christian marital practices.

In using the Old Testament in this way, Clement closed the chasm which threatened to open between the non-Christian past and the Christian present of the newly converted populations. He even reassured his flock that Christ had taken out of Hell the souls of all humanity, of all past ages: "believers and unbelievers, those who praised god and those who worshipped idols." This was not at all what king Radbod had been told!

Aldebert was an even greater challenge than was Clement to a man such as Boniface. For Aldebert represented an older strain of Christianity—the Christianity of the charismatic holy men who had brought the faith to so many regions of western Europe and the Mediterranean. Aldebert was born of simple parents. He wrote of himself as a bishop "by the grace of God": so had the eccentric Patricius. His mother had dreamed of a calf emerging from her side: the mother of Columbanus had "seen the sun rise from her bosom." Aldebert, like Boniface, claimed to have received authority direct from Rome. He claimed to know the contents of a letter dropped by Jesus Christ himself from Heaven, that now lay on the tomb of Saint Peter.

Thus authorized by Jesus and by Saint Peter, Aldebert created his own Christian mission. He was said to have considered pilgrimage to Rome unnecessary. He himself was a living relic. Any place where he preached was as much a self-sufficient Christian "microcosm" as was any other. He set up chapels and crosses in the fields and at springs. In the absence of country churches, Anglo-Saxon landowners in Britain had done the same, by setting up just such crosses on their estates. Above all, Aldebert offered instant penance. There was no need to tell him one's sins through confession. He already knew them all. Preaching in the hills around Melrose, Saint Cuthbert had inspired almost the same awe: the villagers confessed to him because they were convinced, by his mere appearance, that he already knew what they had done. Boniface made himself unpopular by securing Aldebert's condemnation. He had taken away from the people of Francia "a most holy Apostle, a patron saint, a man of prayer, a worker of miracles."

We do not know how widespread Aldebert's preaching had been. But the terms of his condemnation, taken together with the manner in which Boniface had set about his own mission and the way in which his example was remembered by successors, hints at a lively debate on how the process of Christianization was to be continued and who could best act as representatives of the new faith.

In many ways, the erratic Aldebert stood for one vivid strand in a very ancient Christianity. As a wandering holy man, he stood closer to Saint Martin of Tours and to Saint Cuthbert than to the new clerical elite gathered around a man such as Boniface. Boniface, by contrast, was not a charismatic figure. Rather, he radiated "correct" ecclesiastical order. His task turned out to be less to convert the heathen than to clear up anomalies and to put an end to long habits of compromise. He had brought from the "micro-Christendom" of Saxon Britain a blueprint of "correct" Christianity which he was quite prepared to impose on the ancient Christianity of Continental Europe.

Boniface soon learned that, judged by his high standards, Gaul and Italy were no less prone to "barbaric lack of order" than were the supposedly wild woods of Germany. In 743, he wrote to pope Zacharias. He had been told by pilgrims who had visited Rome from Germany that the Kalends of January were still celebrated there:

> in the neighborhood of Saint Peter's church by day and by night, they have seen bands of singers parade the streets in pagan fashion . . . They say that they have also seen there women with amulets and bracelets of heathen fashion on their arms and legs, offering these for sale to willing purchasers.

If "ignorant common people" from the north saw such unabashed, ancient profanity in the very center of Christendom, they could hardly be expected to pay heed to the strictures of their priests at home. It is a characteristic letter. Over the years, the "depaganization" of Christians had come to interest Boniface as much as did the conversion of pagans.

Boniface wrote this letter when he had become a major figure within the Frankish kingdom itself. After 742, the pope had authorized him to act as the privileged counsellor of Pippin and of other "rulers of the Franks," in summoning councils to effect a reform of the Frankish Church. Boniface's position among the Franks was unprecedented, but his powers were ambiguous. He was not popular. Frankish bishops had their own firm views on how best to set up a Christian order.

In northern Francia and in the Rhineland, Boniface was by no means the hero of his generation. He faced determined opposition from bishops who regarded him as an interloper. He returned their scorn with a vengeance. Many Frankish bishops struck him as standing for all that he had left Britain to escape. They were aristocrats. They believed that a man must hunt; and that a man of honor, even a bishop, must, of course, kill with his own hands the killer of his father (the father being also, of course, a bishop!). It hurt Boniface to mix with such people at court, and to share Frankish good cheer with them at Pippin's great feasts. But he had no option. He wrote to his friend Daniel:

> Without the patronage of the Frankish prince I can neither govern the faithful . . . nor protect the priests . . . nor can I forbid the practice of heathen rites and the worship of idols in Germany without his orders and the fear he inspires.

Altogether, correct order was hard to find in Francia. Even books were written in a crabbed hand, which strained his failing eyesight. He remembered a copy of the Old Testament prophets which had been used by his teacher in Britain. "I am asking for this particular book because all the letters in it are written out clearly and separately." By now a blind old man, Daniel replied by ordering the transcription of long passages from Saint Augustine on the need for patience when living with evil men. Written in North Africa, almost four centuries before, now copied by an Anglo-Saxon in Winchester for an Anglo-Saxon working in central Germany, these were what a friend could offer, "culled from the works of ancient scholars, things useful to bear in mind in the midst of so much barbaric lack of order."

Altogether, the Franks had been a disappointment to Boniface. Only the new-won lands gave the missionary in Boniface the opportunities for which he craved. Now an old man in his late seventies, Boniface turned back to the far north. He went on a tour of the mission fields in a Frisia barely pacified by Frankish armies. On June 5, 754, his entourage reached Dokkum, on the edge of the North Sea. With its liturgical paraphernalia and great chests of books, Boniface's progress through Frisia was, as he always intended it to be, a splendid sight, designed "to impress the carnal minds of the heathen." Almost by accident, the great man became a martyr. A band of pirates—hard sea-rovers, not indignant pagans—fell on his party. In the great ironbound treasure chests, which every nobleman carried with him when travelling, they did not find gold, as they had hoped. Rather, they found the heart of Boniface's sense of order. They found texts.

> Disappointed in their hope of gold and silver, they littered the fields with books . . . throwing some into the reedy marshes . . . By the grace of God, the manuscripts were discovered a long time afterwards, unharmed and intact.

In the Episcopal Seminary at Fulda we can still see one of these books. It is a thoroughly ordinary manual. It contains an anthology of Patristic texts, partly concerned with the Arian controversy—that is, with a theological controversy which had happened four centuries previously, far to the south in the Mediterranean, when there was still a Roman empire in western Europe. It was an unpretentious volume, one of the many strictly functional books from which Boniface hoped to build a Christian order on the shores of the North Sea. It has violent cuts across the margins. It may well be the book which Boniface raised, instinctively, above his head, as the pirate's sword descended.

Boniface had died as a martyr. But he had lived very much as a schoolteacher, bringing order and instruction to untidy lands. It is not that the conversion of Germany was without drama. We can glimpse a small part of the process in a later account of the life of an Anglo-Saxon nun, Leoba. Leoba was a kinswoman of Boniface. She and other nuns had been taken by Boniface from Wimborne in Dorset, and placed in Tauberbischofsheim, southwest of Wurzburg. The little community of foreign women did not find themselves among pagans. Instead, they faced a local population which was anxious to have an enclave of "holy" virgins in their midst. They turned hostile only when this reputation for holiness seemed to have been sullied. A crippled girl, who had lived from the food given as alms by the nuns at the convent gate, drowned her illegitimate baby in the nuns' millpond. The villagers were appalled. They claimed that the nuns, these so-called virgin mothers, had disposed of their love-child in the very water which they used both to baptize the villagers and to drive their mill. By so doing, they had polluted the water of the village. Only days of dramatic penitential processions could reassure the villagers that the nuns were "pure" of guilt. The convent was to be a "sacred" place. Only then could it act as a power-house of prayer and a place of atonement. Far from being indifferent to Christianity, the people of the region had been enraged when it appeared that the holiness which they wanted from a convent had been desecrated by the sins of a nun.

Slowly, after proving that it was indeed a "sacred" place, the convent at Tauberbischofsheim gained support.

> Many nobles and influential men gave their daughters to God to live in the monastery . . . Many widows also forsook their homes . . . and took the veil in the cloister.

Tauberbischofsheim was another link in a Christian network, similar to those formed around the convents and monasteries of Ireland, Britain, and northern Gaul in the days of Columbanus and Bede. It was a smaller version of Willibrord's Echternach. These little nodules of local support for places endowed with an aura of the supernatural, such as Leoba's convent, brought about the "grassroots" conversion of Germany more effectively than did the high ecclesiastical policies associated with the leading missionaries.

Apart from these accounts, however, the supernatural was strangely distant in Boniface's world. What he and his followers considered themselves to have brought, rather, was the miracle of preaching and of "correct" instruction. It is revealing to see the extent to which Boniface and those around him linked up, across two centuries, with the tradition represented by Caesarius of Arles. After a long period of neglect, Caesarius' works came to be copied again in Frankish circles. They were copied in women's monasteries in the Rhineland and instantly put to use in Germany. As we have seen, Caesarius had been a tireless preacher and critic of local semi-pagan customs. He had not been a wonder-worker. Caesarius was a significant model for a missionary to have chosen.

In 743, an *Index of Superstitions and Pagan Practices* was drawn up, in connection with Frankish councils over which Boniface had presided. The list shows practices very different from those of the Mediterranean peasantry, which Caesarius had denounced when he preached at Arles. They mention, for instance, the *nodfyr*, the "fire of need." This was fire created anew by rubbing wood, with all other fires extinguished, so as to fortify the powers of the land against cattle-plague. The *nodfyr* was still lit in Marburg in the seventeenth century. As late as 1767, it was used in the once Scandinavian western Isles of Scotland.

These details hint at a sacred landscape of which Caesarius had never dreamed. But the attitude which brought such a list together was significantly similar to that of Caesarius. The document declared, in effect, that paganism, as such, had ceased to exist. All that the bishops had to deal with, now, were "survivals," "superstitions," *paganiae*, "pagan leftovers." The continued existence of such practices merely showed the ignorance and the stubborn attachment to old habits of an unenlightened Christian people. Such people were "rustic" in the true sense of the word. They were undereducated Christians. They were not pagans. In speaking of popular practices in a tone similar to that once used by Caesarius, the *Index of Superstitions* declared that the ancient gods of Germany were already safely dead. The "superstitious" practices of "rustic" believers were no more than lack of instruction. They did not betray the continued, uncanny presence of the old gods.

It is worthwhile to linger a little on the implications of this attitude. It shows that, in this as in so much else, the eighth century marked a significant change in the mental horizons of the elite of the Christian Church. Christianization was no longer perceived as taking the form of an outright clash of supernatural powers. As we saw in chapters 2 and 3, this had been the principal element in all narratives of the triumph of Christianity. But in the eighth century, victory over the gods could be taken for granted. That victory lay in the past. The real task of the Church, therefore, was a *mission civilisatrice*. Education was as important as miracles.

In this, the revival of the preaching texts of Caesarius of Arles was decisive. It ensured that forms of religious instruction which had once been brought to bear on sophisticated urban populations in the late Roman Mediterranean—in the Hippo and Carthage of Augustine and in the Arles of Caesarius—were now applied in central Europe to the populations of an overwhelmingly rural society, gathered around monasteries and served by parish priests.

From Bavaria to Frisia, the generation of Boniface and of his successors was characterized by a plethora of little books. These are neat books, copied in a business-like manner and meant to be carried and consulted. Books of penance were carefully kept up to date to do justice to the prevalent sins and misdemeanors of the various regions in which they were used. We can even guess which one was used by Willibrord among the Frisians, while others were meant for different regions. Books of rituals were equally important. They provided the correct form of words for the administration of Christian sacraments. Some of these even contain the first, hesitant translations into German of the Lord's Prayer and of the convert's baptismal oath that promised to renounce the gods. Most moving of all, in many ways, were collections of sayings culled from all over Christendom. They were brought together in little volumes, so as to create a new Christian "wisdom literature." An almost folkloristic, gnomic lore, more like riddle collections than the encyclopedic anthologies of the seventh century, circulated in Latin among the clergy of Bavaria and other regions.

These books are all well worn. They had been frequently used. When we see them in modern library collections they are, in their own way, as moving as the compact, slashed volume associated with the death of Boniface. For we are looking at the humble tools which passed the message of Christianity, from the great centers of Ireland, Britain, and the Frankish kingdom to networks of monks and priests working in new lands.

For such people, the missionary was no longer the wonder-working, itinerant holy man. He or she (for the convents played a crucial role in the quiet elaboration and distribution of orderly bodies of information) was increasingly perceived as, first and foremost, a teacher. When Huneberc, an Anglo-Saxon nun, wished to sum up the life of her kinsman, Willibald, the first bishop of Eichstatt (whom, surprisingly enough, we have already met, at the end of chapter 13, as a pilgrim wandering through the Holy Land in the first century of Muslim rule—such was the range of these religious exiles!), she chose a loaded phrase. Willibald had been the *populi paedagogits*, the Educator of the Christian people. It was a suitable ideal for a world reduced to order. Whether it came in the form of newly founded bishoprics and monasteries, which cast a net of Christian books and Christian teachers over the new territories, or in the form of an agrarian system based upon a greater measure of control over the lives of the peasantry, by the middle of the eighth century Christianity and order had begun to come in earnest, and hand in hand, to Germany.

THE DEVELOPMENT OF CHRISTENDOM

PART TWO

THE DEVELOPMENT OF CHRISTENDOM

The emergence of a recognizable European culture, at least among intellectual and political elites, and the important role of Christianity in shaping the identity of that culture between the ninth and the twelfth centuries, create new problems for historians. Both secular and clerical elites saw themselves as part of a uniquely Christian society. Nevertheless, it is not at all clear that the warrior nobility and professional clergy had the same idea of Christendom in mind. Moreover, what happens to those who do not fit into the dominant cultural paradigms of either group? This section explores the nature and implications of medieval Christendom.

An obvious place to pick up our story is with the Franks. Although Clovis' Merovingian family was deposed in favor of the Carolingians, the kingdom of the Franks continued to play an ever-growing role in the development of Christian culture throughout Western and Central Europe. The Carolingians took power with the blessing and encouragement of the pope, solidifying the ties between the papacy and the Franks. At the beginning of the ninth century, the rise of the Franks culminated in the empire of Charlemagne, whose territories included all of modern-day France, Germany, and the Low Countries, as well as the northern parts of the Italian and Balkan peninsulas. Defeat at the hands of the Carolingians meant the adoption of Christianity. While the initial conversion of conquered peoples like the Saxons was certainly not a matter of the heart, the Carolingians supported the efforts of missionaries to create a Christian culture among their new subjects. Charlemagne was genuinely concerned with the quality of Christianity in his vast realm. While he lacked the infrastructure to effect direct change among the peasant majority, he expended considerable time and energy reforming and improving the formal church. On the practical level, he issued decrees to standardize worship and more uniformly regulate the lives of monks. He was the patron of an intellectual revival devoted to the recovery, preservation, and interpretation of classic literature, especially the Christian scriptures and writings of the church fathers. Beyond recovering the past, Carolingian courts were the scene of the most creative theological discussions since the late Roman Empire. Most importantly, Charlemagne saw himself as a Christian leader. The Frankish monarchy had long identified itself as the new Israel, with its kings anointed like Old Testament monarchs. Charlemagne saw himself as a new David, the greatest Old Testament monarch, chosen by God to rule over His people, responsible for their spiritual wellbeing. Charlemagne also revived the idea of Rome in Western Europe, when he was crowned emperor of the Romans in 800 by the pope. However, he was not reviving the splendor of pagan Rome under Hadrian or Trajan; rather, he emulated the Christian emperors of the late Roman Empire. Charlemagne did not achieve his vision. His empire collapsed in the midst of civil war and outside invasions. Nevertheless, eleventh- and twelfth-century kings and nobles would appropriate his vision of a Christendom governed by a warrior-king and his noble companions.

The relationship between Christian institutions and the newly christianized warrior elites changed in the intervening centuries as well. As part of the christianization process, church leaders had encouraged the aristocracy, particularly the kings, to see themselves as protectors of the faith. In so doing, popes and other bishops came to depend on the support of the warriors who protected them and helped spread the faith. This situation became acute when Frankish hegemony collapsed. Power devolved to regional and even local landlords, who treated churches and monasteries as part of their personal property, appointing the priests and abbots. Powerful regional dynasties controlled the appointment of bishops, even the bishop of Rome.

Beginning in the late tenth century, church reformers sought independence from secular interference. Initially, several monasteries were founded by nobles who relinquished influence over them. The most important of these was Cluny in Burgundy, now southern France. Monasteries founded on the model of Cluny quickly spread through Western Europe. By the middle of the eleventh century, monks raised on Cluniac ideals came to dominate the church in Rome, with several elected to the papacy. Once in positions of power, they made Cluniac ideals the basis for a churchwide reform movement. Although several popes and many bishops were behind the movement,

it is usually called the Gregorian Reform, after the most famous of the reformers, Pope Gregory VII. The reformers had a sweeping vision. Eliminat-
ing secular interference from ecclesiastical appointments was only the beginning. The reformers envisioned the pope governing a Europe chiefly defined
by its Christian religion. This was revolutionary on two levels. By claiming
the preeminence of eccliastical authority over political power, the reformers
were reversing a two-century trend. By asserting the authority of the pope
over other bishops, they were changing the balance of power within the
church. With this new power, the reformers wished to regulate the beliefs
and behaviors of all Christians in Europe, starting with the elite. Bishops,
monks, and priests were held to stringent moral and professional standards.
Not only were the kings and aristocrats supposed to be publicly Christian and
acknowledge the superiority of church leaders, the reformers expected them
to be genuine, committed Christians.

The goal of the Gregorian Reform was to create a certain type of Christian culture in Western Europe, an entire society modeled on Cluniac monasticism. The breadth of the reformer's success is easy to assess from the surviving evidence, and all current histories of medieval Christianity describe it
at length. The popes and other church leaders who led the Gregorian Reform
left a wealth of written evidence. Correspondence, papal decrees, agreements
with various kings, sermons, theological treatises, and administrative reports
allow scholars to follow the progress, and occasional setbacks, of the reform
in minute detail. We know the thoughts and feelings of the important reformers. We also have the reactions of important figures who opposed the reformers, such as the German emperor and certain powerful bishops. Some
important compromises notwithstanding, the reformers achieved a surprisingly large number of their goals. The depth of their success is more difficult
to ascertain. While the evidence is too thin to draw any solid conclusions as
to how much immediate impact the reformers had on the average European,
there is tantalizing, ambiguous evidence concerning the relationship between the aristocracy and the clerical elite in this period. Because priests or
monks produced almost all the documents surviving from this era, we cannot
read the evidence at face value. The reformers were intent on freeing church
institutions from lay control. They saw secular influence as corrupting and
portrayed the warrior aristocracy, especially the kings, as the enemy. In the
last several decades, however, scholars have begun to reassess the reality of
religious culture among the secular elite.

The Crusades provide an excellent case study concerning the religious
beliefs of the nobility in comparison to the reformers. The First Crusade
arose out of a sermon given by Pope Urban II in the southern French town

of Clermont in 1095. The Christian Byzantine emperor had sent a letter to Urban requesting Frankish mercenaries to help defend the eastern Mediterranean against Muslim Turkish invaders. Instead, Urban called for something like an armed pilgrimage. Scholars have long debated Urban's motives. A former prior of Cluny and Gregory VII's most trusted aide, Urban was an ardent reformer. Most likely, he saw the letter from the Byzantine emperor as a tool for furthering the reform agenda. Papal representatives, providing a model for church leadership over the secular nobility, would lead the Crusade. A larger goal may have been a reunion of Greek and Roman Christians with the pope as the leading figure. Urban and the European royalty certainly saw the call for the First Crusade as part of the reform movement. Urban preached the Crusade in southern France, near the heart of Cluniac monasticism and outside the practical reach of either the French king or German emperor. In addition, no European king participated in the papal-led venture.

Many very powerful aristocrats, however, did respond to Urban's speech. The count of Toulouse, the duke of Lorraine, and the French king's brother led a huge army of French and German warriors. Why did they go? Did their response to papal urgings show the success of the reformers in changing the religious and political culture of Europe? Or were they merely using Urban's speech as an excuse for taking their vicious, predatory behaviors on tour? Both by rereading traditional sources and expanding the range of sources, many scholars have attempted to answer these questions. The first selection in this chapter argues that there were two competing elite Christianities with a clerical elite of bishops, priests, and monks attempting to tame and control a secular, political elite whose Christianity had been compromised by the demands of dynastic competition and the feudal warrior ethos. Important new studies of the nobility in various regions have questioned this assertion and have revealed that many in the military elite were closely allied with the clerical elite. The second selection explains that the nobility of Burgundy, for example, were not only strong supporters of the clerical elite, but were often in the vanguard of religious reform. Focusing on the crusaders themselves, the third selection claims that they were motivated primarily by piety, and only secondarily, when at all, by the material and dynastic benefits of conquest.

What about those people living in Europe who did not fit into this new Christendom? In the final two selections of this section, we will look at two groups who found themselves increasingly marginalized by the end of the eleventh century. Both the clerical and secular elite in the Middle Ages were male dominated. The religious reformers, in particular, were overtly misogynist. The advocates of the Gregorian Reform had imbibed strict monastic values concerning sex. They saw sexual relations, and thus women, as sinful and unclean. The reformers envisioned a male Christendom, led by celibate clergy and celebrating those lay people who abstained from sexual relationships. Even so, our fourth selection describes how wealthy women could retain influence in this Christian culture through the patronage of religious texts. While the clerical and secular elite may have had disagreements over the details, both groups increasingly saw themselves living in a society chiefly defined by Christian belief and practice. The first Crusade was directed against Muslim Turks, but many crusaders participated in violent persecutions and massacres of European Jews on their way to Jerusalem. The final selection analyzes the impact of christianization on the Jewish communities that were a prominent part of the fabric of European society at that time.

Further Reading

Bartlett, Robert. *The Making of Europe*, Princeton, NJ: Princeton University Press, 1993.

Bull, Marcus. *Knightly Piety and the Lay Response to the First Crusade*, Oxford: Clarendon Press, 1993.

Bouchard, Constance Brittain. *Sword, Mitre, and Cloister: Nobility and the Church in Burgundy, 980–1198*, Ithaca: Cornell University Press, 1987.

Cohen, Mark R. *Under Crescent and Cross: The Jews in the Middle Ages*, Princeton, NJ: Princeton University Press, 1994.

Cowdrey, H. E. J. *Pope Gregory VII*, Oxford: Oxford University Press, 1998.

———. *The Cluniacs and Gregorian Reform*, Oxford: Oxford University Press, 1970.

Housely, Norman. *Contesting the Crusades*, London: Balckwell, 2006.

Lawrence, C. H. *Medieval Monasticism*, 3rd ed., London: Pearson Education, 2001.

Moore, R. I. *The First European Revolution: The Making of Europe*, London: Blackwell, 2001.

———. *The Formation of a Persecuting Society*, London: Blackwell, 1987.

Riley-Smith, Jonathan. *The First Crusade and the Idea of Crusading*, London: Athlone Press, 1986.

CHAPTER EIGHT

~

The Knight, the Lady, and the Priest: The Making of Modern Marriage in Medieval France*

Georges Duby

*The eminent French medievalist Georges Duby has devoted his professional life to uncovering the cultural attitudes (*mentalités*) of the French nobility during the tenth through twelfth centuries. Through numerous books, Duby has painted a picture of a self-consciously Christian secular elite, who, nevertheless, resisted the influence of their clerical counterparts. The Gregorian Reforms only exacerbated this situation, according to Duby. One of the chief concerns of the reformers was sexual purity. They demanded celibacy from the clergy and encouraged it among the laity. Since marriage was the norm among the laity, the reformers sought to regulate and sacralize the institution. "Church weddings" are common today, even for those who would not otherwise enter a church. Before the twelfth century, the church had little to do with marriage. Powerful families arranged the marriages of their offspring for political advantage and priests were only marginally involved in the wedding ceremony. Peasant villagers merely set up house together without needing external sanctions. As part of regulating the sexual morals of the laity, the reformers advocated a more intentionally Christian conception of marriage. When the French king Philip I imprisoned his first wife and married another women, Pope Urban II and the reforming bishops of France decided to make an example of him. In the same speech at Clermont in 1095 in which Urban called for the First Crusade he excommunicated Philip for bigamy and incest. Duby uses this incident to*

* © 1983 by Barbara Bray. Introduction © 1983 by Natalie Zemon Davis. Used by permission of Pantheon Books, a division of Random House, Inc. Georges Duby, *The Knight, the Lady, and the Priest: The Making of Modern Marriage in Medieval France,* trans. by Barbara Bray, Chicago: The University of Chicago Press, 1983, pp. 7–10, 15–18.

highlight the differing cultural assumptions of the nobility and the reforming clergy.
According to Duby, what are the limitations of his inquiry into this event? What
does Duby mean when he says that Philip did not think he had done anything wrong
by taking another wife?

Philip I was just as concerned about his own salvation and just as afraid of sin-
ning as anybody else. But his beliefs about right and wrong were different from
those that the reforming clerics were trying to impose. He thought differently
from them about marriage. And he was sure he was guilty of no wrongdoing.

Philip had married Berthe de Frise when he was twenty. His first cousin,
the count of Flanders, had given him her hand: she was his wife's daughter
by a previous marriage. This arranged marriage set the seal on a reconciliation between the king and his vassal and father-in-law.

For nine years Berthe remained barren. But she prayed, and at last a son
was born: Louis, later Louis VI. Heaven had answered the entreaties of
Arnoul, a reputedly holy hermit of Saint-Médard de Soissons whom people
came from far and near to consult on family problems. Arnoul, who like
Berthe was from Flanders, had interceded for her lest she be sent away for not
producing an heir. But despite the birth of Louis, Berthe was repudiated,
though not until 1092, twenty years after her marriage. Her husband then installed, or rather imprisoned, her in the chateau of Montreuil-sur-Mer. This
fortress was part of her dower, i.e., the settlement made by the husband on
the wife when they exchanged vows, and which came in handy if he wanted
to get rid of her later: he could leave her in possession of the property but
keep her sequestered there.

Having thus disposed of Berthe, the king took up with Bertrade, who belonged to the Montfort family and was married to the count of Anjou.

Did Philip seduce Bertrade or she him? Did he take her by force or did she
come to him? Or—and this seems most likely—did he have an arrangement
with her husband?

And what did what we call love have to do with it all? I must say at once
and emphatically that we do not know, and no one ever will. We are almost
entirely ignorant about the men and women who lived in France nearly a
thousand years ago: their mental imagery, how they spoke and wore their
clothes, their feelings about their own bodies. We do not even know what
they looked like.

What was it about Bertrade that attracted Philip? What was the nature of
his desire? We can guess at the answer to such questions in the case of
Charles VI and of his uncle the duke of Berry at the end of the fourteenth
century. But the paintings and sculptures that survive from three hundred

years earlier give us no female form to contemplate except the stylized image of the Virgin Mary, a symbol or theological argument rather than a woman. Apart from this there remain only the lurid, frenzied, broken puppets representing the damned, which priests made use of in their sermons to illustrate the fate awaiting the lustful.

So my investigation of marriage during this period is necessarily restricted to what was on the surface both of society and of institutions; to facts and to events. About the passions that moved body or spirit I can say nothing.

Philip's remarriage caused a sensation, as can be seen from the allusions to it in the few written records that survive. The best chroniclers of northern France—Clarius of Sens, Hugues of Flavigny, Sigebert of Gembloux—all bore witness to ceremonies as solemn and holy as for a real marriage. The lord of Beaugency, issuing a document at that time, did not date it, as was the custom, in terms of the birth of Christ or of the reign of the ruling sovereign; he dated it "the year when Philip took to wife Bertrade, wife of Fouque, count of Anjou." So people were surprised. But there was no sign of disapproval. It would all probably have passed off quite peacefully had it not been for the reformers. Had it not been for Yves, bishop of Chartres.

Yves was fifty years old and had just managed, not without difficulty, to establish himself on his episcopal throne. He replaced one of the prelates dismissed by Urban II in his purge of the superior clergy. The Roman Curia's interference in local affairs had shocked many clerics, including the metropolitan archbishop of Sens, who refused to ordain the new bishop of Chartres. So Yves got himself ordained in Capua by Urban II himself. This was taken to be an infringement of the powers of the king, and in 1091 the interloper was deposed by a synod. But Yves held out, relying on legates and on the Holy Father himself, insisting on the supremacy of papal decisions. Brought up as a rigorist, Yves was already inclined to sympathize with the reformers, and his present difficulties threw him into their camp. He joined them in their confrontation with the old school of prelates, his allegedly simoniac and Nicolaist colleagues, and with their accomplice the king. The see of Chartres became an outpost in the struggle, a wedge driven into the traditional structures of the royalist Church.

Philip's second marriage provided Yves with a good opportunity to launch an attack. The king, wishing the wedding to be an impressive occasion, summoned all the bishops to be present. But the bishop of Chartres declined the invitation, and tried to persuade others to do the same. He argued, in opposition to his enemy the archbishop of Sens, that it was the archbishop of Reims who had the right not only to crown the kings of France but also to consecrate their marriages. He wrote to the archbishop of Reims that he would not go to the wedding "unless you yourself celebrate and perform it, with your suffragans assisting and cooperating." But he also gave a warning: "This is a dangerous matter. It could do great harm both to your reputation and to the honor of the realm." Moreover, "Other and secret reasons of which I may not speak at present prevent me from approving this marriage." He addressed another, more outspoken letter to Philip himself: "You will not see me in Paris, with your wife of whom I know not if she may be your wife." The wording is important. Men like Yves were skilled in rhetoric and practiced manipulators of language. When he used the word *uxor*, Yves was recognizing that Philip and Bertrade were already husband and wife: for him the nuptial ceremony was merely an additional celebration. "I shall not come," he went on, "until I know if a general council has found that you and your spouse are legitimately divorced, and that you and her you wish to wed may legitimately be married."

What Yves was saying here was that only churchmen were competent in such matters, that the authority of bishops was subordinate to that of councils, and that the matter in question turned on two separate issues. Did Philip have the right to repudiate his first wife?—a question that carried an imputation of bigamy. And had he the right to marry the second?—a query that raised the issue of incest. And until the matter had been cleared up there could be no marriage, only concubinage. But was it decent for a king to live in that state? Yves insisted on this point in order to justify his not going to the wedding. He was not failing in his duty; on the contrary. On the temporal plane he was acting as a loyal counselor when he declared this marriage to be detrimental to the crown. On the spiritual plane he was acting as a vigilant director of conscience when he declared it to be detrimental to the king's salvation. The letter ended with a little sermon on lust, illustrated by Adam, Samson, and Solomon, all of whom were ruined by women.

Philip took no notice. The union was celebrated in due form and blessed by the bishop of Senlis in the presence of all the bishops in the royal domain. The archbishop of Reims had given his approval, and so apparently had Cardinal Roger, papal legate to the north of France. But Yves persisted. He assembled a file on how to "bring about a divorce between Philip and his new wife." He sent it to the pope, who replied with letters and a circular to the prelates of France forbidding them to crown Bertrade queen. There was also a reprimand to the archbishop of Reims and a warning to the king. If he did not cease all relations with the woman he had "by way of wife," he would be excommunicated.

The bishop of Chartres had already decided to break with the king. He withheld vassal service and did not bring his knights to the great assembly at which the king arbitrated a quarrel between the sons of William the Conqueror. This made him guilty of a felony, and he fled. By the end of 1093 he was to be found among the retinue of the pope. At this point the whole matter might have been smoothed over, for Berthe died, and so Philip was no longer committing bigamy. But we must not forget that Philip was anxious about the salvation of his soul. It is more uncomfortable for a king than for an ordinary man to be told he is living in sin. Philip gathered together in Reims as many prelates as he could—two archbishops and eight bishops. They all confirmed the royal marriage. They went further and talked of trying Yves of Chartres. The Council of Autun was the answer.

The excommunication of the king of France was a very serious matter, but it was part of an overall plan: the Roman Curia's all-out offensive aimed at carrying through the reform. The pope was to tour southern Gaul, but to win the day in the north it was necessary one way or another to deal with the king.

All the contemporary judgments that survive have come down to us because they were recorded in writing—and the writing was done by priests or monks. In those days the Church had an exorbitant cultural monopoly. It alone could create enduring objects capable of lasting through the ages. The men who provided our only sources of information were among the best educated of their day—the best, that is, in terms of what the academic and ecclesiastical culture of that age had to offer. And they were all men putting forth accepted opinions; the texts that were preserved and copied over and over again were texts that toed the line. We know, from his carefully kept correspondence, the thoughts of the bishop of Chartres on this topic. But about those of the bishop of Senlis, who officiated at Philip I's remarriage, we know nothing.

What chiefly concerns us, the way the knights lived and thought, can be seen only through the eyes of the priests, and of the most conformist among them, those who were canonized by the Church like Saint Yves of Chartres.

How many others, we might wonder, felt as these men did and in the name of the same principles? How many regarded the king's behavior as wicked and sinful, harmful to both his soul and his body, and ultimately injurious to his kingdom? For we must not forget that the rigorists were not condemning a single case of profligacy between a man and a woman (or rather the profligacy of one man, for they were concerned only with him). What they were considering was the joining of a man to a woman in a way that enabled the two to present themselves as man and wife. They were considering a union everyone thought of as a kind of marriage—permissible or otherwise. Their judgment would have been less severe if they had not been dealing with a solemn and official union necessarily subject to laws that must not be broken. If those laws were broken, the culprits must be solemnly reprimanded.

In these circumstances the very partial sources on which we have to rely reveal only one thing: the precise rules laid down by the rigorist Church to determine what constituted a *legitimum matrimonium*, or lawful marriage. Clearly these requirements were not insisted on by the majority of churchmen at the time and in the region of which we are writing. We have only to look at the bishops, all of whom except one turned up for the king's second marriage in Paris. They cannot all have been adventurers, toadies, or timeservers. Consider too how little store they later set by the sentence of excommunication, and how ready they were to annul it despite the pope's threats and remonstrances. The fact was that their moral values were different from those of the rigorists, and did not require their moving heaven and earth to separate Philip and Bertrade.

As for the nobility, we know practically nothing about what they thought. But is it really likely that where their own interests were at stake they took the sterner view? We have only to look at William of Anjou driving the reforming cardinals out of his capital, and the attitude of Fouque of Anjou before he became an instrument of papal intrigue.

When we come to Philip I himself, can we really imagine he was "impious," or even inattentive to the gaggle of priests who were always snapping at his heels? Can he really have been negligent of the king's "majesty," when he never stopped struggling against his rivals, the feudal princes? He held out for twelve years, keeping up appearances but never abandoning the woman he regarded not as his concubine but as his wife. Can we not assume this was because he also had principles? They might have been different from those of Yves of Chartres, but they were no less exacting.

I do not say that *amor* did not enter into it at all, but I do suggest that when Philip dismissed his first wife, then took and kept another, he was not giving way to senile passion but applying a set of moral standards. These rules were related to lineage; he was responsible for a patrimony. This of course included his "domain," the lordships that had belonged to his ancestors. It also included the "crown," which had been incorporated into these. But first and foremost it included the glory of his race—and all that had come down to him from his father and was his duty to hand on to his lawful son.

In 1092 Philip had only one son, a boy of eleven. In those days eleven was a vulnerable age, and the child was delicate. Suger hints at this in his life of Louis VI, where he says that William Rufus, king of England, "hankered after the kingdom of France, if by some mischance the sole heir should die."

Philip could hope for no more children from Berthe: it was time for her to go. Robert le Frison, count of Flanders, who had given Philip Berthe's hand twenty years before, was preparing himself for death in the monastery of Saint-Bertin, and the danger posed by the "hatred" a repudiation would incur in that quarter was for the moment diminished. And indeed it proved to be of short duration. Philip married Bertrade.

It was a good choice. At a time when the Capetian monarchy was much depleted, the king's first priority was to consolidate the reduced territory he was ruling as best he could from Paris and Orleans. The need was not to make brilliant alliances with great families of royal descent, but to lessen the power of the political groupings growing up around the chateaux of the Ile-de-France.

Montfort was a key fortress on the approaches to Normandy, the king's most vulnerable flank. And it was held by Amaury, Bertrade's brother. She herself was descended through her mother from Norman princes and from Richard I, the "pirate" count. She had already proved her fertility by giving sons to the count of Anjou, and she bore Philip three children, two of whom were boys. But it was necessary for those two sons to be legitimate, so the fate of the king's whole line depended on the status accorded to his consort.

If Bertrade were regarded as a mere concubine, her sons would be bastards and Philip's rivals could indulge in all kinds of hopes. These rivals included, as we have seen, William Rufus, who according to Suger "set at naught the rights of Bertrade's sons to the succession." But if the second marriage were held to be legal, then the danger of escheat receded. So it was natural that Philip, who might easily have found another way of satisfying whatever desire he felt for Bertrade, should do all he could to make their nuptials a striking and duly solemn occasion, and that, until his eldest son had proved his virility, he should refuse to estrange himself, even if only for appearance's sake, from the mother of his younger sons. It may have been love that made him decide not to part with Bertrade. What is certain is that his duty as king obliged him to keep her, come what might.

Philip, in his fifties, a time of life at which all other French kings had died, was bound to have been haunted by fears of hell. He must have hoped that the bishops might intervene and officially cleanse of sin the physical intercourse he indulged in, no doubt with pleasure. The fact was, he did not think, and other people did not think, that he was doing anything wrong.

~

CHAPTER NINE

Knightly Piety and the
Lay Response to the First Crusade*

Marcus Bull

One thousand years later, the Crusades remain fixed in our popular imagination. Scholars continue to debate the motives of Urban II and those who went on Crusade. In recent years, the picture of the knight in shining armor has gone out of fashion. Instead, the crusaders are depicted as the vanguard of European imperialism. In both cases, the crusaders are imagined for the sake of the present. Recently, many historians have taken the more productive approach of discerning how the crusaders perceived themselves. One of the most prominent among them, Marcus Bull, believes that crusading knights responded to Urban's call out of a sense of Christian piety. Urban II and his contemporaries did not use the term "crusade." Urban preached an armed pilgrimage that would serve as penance for those who participated. After an exhaustive analysis of the available evidence, Bull argues that Urban knew his audience very well. Crusaders responded primarily to the penitential rewards of an armed pilgrimage. Bull describes an aristocratic class intimately connected with the leaders of church reform. According to Bull, what role did penance play in the piety of southwestern French nobility? How was the first crusade a penitential act? What are the limits of Bull's thesis? Does he contradict Duby? Why, or why not?

It is the central argument of this study that the first crusaders' pious motivations, the main element among all the reasons why men went on the First

* © 1993 Oxford University Press. Marcus Bull, *Knightly Piety and the Lay Response to the First Crusade*, Oxford: Clarendon Press, 1993, pp. 5–6, 282–287.

Crusade, were moulded by contacts with religious communities. It has just been seen that laymen supported ecclesiastical bodies for their own good, particularly their spiritual welfare. Participation on crusade was motivated by the same concern. In the broadest terms, therefore, one might possibly argue that benefaction of churches and crusading were no more than parallel pursuits, tending to the same aim of salvation but formally distinct one from the other. In fact it becomes evident on close examination of the evidence that the two activities were intimately, even organically, linked. To examine how this could be so, it is first necessary to understand precisely what Pope Urban II offered the faithful when he launched the First Crusade.

As it was recorded on behalf of Bishop Lambert of Arras, the second canon of the Council of Clermont (the "indulgence") was predicated on the supposition that the faithful would respond to the prospect of spiritual rewards couched in the language of penance: "Whoever for devotion alone . . . shall set out for Jerusalem to liberate the church of God, to him may that journey be reckoned in place of all penance." There is further evidence for an emphasis upon penance in crusade preaching. In September 1096 Urban II wrote to the clergy and people of Bologna proposing the crusade as a "total penance for sins for which they shall have made true and perfect confession." It should be noted that the terminology of Urban's few surviving pronouncements concerning the crusaders' spiritual rewards is not entirely consistent. In December 1095 he wrote from Limoges to the faithful of Flanders proposing the crusade "for the remission of all sins" and making no explicit mention of penitential acts. The apparent inconsistency, however, was only the result of the imprecision of the formula *remissio peccatorum*, not of muddled thinking on the pope's part. What Urban stated was that participation on the crusade was a satisfactory penance, a task so arduous that it would expunge the consequences of all confessed sins.

The nature of Urban's promise has generated a good deal of controversy, much of it coloured by the hindsight of how the mature crusade indulgence slowly developed in the twelfth century and became fixed in the thirteenth. To express matters in their simplest terms, what Urban did not offer was the later medieval indulgence, the extra-sacramental remission by the church, by means of the inexhaustible fund of good built up in the Treasury of Merits, of the temporal punishment due for sins. This developed idea presupposed a clear distinction between the punishment which attached to sin in this world and in the afterlife prior to entry into Heaven and the guilt of sin, which could be forgiven through sacramental absolution. The later indulgence also rested on the practice which gradually emerged in the eleventh and twelfth centuries whereby a confessor would absolve a penitent after confession but before the performance of the penance he had enjoined. This sequence in part reflected the extension into pastoral routine of concerns expressed by twelfth-century theologians that proper emphasis should be placed on the penitent's intention, not his mechanical actions, and further that no human act, however onerous or time-consuming, could even begin to match the offence done to God by sinful conduct: however assiduously the faithful performed their penances, there would always be a balance of punishment in this world and the next (that is, in "Purgatory," the substantive used from the twelfth century to label the "middle place" between Heaven and Hell). The core of the penitential act by this stage was consequently the sinner's contrition, expressed in confession, and the confessor's mediation of Grace through absolution. In effect, the sinner was throwing himself on God's mercy. The performance of the penance was not an empty gesture. It served as an earnest of intent to demonstrate the penitent's submission to the church's discipline, and it was a step in the right direction towards easing the punishment of sins. But it was not the cardinal event in the penitential sequence.

Before this system developed, the sequence of events involved in confession had been subtly but significantly different. The sinner made confession, whereupon the confessor, quite possibly using a penitential as a guide, ordered that he perform a suitable penance. The penitent duly completed what was required, anything from a fast to years on wandering pilgrimage. Finally, the confessor, satisfied that the penance had been acquitted, granted absolution. In this system the granting of sacramental absolution was tantamount to the church stating that the penitent had erased the sins he had confessed (deliberately concealing sins from the confessor was itself sinful); he had "satisfied" the debt which his sins had created. Pursuing the rationale of this system to its extremes, it would have been technically possible for an individual to go straight to Heaven provided that he confessed every sin which he ever committed, performed every penance completely, and dropped dead at the instant of sacramental absolution. In such circumstances he would have been in the same position as an infant who died immediately after being cleansed of Original Sin by baptism. It was, however, supremely difficult for anyone, and virtually impossible for a layman, to keep an accurate tally of every sin and maintain the necessarily heroic levels of spiritual cleanliness over a lifetime. If anyone managed it and did so publicly, then he might become recognized as a saint—and the church canonized very few laymen indeed before the thirteenth century. The motive force behind the system of satisfactory penances was not, therefore, that it made people believe that there was a short cut to eternal salvation, but rather that it encouraged the faithful to do as much as they could to limit the pains which they would suffer after death. Urban's proposal to the first crusaders belonged to this earlier system of ideas.

Or, to be more precise, it was an extension of it. It is impossible to fix upon a precise date when the old penitential discipline gave way to the new, given that the problem was not the subject of one definitive piece of legislation, and that considerable regional variation in practice must have resulted from the progressiveness or otherwise of local senior clergy. What is reasonably clear, however, is that the First Crusade fell somewhere within the period of transition. Much of the uncertainty which has surrounded the First Crusade "indulgence" stems from the vagueness which surrounds the changes in the church's practice, with scholars attempting to project Pope Urban's meaning forward in time to conform with later penitential observance. The issue becomes much clearer if we consider that the First Crusade "indulgence," far from being obscured by the uncertainty surrounding penitential discipline, was the direct result of it. In other words, Urban was drawing upon the old idea that penances could be satisfactory, but also addressing emerging anxiety that normal penitential forms were unattractive or fell short of appeasing God. (Laymen no doubt rationalized the unattractiveness of penances as their inefficacy.) The crusade was in effect a "super-satisfaction." The concerns to which Urban responded did not only come from intellectuals worried about the quality of sin, but also from the ordinary faithful. Their quarrel was not with the idea that penances could be satisfactory; rather, they felt that they had fallen behind in the performance of their penances so much that it would be impossible to acquit themselves before death. Professor Hans Mayer has attempted to rebut the argument that the First Crusade was a satisfactory penance by maintaining that no penance could have been as arduous an undertaking as participation on the crusade. Of any single penance this is true. But this argument misses the fundamental point that the crusade was not a substitute for any one other penitential act but for all penances, both those outstanding before the crusade and those enjoined by potential crusaders' confessors shortly before departure. Thus, according to a Montecassino chronicler, who was very probably drawing on ideas which were voiced within Urban's close circle, the pope suggested the crusade to certain penitent French princes who "could not perform a fitting penance for their innumerable offences amongst their own people," not least because they felt that laying aside their arms during periods of penitential performance placed them at a disadvantage among their peers.

It is therefore unnecessary to posit a situation in which the pope and senior clergy declared a limited indulgence comprising a commutation of penance, whereupon the popular preachers of the crusade and the faithful connived at misconstruing what was on offer as forgiveness of all sins. At this stage there was no clear distinction between canonical punishment—the penance—and the temporal penalties in this world and the next created by sin. Pope Urban knew his audiences too well, and spent too long among them in 1095–6 at the head of a mobile curia drawing on local expertise, to have let the fundamentally important spiritual reward element of his crusade message grow out of control. For Urban and the faithful who responded to his appeal, *remissio peccatorum* was equivalent to *remissio poenitentiae* because of the super-satisfactory quality of the expedition. Thus Guibert of Nogent's description of the crusade, noted at the beginning of this study, as "a new way of attaining salvation" recalled the novelty not only of the idea of an armed pilgrimage to Jerusalem, but also of the way in which the crusade opportunity cut through the existing norms of penitential discipline.

It follows from the foregoing that the crusade appeal was directed at laymen who were acquainted with the demands of penitential practice. It is now necessary to examine whether this familiarity was linked in any way to the relationship between the faithful and religious communities.

It is very difficult to know how often individual eleventh-century nobles and knights subjected themselves to penitential discipline, and still harder to generalize about the practices of whole social groups. Charters are not an ideal source, for, as has been seen, they usually recorded only one aspect of a layman's relations with the church, the formal grant of property, and did not consistently mention the circumstances behind a property transaction. The most informative documents deal with formal, public penances. Although penances of this sort must have formed a minority of all cases, it is useful to begin with them.

An interesting case from southern Gascony demonstrates some of the salient features of public penances. In about 1034 Count William of Astarac was persuaded by Archbishop Garsia II of Auch that he had married within the prohibited degrees and that this placed him under the penitential discipline of the church. The penance imposed upon him comprised abstinence from meat on Mondays and Wednesdays and from meat and wine on Fridays, the feeding of one hundred poor folk annually, the washing of twelve paupers' feet on Good Friday, and the distribution of alms. Further prescriptions dealt with periods of sexual abstinence. The penance had three significant features. First, the possibility of commutation was allowed from the beginning. Abstinence from wine on Fridays was considered equivalent to giving 3d. to an unspecified number of the destitute, and forty days fasting might be replaced by the giving of 5s. in alms over the same period. Archbishop Garsia's penitential ordinance expressed the penances in the plural, which suggests that he attempted to frame general rules for all those guilty of consanguinity in the light of a particular cause célèbre. An undated fragment appended to the penitential decree in the cartulary of Auch, however, suggests that bargaining and compromise were normal, at least when the penitent was a powerful figure. Although no penitent is named in it, this fragment is in the singular. It refers to far longer periods of sexual abstinence (Lent, Advent, and five days per week) than the general ordinance, and its provision for the poor is less exacting (three paupers to be fed and clothed indefinitely). It most probably represents an early draft of Count William's penance before it was subjected to negotiation. This illustrates an important feature of penitential discipline: that penances, once enjoined, were not immutably fixed. A penitent might avail himself of a number of approved actions which were considered to be of equivalent value. This factor will be of fundamental importance when we come to consider the reasons why laymen gave properties and rights to religious communities.

The second important feature of Count William's penance is that it reveals some understanding of the difference between lesser and graver errors. This did not simply involve a contrast between venial and mortal sins, an idea which became more refined in the twelfth century and turned upon the intrinsic quality of the fault. Rather, a working distinction was used based on public notoriety. Garsia's ordinance argued that, just as serious wounds require dressing, so there was a correspondence between the gravity of faults and the means required to compensate for them; whatever had been committed openly, therefore, could only be remedied likewise. In other words, Count William's actions belonged to a species of conduct beyond the scope of everyday, lesser faults which could be dealt with by private confessors (and consequently were much less likely to be put in writing). This serves as a warning that the surviving documents are likely to present a "top-heavy" picture of laymen's sinful careers, and that it would be unwise to underestimate the capacity of laymen to become burdened by a long sequence of individually private, and often relatively minor, sins.

Thirdly, the imposition of this form of penance was reserved for bishops. A verbose account of Count William's dealings with the archbishop, in the name of "Odo the Deacon," expounded the jurisdictional authority of Garsia's actions. It recalled the Petrine Commission, the Power of the Keys, and the power to bind and loose.

CHAPTER TEN

~

Sword, Mitre, and Cloister: Nobility and the Church in Burgundy, 980–1198*

Constance Brittain Bouchard

The monastic and ecclesiastical reforms begun at Cluny and culminating in the Gregorian Reform emphasized freeing church institutions and personnel from corrupting secular influence. The conflict between Gregory VII and the German emperor Henry IV and the excommunication of Philip I of France by Urban II reinforce the notion that the reformers and the nobility were at odds concerning the sort of Christian society Western Europe ought to be. Looking past popes, emperors, and kings, however, reveals a different situation. Constance Brittain Bouchard, for instance, has focused on the religious behavior of the Burgundian nobility between the tenth and twelfth century. Burgundy, now southern France, was the home of Cluny and the epicenter of religious reform in that period. Although the nobles themselves have left very little evidence of their beliefs, Burgundian monasteries kept meticulous records, called charters, of their dealings with the local aristocrats. Based on these records, Bouchard claims that cooperation, not conflict, typified the relationship between the nobles and reforming churchmen in Burgundy. This cooperation was possible because of the close familial ties between the secular and ecclesiastical elite in Burgundy. Burgundian counts and castellans were the fathers, brothers, uncles, and cousins of the Burgundian bishops and abbots. It seems implausible that conflicting worldviews could exist between groups so closely related, both geographically and biologically. In fact, monastic charters show that the Burgundian nobility played a large role in supporting and furthering monastic reform in

* © 1987 Cornell University Press. Used with permission of the publisher, Cornell University Press. Constance Brittain Bouchard, *Sword, Mitre, and Cloister: Nobility and the Church in Burgundy, 980–1198*, Ithaca: Cornell University Press, 1987, pp. 125–138, 102–104, 106–107, 110.

their territories. Far from being in conflict, the secular and clerical elite of Burgundy worked together toward religious reform. In the selection below, what do the monastic charters reveal about the piety of the Burgundian nobility? Do Bouchard's findings contradict Duby's conclusions?

Much of the monastic reform of the late tenth and eleventh centuries was similar to that carried out by Cluny in the tenth century. Very few completely new monasteries were founded in Burgundy, and those few were generally the foundations of dukes or counts. New monastic communities were most commonly founded when a nobleman gave a church he had owned (or even his castle chapel) to a monastery of renowned regularity of life. Cluny helped establish more new communities of monks in the first half or three-quarters of the eleventh century than did any other single Burgundian house in the same period. Sometimes the church in which monks were set was an abandoned monastery, sometimes a chapel or rural parish church that had not before been served by monks. Some of these churches became priories, while others, though staffed at least in part by monks from the mother house, retained their independence and their own abbots. Often only a few monks might settle in the church, too few to have sustained it had it been an independent monastery but enough to establish the mother house's claim to it and to offer prayers for the house's noble founder. A tiny church supporting only a few monks was known as a cell; monks might be rotated in and out of it from the mother church. Many other churches given to monasteries remained parish churches or chapels and housed no monks.

Both secular nobles and bishops gave churches in their control to the great reforming houses as dependencies. A donor usually gave a church he held to a nearby monastery; almost all the churches Cluny received in the eleventh century, for example, were located in Burgundy. If the nobleman who helped establish a new body of monks was very powerful, he might also establish other houses, and if he was a simple castellan he might establish only one house on which his descendants' pious generosity would be focused for generations, but in any case such reforms were a matter involving only a man's family, not his neighbors. The following examples are taken from the late tenth and early eleventh centuries, a period in which a number of old Burgundian houses were restored.

St.-Bénigne of Dijon was, after Cluny, one of the most important reformed monasteries of Burgundy. A very old house, it had fallen into what an eleventh-century chronicler called an "ambiguous position" after the Viking and Magyar invasions. It was reformed in 990 by Otto-William, count of Burgundy, and his brother-in-law Bruno, bishop of Langres. They asked the abbot of Cluny to send them twelve monks, headed by Otto-William's cousin William, a monk at Cluny who became the first reformed abbot. The necrology of St.-Bénigne commemorates Bishop Bruno as having reformed the house with "the great help of Count Otto-William of Burgundy." St.-Bénigne, reformed to Cluny's *ordo* but not her direction, quickly became the center of its own reform movement. For example, shortly before 1000, Duke Henry of Burgundy, Otto-William's stepfather, gave St.-Bénigne the church of St.-Vivant of Vergy, and Abbot William established a priory there. Otto-William's son, Count Raynald of Burgundy, gave St.-Bénigne a small church in the castle of Vesoul, and four monks were set there. St.-Bénigne continued to receive gifts from the counts and dukes of Burgundy throughout the eleventh century.

St.-Germain of Auxerre, like St.-Bénigne an old house, owed its reform to the concern of noble families long associated with the house. It had been originally founded in the fifth century as a basilica in honor of Saint Germain, bishop of Auxerre. It became a monastery in the sixth century and produced a number of scholars and bishops of Auxerre over the next three centuries. In the late ninth century, however, it lost both its regularity and its independence. Hugh, called "the Abbot," of the great noble family of Welfs which produced the kings of imperial Burgundy and who himself was the uncle of Charles the Bald, took the direction of St.-Germain by 853, even though less than twenty years earlier Louis the Pious had granted the monks the right to elect an abbot from among their own members. Hugh was succeeded by Lothair, son of Charles the Bald, and though he seems to have adopted the monastic life himself, after his death the monastery was given to Count Boso, a *fidelis* of the king. In the tenth century, St.-Germain was headed by the dukes and counts of Burgundy, beginning with Richard le Justicier, Boso's brother, who had himself married a woman of the Welf family. St.-Germain might thus be considered a classic example of decadence, of a house suffering "in the hands of the laity." But it was the nobles controlling St.-Germain who brought about its eventual reform. In the 980s, Duke Henry of Burgundy, who had been lay abbot of the monastery for some twenty years, decided to reform St.-Germain. Not surprisingly, after over a century of lay rule there were few monks left at St.-Germain, and those there did not follow a strictly regular life. Henry and his half brother Heribert, bishop of Auxerre (971–996), asked Maiolus, abbot of Cluny, to send them a monk versed in strict observance of the Benedictine Rule who would restore the abbey's reputation. Maiolus agreed, and, restored to Cluny's discipline under their new abbot, though not made a dependent of Cluny, the monks of St.-Germain flourished for close to a century.

But St.-Germain did not remain reformed. About a century later, the abbot, who had acquired his position at a very early age, fell into some sort of "iniquity," according to contemporary sources. The house was once again restored to a strict observance of Cluniac customs, but not by the abbot of Cluny. This reform was carried out by Bishop Humbald of Auxerre (1095–1114), whose first act as bishop was to have the current abbot of St.-Germain dismissed, and by Counts William of Nevers and Stephen of Blois, the second of whom held the advocacy of St.-Germain in fief from the duke of Burgundy. The new abbot was a Cluniac monk who was nephew of the abbot of Cluny, but before assuming his office he was absolved, at the insistence of the bishop of Auxerre, of his allegiance to his uncle and to Cluny. It is clear that on the two occasions, a century apart, that St.-Germain was reformed, it was at the initiative of secular lords and bishops; these lords saw Cluny as an appropriate house from which to obtain reforming abbots, but Cluny herself neither initiated the reform nor brought St.-Germain into her order.

Another important reform that took place at the very end of the tenth century was that of Paray-le-monial. This house, one of the few new tenth-century foundations, had been founded in 973 (under the name Orval) by Lambert, count of Chalon-sur-Saône. He founded it on his own land, at his own expense, "with the help of Maiolus, abbot of Cluny," according to the foundation charter. Maiolus sent monks from Cluny to live there, and Lambert specified that the house would be free of all "secular domination," but the house was not made a dependency of Cluny. It maintained its own abbot and turned to the count of Chalon rather than to the abbot of Cluny for protection. After Lambert's death around 978, Count Geoffrey Greymantle of Anjou, who married Lambert's widow and acted as count of Chalon, and Lambert's son Hugh all gave a number of churches and pieces of land to Orval. But within twenty-five years of its foundation, Orval already required reformation. It was reformed in 999 by Lambert's son Hugh, count of Chalon.

Hugh was a powerful count who also acted as bishop of Auxerre for forty years at the beginning of the eleventh century (999–1039). He is often referred to in the charters of the time as "both count and bishop." As count, he fought the king in the Burgundian wars of 1002–1004. As bishop, he rebuilt the cathedral of Auxerre and helped restore lost property to several churches in his diocese. In both his capacities, as count and bishop, he proved himself a patron of reform and a close friend of the monastery of Cluny. It was in his role as count rather than bishop—Paray was in his county but not his diocese—that he reformed the house. The reformation charter spoke vaguely of "brotherly love declining and iniquity increasing"; Hugh, the charter said, saw that "worldly deeds will lead to ruin" and that "this house had not been able to remain in the state in which his father had established it." Though the monastery had been declared free of secular domination when founded, there was no question but that it was Hugh's to dispose of as he would, and he gave it to Odilo, abbot of Cluny, as a dependent house. Henceforth it did not have an abbot of its own but rather a prior, answerable to Cluny. Hugh had his uncle Robert, his half brother Maurice, Count Otto-William of Burgundy, and Otto-William's son Gui all confirm this reform. Unlike St.-Bénigne and St.-Germain, then, it became a priory.

The regularity of Paray was now assured. It continued to receive gifts from the counts of Chalon throughout the eleventh and twelfth centuries. Over the next forty years Hugh made numerous gifts to the monks, many of which were confirmed by his nephew Theobold, who succeeded him as count of Chalon and continued his generosity after Hugh's death. That Hugh asked for confirmation from Theobold rather than the canons of Auxerre again indicates that these gifts were made in his capacity as count, not bishop. After Theobold succeeded as count he again confirmed the abbey's rights and possessions; his daughter Ermengard, lady of Bourbon, as she was dying, gave Paray land that had been part of her dowry; and Theobold's grandson, Gui of Thiers, count of Chalon, confirmed all of his predecessors' gifts to Paray when he left on the First Crusade. His descendants in the twelfth century reiterated and reconfirmed the house's rights and privileges.

St.-Marcel-lés-Chalon, a house originally founded in the sixth century but which was in ruins in the tenth century, provides another example of reform on the eve of the eleventh century. The house was reformed when Geoffrey Greymantle, Hugh's stepfather and acting count of Chalon, gave St.-Marcel to Cluny at the end of the tenth century, to become a priory. Geoffrey did so with the assistance of Abbot Maiolus of Cluny and Duke Henry of Burgundy. "The religious life was almost extinguished" there when Geoffrey reformed it, according to a charter drawn up two generations later. In 999, Geoffrey's stepson, Hugh of Chalon, confirmed the reform of St.-Marcel at the same time he gave Paray to Cluny.

The reforms detailed above, and others that took place from the end of the tenth century through the late eleventh, were carried out at the initiative of and with the consent of counts, viscounts, and bishops from powerful families. The bishops who helped further the cause of monastic reform were not themselves "reformed," at least in the later eleventh-century sense of the term. Bruno of Langres had been appointed bishop by his uncle the king when still five years too young to be canonically elected; and Hugh, simultaneously bishop of Auxerre and count of Chalon, played a personal and active role in the Burgundian wars of the early eleventh century.

Ecclesiastics did not have to pursue the austere monastic life themselves in order to support it.

This establishment of bodies of reformed monks produced a large number of dependent houses for the great Burgundian monasteries. In 931 Pope John XI had confirmed Cluny's right to place the monasteries it had been given under the authority of Cluny's abbot, and by 937 there were already seventeen such dependent monasteries listed in papal confirmations of Cluny's possessions. This figure had increased to thirty-seven in 994 and over sixty by 1048, and even so these figures do not include those houses like St.-Bénigne which retained their own abbots nor the many churches given to Cluny where no monks were set. The number of Cluniac priories continued to increase in the twelfth century; the figure for the end of the century has been estimated at anywhere from a few hundred houses to a thousand, depending on how one defines "Cluniac."

~

CHAPTER ELEVEN

Under Crescent and Cross: The Jews in the Middle Ages*

Mark R. Cohen

Jews had lived in Europe for centuries. Jewish communities flourished around the Mediterranean coast during the Roman Empire. When the Romans brutally crushed a Jewish revolt and destroyed the Temple in 70 A.D., displaced Jews moved throughout the known world, including Western Europe. While Jews resisted conversion and christianization, they enjoyed a relatively stable existence in early medieval Europe. Jews were particularly valuable to the early medieval economy. The former western provinces of the Roman Empire were undeveloped and isolated from interregional trade. Moreover, New Testament and Roman attitudes toward profit and trade discouraged early medieval Christians from engaging in mercantile activities. Jews had no such compunctions and tended to be better educated and more connected to the wider world. Two parallel developments in medieval Christian culture irrevocably changed the status of Jews in European society. First, an increasingly tolerant attitude among Christian scholars toward merchant activity and profit deprived the Jews of any cultural advantage in the commercial sphere. Second, the rise of a self-consciously Christian culture in Western Europe in the eleventh century left no secure place for non-Christians in European society. Many of the knights who answered Urban's call for an armed pilgrimage to purge the Holy Land of Muslims began their journey by attempting to purge their own territories of Jews.

While the previous selections focused on the attitudes of the Christian nobility, the following selection focuses on the experiences of medieval Jews. By employing

* © 1994 Princeton University Press. Reprinted by permission of Princeton University Press. Mark R. Cohen, *Under Crescent and Cross: The Jews in the Middle Ages*, Princeton: Princeton University Press, 1994, pp. 121–125, 129–131.

*the anthropological concepts of hierarchy and marginality, Mark R. Cohen believes
we can better understand the precarious status of Jews in medieval Christendom.
What do the terms "hierarchy" and "marginality" mean? What is the difference between "status" and "class"? How do these concepts give us insight into the situation of medieval European Jews?*

In *Homo Hierarchicus*, the French social anthropologist Louis Dumont,
studying the caste system in India, draws some important implications for
the social order of premodern societies. Dumont argues that the fundamental idea unifying societies composed of a multiplicity of groups and sta-
tuses is hierarchy, that hierarchy, more than power, determines how the elements of such a society interact. Hierarchy is "the principle by which the
elements of a whole are ranked in relation to the whole, it being understood
that in the majority of societies it is religion which provides the view of the
whole, and that the ranking will thus be religious in nature." The hierarchical relationship is that "between encompassing and encompassed or
between ensemble and element." Paradoxically, the elements of caste
systems—and, by extension, the components of any stratified society—
manage to coexist more or less harmoniously precisely because each knows
that it and all the other subgroups of the population are part of a totality.
Differences are accepted as natural in a fully formed, or "ideal-type" hierarchical society, of which the Indian caste system is the best-known example.
This, Dumont says, explains the tolerance toward others often noticed
among Indians or Hindus. "It is easy to see what this feature corresponds to
in social life. Many castes, who may differ in their customs and habits, live
side by side, agreed on the code which ranks them and separates them. They
will assign a rank, where we in the West would approve or exclude. . . . In
the hierarchical scheme a group's acknowledged differentness whereby it is
contrasted with other groups becomes the very principle whereby it is integrated into society."

Medieval Christians had ways of talking about the social order and the
place, daily, of the infidel or nonconforming Christian in that order. They were
conscious of status rather than class. Thinkers spoke in terms of hierarchies—
who was above whom. At the beginning of his history of the hierarchical concept of the "three orders" (those who pray, fight, and labor) in medieval Christendom, Georges Duby quotes the words of Pope Gregory the Great to describe
the "necessary inequality" of the social order:

> Providence has established various degrees and distinct orders [*ordines*] so that,
> if the lesser show deference to the greater, and if the greater bestow love on the

lesser, then true concord and conjunction will arise out of diversity. Indeed, the community could not subsist at all if the total order of disparity did not preserve it. That creation cannot be governed in equality is taught us by the example of the heavenly hosts; there are angels and there are archangels, which are clearly not equals, differing from one another in power and order.

Jeffrey Burton Russell's description of the principle of "right order" in medieval Christian society complements Dumont's formulation:

> There were three social hierarchies, the feudal-manorial, the urban, and the ecclesiastical. Within this ordered society, every institution and every person had *libertas*. The meaning of *libertas* was quite different from the meaning of 'liberty' now. It meant the right—and the duty—of an individual to occupy his proper place in society.

In terms of its social structure, medieval Islam is less easy to define than Christendom. A considerable body of modern scholarship has endeavored to show how analogies with the West frequently do not work. Feudalism and corporation are fundamental characteristics of European society now generally believed to have been absent in Islam, at least in the form known in the West, and in the classical medieval centuries. On the other hand, the notion of hierarchy—while neglected—can aptly be applied to Islam. At the beginning of a discussion of "Islam and the social order," a leading Islamic historian regrets that "the problem of the hierarchies is one of those rarely touched on by orientalists except from the slightly different angle of 'social classes'." Few orientalists, however, would dispute the notion of hierarchy as appropriate in an analysis of the position of non-Muslims in Muslim society.

To hierarchy, which marked the social order of the two societies in which the Jews lived during the Middle Ages, must be added the element of marginality. As refined by certain sociologists, "marginality theory" describes a type of hierarchy in which members of a group "(1) do not ordinarily qualify for admission into another group with which, over varying lengths of time, it is more or less closely associated; (2) when these groups differ significantly in the nature of their cultural or racial heritage; and (3) between which there is limited cultural interchange or social interaction." In a "marginal situation"—unlike caste systems with their ideal of permanent or total group exclusiveness—there is some permeability of the barriers (or boundaries) separating elements in the hierarchy. While both marginality and exclusion engender or reflect intergroup tensions, marginality expresses a less alienated relationship between the subordinate group and the larger society.

The concept of marginality that best describes the position of the Jews in the Middle Ages is one that "refers to the fairly long-lasting, large-scale hierarchical situation in which two or more groups or even nations exist together."

> The groups vary in degree of privilege and power and there is inequality of status and opportunity. The barriers between the groups are sufficient to prevent the enjoyment by the subordinate group, or groups, of the privileges of the dominant, non-marginal group, but do not prevent the absorption by the former or the latter's culture.

Not infrequently, subordinate strata resist the absorption of some feature of the dominant group's culture that is incompatible with their own value system. This, too, fits the Jewish condition in the medieval diaspora.

The Jews can be said to have begun at the bottom of the hierarchy in Christendom, but in a marginal situation. As the historian Bernhard Blumenkranz has shown, there was considerable social interchange between Jews and Christians during the centuries between the Barbarian invasions and the rise of the crusading spirit in Latin Europe. Spatially, the Jews were not excluded; they lived relatively close to and peacefully with their Christian neighbors. The Jews probably engaged in amicable debate about religion with learned Christians. Here and there, Jews held public office. In time of warfare, they could be found standing side by side with Christian comrades in armed defense of their towns. The Jews maintained their own cultural identity by resisting attempts to convert them and by rigorously enforcing Judaism's ancient taboo against marriage outside the Jewish community.

Even in this relatively tranquil period in Christian-Jewish relations, however, the idea of excluding Jews from Christendom was not absent. In an oft-cited letter of Pope Leo VII (r. 936–39), appointing a certain Frederick archbishop of Mainz, the pope responds to Frederick's query "whether it is better to subjugate [the Jews] to the holy religion or expel them from your towns." The pope responds by urging his vicar to strive to convert the Jews through preaching (though not by force). If, however, they refuse to accept baptism, the archbishop possesses delegated authority to expel them, "for we ought not to associate with the Lord's enemies."

Until the eleventh century, Pope Leo's view had little practical import. The church retained only limited influence over mundane, or even spiritual, affairs in the world at large, and Jews enjoyed substantial support from secular rulers interested in exploiting their economic utility. True, a Latin source relates that the German emperor Henry II expelled the Jews from the town of Mainz in the year 1012. They were allowed to return several weeks later, though, and there is no evidence that Henry's act was more than a local affair. It is thought that he was retaliating for the apostasy earlier that year of a deacon and cleric named Wecelin. Nonetheless, the event of 1012 was a harbinger of the more definitive and traumatic expulsions to come during the High and late Middle Ages. It underscored the tenuous dependability of the Jews' presumptive right to reside among Christians.

With the rise of the crusading spirit and the deepening of Christian consciousness and piety in the population at large beginning in the eleventh century, Jews were gradually excluded from society. As infidels, they were considered "outside the church" (*extra ecclesiam*); practically speaking, this meant they were not subject to ecclesiastical jurisdiction. In his *Decretum*, Gratian, the great canonist of the twelfth century, reinterpreted a Pauline saying in the New Testament to support this position:

> Their [the infidels'] punishment, however, is left for divine judgment alone, when we cannot exercise discipline over them, either because they are not subject to our law or because their crimes, although known to us, nevertheless cannot be proven by clear evidence. As for those who are not of our law, the Apostle says in the First Epistle to the Corinthians; For what does it concern me to judge those who are outside [*his qui foris sunt*] God will judge them.

Canon law grouped Jews together with other peoples, especially pagans and heretics, with whom contact was discouraged. As we have seen, this clustering of Jews with other subordinate groups, implying guilt by association, was already present in Christian-Roman Jewry law. Medieval canon law included precepts excluding these outsiders from the rights held by Christians in courts of law. Gratian's *Decretum* declares that "pagans, heretics of Jews cannot sue Christians." Probably influenced by Roman and canon law, Germanic law disqualified Jews, along with heretics and unbelievers, from "being spokesmen of a man and of standing in court against a Christian."

Common, too, was the tendency to lump Jews together with lepers, an association that reinforced their status as outsiders. At about the middle of the thirteenth century, as we have seen, the ecclesiastical decree of the Fourth Lateran Council, requiring that Jews exhibit an identifying sign on their clothing, began to be implemented. Secular rulers responded, albeit unevenly, to the church's call, ruling that Jews must sew different distinguishing marks on their outer garments. Because special attire was prescribed for abhorrent groups such as prostitutes, Christians could not help but consider the Jews' special sign as also a mark of degradation and exclusion. Symbolically, too, descriptions of the role of the Jews in the ceremony of welcoming a king or bishop upon his entry into his city turn from integrative—with "the Jews as part of the community like any other, and often dispersed among it"—to exclusionary beginning in the twelfth century, "a change in the welcoming ritual, whose effect was to exclude them from the political community."

We may conclude that, over time, Jews, as they came to be excluded from the hierarchy of the Christian social order, lost the benefits of their marginal situation. By the thirteenth century, Jews in the Latin West no longer conformed to Dumont's model of hierarchy based on relations "between encompassing and encompassed or between ensemble and element." Neither Christians nor Jews felt that the latter were integral to society, that they were an encompassed element of the encompassing whole. By that time, the universalism of the encompassing whole had been tempered by a "Christian particularism, the primitive solidarity of the group and the policy of apartheid with regard to outside groups." None of the complex models subdividing Christendom into socioprofessional "estates" which increasingly came to characterize the social order from the beginning of the thirteenth century had any place for the Jews.

True, the centuries-old Augustinian tradition that Jews have a role to play in Christian soteriology (as witness to the superiority and chosenness of the Christian faith) continued to assure the Jews of their low rank in the hierarchy of Christian society. The Augustinian theology, however, faced powerful countervailing political, economic, and social forces. The Augustinian tradition did not protect the Jews of the late Middle Ages from exclusion. Once they were no longer tolerated on even the lowest rung of the Christian hierarchy, the groundwork was laid for the widespread expulsionary policy of the thirteenth to fifteenth centuries.

Some Jews lived in rural areas, where they engaged in agricultural pursuits, both in Islamic lands and in Europe. The vast majority, however, inhabited towns. A comparison of the Jew as townsman in Christendom and in Islam yields insights into why the Jewish-Muslim relationship generated less hatred and persecution than the encounter between Christian and Jew. Scholars no longer believe that the Barbarian invasions destroyed the urban life of the Roman Empire. Although a decline had indeed begun by the period of the late empire, towns continued to exist in attenuated form. The legacy of Roman urbanism was an underlying element of urban growth during the Middle Ages.

On the whole, life was predominantly rural and agricultural. By the early Middle Ages, "the former Roman centres [had] turned into islands amidst a world which [had] become predominantly rural." Although the "town as a residential centre had survived the age of tribal migrations in some particularly important sites of the Rhine, Meuse and Moselle valleys, . . . the distinctively urban way of life with its special contribution to civilization had not survived." The trading centers (called *wiks*) that appeared for a period of two centuries during the Merovingian and Carolingian periods "constituted alien enclaves within the Carolingian world rather than organically belonging to it."

Oriental long-distance traders (Jews and Syrians; later, Jews alone) could be found living in settlements that were much diminished in area and population, as well as political and cultural importance. Traders were an alien, mercantile presence within a social environment itself considered alien by the larger society.

Only as trade began to revive in the tenth century, and as the commercial revolution took hold in the eleventh, did commercial urban centers sprout anew (or expand on old foundations). Most of the Christian inhabitants of these settlements were traders accustomed to considerable freedom, which was fundamental to their profession. They were also equipped with a body of customs—the "Law Merchant." Hence, in many places, merchants petitioned the monarch or feudal seigneur for urban liberties exceeding those granted most others in society. Later, organized burghers demanded formalization of self-government in the form of charters. Many central authorities—be they royal, aristocratic, or ecclesiastical—opposed the evolution of towns into independent "corporations," legal bodies with their own laws and customs and a judiciary separate from the court of the overlord. The struggle to achieve emancipation from the lord of the town had some successes beginning in the twelfth century, a process that complicated the normal feudal arrangement. In England, the pattern of town origin and growth in the early Middle Ages may have differed somewhat from that on the Continent. There were no Jews in England, however, before the Norman Conquest of 1066. By that time, the process of evolution (toward some measure of formal corporate independence and self-government) resembled social developments in northern Europe—often to the dismay of society as a whole and against the trend toward centralized feudal authority which, in England, was the monarchy.

A stigma attached to the innovation represented by the town. Towns "were new things in the scandalous sense which was given to this adjective in the middle ages" and "a centre of what feudal lords detested: shameful, economic activity." As Ennen observes, the town of northern Europe did not fit into the classic social order of medieval society based on an agrarian relationship between noble and peasant. Urban autonomy, codified in town charters, placed the town outside feudal law. The sworn assemblies of traders that took control of urban affairs throughout Europe beginning in the twelfth century and demanded rights from royal or episcopal overlords represented a revolutionary force.

Presumably, the presence of settled Jews in the suspect, emergent towns of Europe added to the religious and economic background of anti-Jewish sentiment. Moreover, within the urban settlement itself, the Jew was something of an anomaly. While other townsmen fought for and took pride in achieving independence from the lord of the town, Jews continued to hold charters from their overlords and, in some places, to be exempt from municipal jurisdiction. Direct dependence on the king, a baron or duke, or some other authority, reinforced the image of Jew-as-outsider. Moreover, their charters included concessions of self-government, which exacerbated differences between the urban Christian bourgeosie and the semi-autonomous Jews in their midst. True, as some believe, Jews in some of the towns held rights roughly equivalent to those of Christian burgesses. As we have seen, however, even in places where Jews appear to have experienced technical "citizenship," they were excluded from municipal offices and subjected to special taxes—handicaps which diminished their honor in a society in which honor mattered very much.

Yet another anomaly contributed to the exclusion of Jews from the normal social order. They could not partake in that fundamental ritual of urban self-identity, the oath Christian burghers swore, promising obedience to municipal authority and adherence to obligations designed to ensure urban peace. Similarly barred from receiving homage, the Jew had no firm place in either the feudal system or the urban commune.

By and large, Jews in European cities lived separate from Christians, usually in a street or section called a "Jewry," "*Jüdengasse*," or "*rue des Juifs*." They chose to live this way for convenience and for the greater sense of security it conferred. Residential seclusion began to impinge on Christian-Jewish relations when the church, wishing to prevent contact between Christians and Jews, especially after the thirteenth century, legislated restrictions on where Jews were allowed to live. Especially during the later Middle Ages, when popular fear and hatred of the Jews grew in intensity and popular antisemitic stereotypes proliferated, the Jewish quarter became a mysterious, frightful place, increasingly the target of terrified, antisemitic Christian mobs. As a sign of the estrangement of Jews from Christian burghers, some towns in the High and later Middle Ages sought from their overlords—and were granted—the privilege of not tolerating Jews. In short, Christian townspeople were allowed to exclude or expel Jews.

Were the Jewish communities themselves—with their charters, leaders, charitable works, and rabbinic law courts—corporations, a kind of town within a town? If they were, how did this fact affect their status? Baron has articulated the view (part of his anti-lachrymose conception of Jewish history) that the Jewish community "was recognized by law as a corporate body apart, entitled not only to regulate its purely religious activities, but also to adjust many civil and political affairs to suit its own needs and traditions." This, Baron believes, offset some of the disadvantages Jews suffered at the hands of Christians. At the same time, Baron recognizes that the peculiar position of the Jews—caught, as they were, in the complexity of overlapping and sometimes arbitrary and self-interested application of the different "laws" to which they were subject—detracted from the "normalization" that corporate status might otherwise have bestowed on them:

> Like the other corporate groups, it lived on the basis of specific privileges which regulated its basic rights and duties, leaving amplification and implementation to local customs. As a rule, the Jewish community enjoyed even fuller self-government than most other corporations. At the same time its rights were often less clearly defined, or willfully disregarded, while its duties were arbitrarily expanded to suit the wishes of rulers . . . In short, the late medieval Jewish community simultaneously appeared as one of the many corporations within the European corporate system and as a corporation of its own kind in many ways placed outside the framework of general society.

Kenneth Stow argues that the Jewish community in the Middle Ages did not constitute a corporation. It was not, he says, integrated into the normal structure of medieval corporate society in the sense of having freedom, independence from outside control, autonomy, and security. However, even Baron does not make such an extravagant claim, nor does Kisch, whose formulation is more to the point. "Developmentally," Kisch asserts, "the Jewish 'corporate bodies' do not represent phenomena analogous to the craftsmen's guilds or other medieval corporations. Rather, did their legal and political status develop from that sum total of basic rights, privileges, and duties accorded them or imposed on them by the holders of political power."

Corporate identity did not extend to the privilege of bringing actions as a community against wrongdoers. In many ways, corporate identity worked in reverse: corporate appearance often encouraged Christian ruling authorities to assign collective responsibility, and even collective punishment, to an entire Jewish community for the real or imagined hostile acts of individuals.

More commonly, Jewish corporate status enabled rulers to amass considerable sums of money from their Jewish subjects, money exacted from the community as a whole. Finally, the aspect of corporation dovetailed with the desire of the Catholic church to segregate Jews and thereby reinforce their status as inferior.

CHAPTER TWELVE

~

Women's Role in Latin Letters From the Fourth to the Early Twelfth Centuries*

Joan M. Ferrante

The Christian culture that gave us the Gregorian Reform and the Crusades was decidedly masculine. The reformers, emphasizing sexual renunciation, depicted women as the occasion for sin. The nobility embraced a militant Christianity, choosing as their role models the violent warrior-kings, David, Constantine, and Charlemagne. Women had few formal roles in this society. The Gregorian Reform made the celibate priest, who alone could perform the essential rituals, the center of religious life. While queens and noble wives could wield considerable influence under certain circumstances, they could rarely rule. Nevertheless, women played a larger informal role in society than was once thought. Due to the nature of the sources, the role of women in Christendom is difficult to assess. With a few notable exceptions, the male clerical elite produced our sources. If we limit ourselves to a modern notion of authorship, we are limited to a few female authors such as Heloise and Hildegard. However, if we expand our notion of how texts are produced, we can discern the influence of women. According to Joan Ferrante, women were both patrons of and collaborators for medieval religious literature. Scholars addressed weighty essays to women and dedicated significant theological works to them. In many cases, the women set the agenda for the work. The following selection describes the involvement of women in religious literature in the Carolingian court and during the time of the Gregorian Reforms. What is the difference between a patron and a collaborator? Why is this distinction important to Ferrante? What roles

* © 1997 Indiana University Press. Joan M. Ferrante, *To the Glory of Her Sex*, Bloomington: Indiana University Press, 1997, pp. 39–40, 43–44, 54–56.

do women play in the creation of these texts? What does this tell us about the religious attitudes of these women? What does it tell us about the religious attitude of the male scholars?

The presence and probable influence of women in the beginnings of vernacular literatures, particularly Provençal and French, has been much discussed, but the fact that women also influenced literature in Latin, religious and secular, throughout the Middle Ages, probably more than we can trace, has had less attention. As I read through the letters, I was struck by how frequently men mentioned that the work they were sending was written at the request of the woman they were sending it to. I began to see that the women friends and colleagues who asked for commentaries on specific texts or who asked questions that could be properly answered only in treatises were as instrumental in the production of those works as the women who commissioned panegyrics or histories or later romances. Without the man's letter, *we* might have no *idea* of the source; with it, we can see something of a collaborative effort. The woman might set the man a program of activity, forcing him to work out his ideas or do more research, or she might frame the structure of his work by the questions she asked; and he responded because the subject interested him and he trusted her to be a sympathetic audience to ideas as he developed them or to be a purveyor of his ideas to a wider public. This led me to a much broader view of women's role in literature written by men, of collaboration as well as patronage.

The two are not necessarily exclusive. Friends and colleagues, even family members, solicited texts and offered various kinds of support (such as gifts or copying manuscripts); formal sponsors sometimes worked closely with the writer, suggesting material, offering information. The woman's role varies from actively soliciting religious works by asking specific questions, requesting commentaries on particular texts, or commissioning a work of history, biography, or romance with a particular slant or plot, to simply receiving works which were dedicated to them in the hopes of or in gratitude for favors. No matter what her role, the woman addressed could and often did exercise some influence over the work produced. The work is usually the product of the writer's and the sponsor's mutual interests, whether intellectual and religious or political, to further knowledge and understanding or support a cause. Even when the writer's interests are very personal—his own advancement—his choice of sponsor involves a political judgment that her favor will be valuable to him. The letters of dedication which describe the relations between writer, patron, and the text, are, of course, written according to conventions which have been thoroughly studied. But since writers do not normally use irrelevant *topoi*, it is possible to determine from those they choose to employ what their situation is.

The relation between writer and patron differs somewhat from one category to another. The religious works for women are usually exchanges between intellectual equals, or at least colleagues and friends who are engaged in the same enterprise and who respect each other's minds. When a woman requests a rule for women, she asks to be identified as different from a man, but when she asks for an exchange of ideas, she asks and is answered as an equal. In the secular works, histories or romances, the patron is clearly in a socially superior position; her taste, her views, sometimes her political agenda, are privileged.

I will discuss collaboration between women and writers in three areas. In this chapter, I consider religious (Latin) texts whose authors address them to the women who had set the subject matter of the discourse by the questions they posed or had determined the form of the material by particular requests, whether guides or rules for the spiritual life, sermons, or treatises on theology or scripture. In chapter 3, I look at historical narrative, Latin histories and biographies, commissioned by or dedicated to a particular woman, who is addressed by name in an accompanying letter or preface. In chapter 4, my focus is on courtly literature in French, translations of histories from Latin and newly composed romances, from the twelfth and thirteenth centuries, in which the woman patron is directly addressed in the text. One assumes there were many more texts written for women which have lost all trace of the addressee, but I will discuss only works which are clearly identified. Like the histories, the romances for women patrons implicitly argue for women's claims to inheritance and power. Indeed, in all three areas, religion, history, romance, the works I discuss here assume the mental and moral capacity of women to act responsibly in their public world.

A work that was close to Alcuin's heart was inspired by Charlemagne's sister Gisla and his daughter Rotrud. Gisla was abbess of the distinguished double monastery of Chelles, and Rotrud, who joined her there, had been tutored in Greek in preparation for a Byzantine marriage, which never occurred. They asked Alcuin for a commentary on the gospel of John, which he answered first in brief and eventually at length he appended their letter of request to the full commentary as a prologue, so future readers would recognize the zeal of their devotion and the occasion of his obedience, providing us with one of the few such requests from women extant. Their letter declares their burning desire to study scripture inspired by his expositions, "after we drank some of the mellifluous knowledge with your wisdom expounding it," knowledge that is to be preferred to all the wealth of the world and is the only true wisdom. They beg him to share his wisdom with them, telling him exactly what they want: "reveal to us the venerable sense of the holy fathers, collect the pearls of many . . . and feed the poor of Christ." But not just the fathers; they want a comprehensive survey of scholarship on the subject: "enter the treasury of the holy doctors and bring forth for us, as a most learned scribe . . . the new and the old." They have Augustine's explanations, which they say are "in certain places much more obscure and embellished with greater circumlocution than can enter the weak intellect of our smallness" (*"quam nostrae parvitatis ingeniolo intrare valeat"*). But despite the humility *topos*, they do not hesitate to imply a comparison with the women Jerome wrote for ("that most brilliant doctor of divine scripture in the holy church, most blessed Jerome, in no way scorned the prayers of noble women, but dedicated many works on prophetic obscurities to their names"), or even with Christ's disciples ("his grace will be yours on the road of this labor who, to the two disciples going on the road [to Emmaus] added himself as the third companion and opened meanings to them that they might understand holy scripture").

In his letter of dedication, Alcuin says he had wanted to do this commentary for thirty years but did not get to it until their good intention excited his pen and called it back to the zeal of writing. He laments his own smallness before the task (equally formulaically, using the same *parvitas* they had used). He speaks at some length about the doctrinal importance of John's gospel and its difference from the other three gospels and cites Augustine, Ambrose, Gregory, Bede, and others. He offers what he has found for them to taste and see "if it has a catholic savor," and sends his only copy to them asking if they deem it worthy to have it transcribed, that is, to publish it for him, with instructions for the copying and editing.

Rabanus Maurus dedicated two biblical commentaries to empress Judith, the second wife of Charlemagne's son, but they seem to have a political significance as much as a religious one. They are both on books about forceful women, one on Judith, the biblical heroine and the empress's namesake, the other on Esther, a biblical queen, "one your equal in name, the other in dignity," whose extraordinary virtues he says make them models for men as well as women, but whose actions make them particularly apt models for the empress. Though he does not say so, Rabanus strongly suggests that he intends Judith to identify with the historical experiences of both women, one who went out aggressively to destroy the enemy of her people, the other who persuaded her husband to change his policy toward them. Rabanus tells the empress in the dedication to the book of Judith that "your prudence has conquered enemies already and if you persevere in good, you will happily overcome them all in your conflict (*agone*), provided you implore divine help." Judith (like Esther) is presented consistently as a type of the church, and Rabanus may well have been encouraging the empress to identify herself directly with church interests like her namesake, though he may also have supported her political maneuvers. He brings a number of other women into his commentary who are extraneous to the story but in whom Judith might have seen models: Semiramis was the queen of all Asia after her husband's death and founded the city of Babylon, making it the capital of the Assyrian kingdom—she is the first person mentioned who founded a city; Rhea Silvia, the mother of Romulus (who founded Rome), is also mentioned; Themaris and Priscilla are mentioned as believers in connection with Paul in Acts. The Old Testament Judith is called "*Judith nostra*" frequently, as though she belonged particularly to Rabanus and the empress. The passages on her beauty and wisdom, admired by all, and her counseling the people as the church teaches its children with maternal affection and magisterial authority must be heard as echoes of the praises Rabanus and others lavished on Judith for her wisdom, her beauty, and the care she took over the education of her son. In the dedicatory letters, Rabanus praises her wit, her imitation of holy women, and her learning. He alludes to what Jerome found in the Hebrew but omits Greek references, which an eager reader might supply for herself after examining the preceding: "you, most noble queen, since you well understand the divine mysteries in expositions, will rightly assess what is to be perceived in the rest." In the last chapter of the Judith commentary, we are told the Lord gave the enemy into the hand of woman, who was destined in Genesis to trample his head.

In the eleventh century, Peter Damian wrote a considerable amount of biblical commentary for royal and noble women, some of whom became nuns. Indeed, he included so much material on the Bible in his letters to women that excerpts from them are cited among his biblical commentaries. Letters to countess/duchess Hermesinde, countess Blanche, countess Adelaide, and the empress Agnes are cited throughout the Old Testament commentaries that were culled by a disciple from Peter's letters and sermons. But the most intellectual of Peter's letters to women is one he wrote to one of his sisters in response to her weighty questions about what existed before creation and what would exist after the end of the world. Though, like Jerome, he says she draws him to unknown things and compels him to teach what he has not yet learned, he does not discourage her curiosity; he says it is fruitful to inquire, that the mind cannot be free from thoughts, and wickedness cannot hold a mind that is engaged in sober cogitation on useful things. He talks about infinity and the finite, referring her to Augustine's *City of God*, Jerome on Daniel and the Apocalypse, and his own letter to Blanche about the day of judgment.

Empress Agnes, when she became a nun, inspired works on the religious life, one from Peter Damian on contempt of the world (*De fluxa mundi gloria et saeculi despectione*) which compares her favorably to the queen of Sheba— Agnes, who came in humility for the wisdom of Christ, is "truly the queen of Sheba. She is herself an example of proper contempt for the world, having exchanged her crown for a veil, her purple for sackcloth, a scepter for a psalter in contrast to worldly rulers who came to bad ends; the list of men and women includes the suicides of mighty queens, of Cleopatra and of Semiramis, who had subjected many kingdoms to herself." John of Fecamp compiled a collection of scriptural passages on the religious life at Agnes's request, which he sent with some comments, adding something on the life and customs of virgins for the instruction of the nuns in her monastery. He too sees her as "a shining example of holy widowhood" to other noble matrons. Recognizing the hostility she had faced, he answers the barking dogs who are her enemies with a description of her pious works as she travels through Italy and France. He asks her to control the publication of the work, making sure that if others want to have it, they transcribe it diligently, neither adding nor omitting. And he wishes her God's comfort in her dual life, active as a Martha and contemplative as a Mary.

In the same period, Goscelin wrote a *Liber confortatorius* in four books for a little-known recluse of Angers, Eve, whom he had known from her earliest years at Wilton. He worried about her moving to the austerity of the recluse life, then came to see it as the right decision and wrote this book to support and praise her. His tone is friendly rather than formal or polemic, growing naturally out of trust and direct contact. The work reveals his strong attachment to her, his grief over their separation—he is so overwhelmed by grief as he writes that he has to stop and sit in the church, weeping—and his desire to make up for the distance by writing, that is, he seems to be consoling himself more than her. This is particularly obvious in the first of four parts, in which he reminisces tenderly about their life together, his teaching, her lending him books, his sending her a fish, their correspondence, and her departure, leaving her parents and especially him desolate. He compares theirs to the separations of other intensely loving pairs, a list that includes David and Jonathan, John and the Virgin, Peter and Paul, Orestes and his friend, abbess Modesta and her sister Gertrude.

Goscelin uses classical as well as Christian allusions and examples throughout the work, testifying to Eve's education and their shared interests, "our" Boethius, Horace, Seneca, and Virgil, who teach the joys of the austere life and the liberty to be attained in it. Her window can provide a library, which should include the lives of the fathers, the confessions of Augustine, the histories of Cassiodorus and Eusebius, the *City of God*, Orosius, Boethius. Like Aeneas, she has found a place where she can rest despite her struggles, but where she also has her own living model, a woman recluse who, Goscelin says, prepared the place for her and watches over her, "*Benedicta domina.*" Benedicta is one of many positive women models Goscelin offers to Eve. In the struggle against temptation that is the subject of the second part, Goscelin mentions Perpetua and Sara, St. Blandina and the captive woman who converted the Iberians, while he warns her against the sins of Adam (gluttony, vainglory, and greed). As encouragement for combat with the old seducer of (the first) Eve, there are more examples in the third part, including Jerome's friends Paula, Eustochium, and Blesilla, scholars and saints of the simple life, what Jerome called "*sancta rusticitas et docta sanctitas.*" In the last part, on triumph, Goscelin contrasts his own experience, when he was assigned to a place he could not bear but came to love, with that of Eve, who, disdaining the easy life of a nun, should be content with that of a poor recluse. He ends with the eternal joys that await her after the Last Judgment, when all the saints will come together, among them queen Edith and the souls from Wilton, and Goscelin will see his dear daughter again, though in his unworthiness he will be far from her.

THE APOSTOLIC LIFE

PART THREE

THE APOSTOLIC LIFE

Instead of skipping several centuries, as we did between sections one and two, this section picks up where the previous one left off. The twelfth and thirteenth centuries saw drastic change throughout European society, especially in religious culture. Unlike the Gregorian Reform, implemented by the clerical elite, lay people often took the lead in the religious developments of this period. A new form of spirituality emerged, based on imitating the itinerant preaching and poverty exemplified by Jesus and his disciples. The *vita apostolica*, as it was called, challenged many of the assumptions held dear by the reformers of the previous century. At the same time, a competing religious worldview, calling itself Christian but rejecting both Trinitarian doctrine and the institutional church, provided an even greater challenge. Some scholars argue that the changes in European Christianity during this period were as profound as those of the sixteenth-century Reformation. Such rapid change does not occur without precedent. Two factors especially warrant our attention: underlying demographic and economic changes beginning in the eleventh century and unintended consequences of the Gregorian Reform.

Early medieval Europe was overwhelmingly agrarian. Wealth was based almost entirely on land. While coins existed, money was used little. Precious metals and other valuable objects were used for display and gifts, not investment. Although the aristocracy provided a limited market for long-distance trade in luxury items, most economic activity was local. There were few towns. Beginning around the year 1000, the population of Europe began to increase rapidly, doubling over the next few centuries. Innovations in agricultural technology increased the productivity of the land. Markets and towns arose in various regions. These developments had a profound impact on medieval society. While most Europeans remained in agricultural villages, new classes of people appeared to occupy the new "ecological niches" in this changed society. Merchants and craftsmen (small-business owners in our world) populated the new towns and managed the ever-increasing commercial activity. Both the secular and clerical aristocracy presided over increasingly more sophisticated institutions requiring lawyers and other civil servants. A new middle class, educated and self-confident, would provide the stimulus for the religious changes of the twelfth and thirteenth centuries.

Tightening our focus onto the trajectory of religious trends, the success of the Gregorian Reform inadvertently provided the context for the challenges the institutional church faced in the twelfth and thirteenth century. During this time, Western Christianity became a virtual papal monarchy. The bishop of Rome presided over the wealthiest and most sophisticated government in Europe. Not only was the pope the unquestioned leader of the Western church, he was the leading figure in all of European society. The papacy used this influence to more sharply define and enforce right beliefs and practices. The parish system came to fruition, giving the clerical elite unprecedented (though imperfect) access to ordinary Christians. Cathedral schools, and eventually universities, produced theologians and canon lawyers to articulate the doctrines and practices that would define Christendom. It is no coincidence that this period also saw the beginnings of dissidents and heretics. As the Western church drew a brighter line between correct and incorrect forms of Christianity, some previously uncontroversial groups would find themselves on the wrong side of the line.

The success of the eleventh-century reformers was cultural as well as institutional. A morally pure clergy was at the heart of church reform from Cluny to Gregory VII. New monastic groups such as the Cistercians and Carthusians demonstrated the continuing appeal of rigorous monasticism. The influence of monastic ideals on secular priests, priests who served in the world, is evident in the creation of regular canons. Priests who staffed cathedrals and other large churches in Europe were known as canons. Regular canons were those priests who wanted to live a communal, regulated life like monks while they ministered to the laity. The reforms were also successful in changing the attitudes of the laity. Rigorous monastic communities such as the Cistercians were very popular among aristocratic donors. There is also evidence that ordinary Christians in both rural villages and towns were becoming more demanding of their priests. Ironically, the reformers had done such a good job of instilling their values into at least some of the laity that they began to push the institutional church to further reform.

It is at this point that broader social trends and religious reform come together. Early medieval Christianity had drawn heavily from the Old Testament. Like Israelite religion, European Christianity before the twelfth century was primarily formal and communal. Christians gathered for rituals performed by priests and lived in a society ruled by a divinely sanctioned warrior aristocracy. Communal rituals would continue to play central roles in medieval Christianity, but they would share the spotlight with more personal and less formal expressions of Christianity. The new, educated urban elite identified with the New Testament more than the Old Testament. We need to be careful here. Early medieval Christians did not ignore the New Testament. Indeed, to be a Christian presupposes a belief in the truth of the New Testament. Nevertheless, many twelfth-century Christians were reading the New Testament with different lenses. Instead of focusing on depictions of Jesus as the son of God, reigning in heaven and judging man, they focused on the human Jesus as a role model. They did not see Jesus and the Apostles as priests or monks, but as itinerant preachers without significant possessions. This apostolic life captured the religious imagination of the time. By the end of the twelfth century, the poor, itinerant preacher became a fixture of the European religious scene and a problem for church authorities. German historian Herbert Grundmann's study of the apostolic life movement, published over seventy years ago, is still the classic treatment of the topic and provides the first selection for this section.

Urban Christians were more apt to identify with the New Testament because the New Testament world was much like their own. Jesus and his apostles, particularly Paul, ministered in towns. While their audience included farmers and shepherds, the New Testament also mentions tax collectors, lawyers, and scholars. Given the many parables about money and commerce, Jesus' audience seems to have included a significant number of merchants.

While the exploits of Old Testament heroes such as Joshua and David made perfect sense to agrarian warlords, the urban milieu of the New Testament resonated with the denizens of the rapidly growing medieval towns. In the second selection, Lester Little describes the social significance of the *vita apostolica* in the new medieval towns.

The response of the papacy to the apostolic life evolved between the late twelfth and early thirteenth centuries. At the III Lateran Council in 1179, a group called the Waldensians asked the pope for approval of their version of the apostolic life. Their founder, a businessman from Lyons named Valdes, had renounced his wealth and gathered a small group of followers to emulate

Jesus and his disciples. Valdes and his followers believed that they were called to preach and produced their own vernacular translations of the Bible. Following the precedent of previous church authorities, Pope Alexander III approved of their lifestyle but would not authorize their translations or sanction their preaching. Most Waldensians rejected the ruling and broke with papal authority. Within a generation, the papacy began to reevaluate its response to the apostolic life. Groups like the Waldensians and Cathars (which are discussed in this section) attracted followers because of their adherence to the apostolic lifestyle. In order to compete successfully, the church sanctioned its own version of the apostolic life.

The most important example of this is the creation of the Dominican and Franciscan orders. Instead of the traditional monastic life, Dominicans and Franciscans lived the apostolic life of poverty and itinerant preaching under the authority of the papacy. To distinguish them from traditional monks, they are often called friars or mendicants (Latin for beggars). The story of Francis of Assisi, the founder of the Franciscans, bears significant resemblance to that of Valdes. Francis was the son of a successful Italian merchant. Converted to the apostolic life, he gathered a small group of followers for a life of poverty and preaching. Unlike Valdes, Francis encountered support from church authorities. His local bishop, and eventually Pope Innocent III, approved of Francis' group. Francis himself differed from the Waldensians in two significant ways. First, Francis acknowledged the authority of the institutional church. Second, the early Franciscans were careful to encourage poverty without condemning the wealth of the institutional church. The issue of voluntary poverty would continue to cause tension within the Franciscan order and between the order and the papacy. Even so, the Franciscan movement became tremendously influential throughout Christendom, and Francis became the Middle Ages' most famous saint. Dominic of Guzman, the founder of the Dominicans, was not a lay convert to the apostolic life. He was a Spanish priest who wished to combat heretical movements in southwestern Europe. He believed that it was the lifestyle, not the ideas, of the Cathars and Waldensians that made them attractive. For the church to be successful, it had to exemplify the apostolic life as well. He created the Order of Preachers, usually called Dominicans, to carry out this mission. For Dominic and his order, voluntary poverty was not an end in itself, but a means to legitimate their preaching.

Dominic's main concern was not groups like the Waldensians, who had basically orthodox beliefs but rejected church authority. By the beginning of the thirteenth century, a group called the Cathars had become very popular in Southern Europe. Cathars called themselves Christians, but held to a set of beliefs very different from the Trinitarian Christianity that dominated Europe. Cathars were dualists. They believed in two opposing forces, one evil and one good. The evil force, often equated with the God of the Old Testament, had created the physical world. Since Cathars considered the physical world as evil, they rejected the value of all physical things. The Cathar elite, called *perfecti*, renounced sex and refused to eat any animal products, because they were the product of sexual reproduction. They vehemently opposed rituals such as the Eucharist, in which bread and wine were believed to become the physical body of Jesus. Because of their disdain for the physical world, Cathar *perfecti* often seemed to live a more apostolic life than Christian priests and monks. The final selection in this section describes how the Cathars and Dominicans competed with each other to be the most apostolic in their ministries.

The apostolic life resonated with both men and women. It was almost impossible, however, for medieval women to live out the apostolic lifestyle of preaching and poverty. Women such as Claire of Assisi worked closely with Francis in the early days of the Franciscan movement. Nevertheless, Claire and her followers ended up living a cloistered life like traditional nuns. The life of Valdes is instructive concerning the role of women in the apostolic life movement. Both a husband and a father at the time of his conversion, he placed his wife and daughters in convents so he could live the life of a wandering preacher. While a man adopting a lifestyle of itinerant begging may have been subversive in medieval society, a woman doing it was unthinkable. Since authorized preaching required formal education, women could not be authorized to preach. Voluntary poverty was not an option for women, who rarely had the right to give away even their own property. The third and fourth selections in this section deal with a phenomenon peculiar to deeply religious women during this period. Many female saints and mystics of this period were known for extreme fasting. Both of the selections explain how the fasting behaviors fit into the religious and cultural developments of the time. Because of their different methodological approaches, they draw differing conclusions.

Further Reading

Barber, Malcolm. *The Cathars: Dualist Heretics in Languedoc in the Middle Ages*, Harlow, England: Longman, 2000.

Bell, Rudolf. *Holy Anorexia*, Chicago: The University of Chicago Press, 1987.

Bolton, Brenda. *The Medieval Reformation*, New York: Holmes & Meier, 1983.

Bynum, Caroline Walker. *Holy Feast, Holy Fast: The Religious Significance of Food to Medieval Women*, Berkeley: University of California Press, 1987.

――. *Jesus as Mother: Studies in the Spirituality of the High Middle Ages*, Berkeley: University of California Press, 1982.

Grundmann, Herbert. *Religious Movements in the Middle Ages*, trans. Steven Rowan, Notre Dame, IN: University of Notre Dame Press, 1995.

Lambert, Malcolm. *Medieval Heresy: Popular Movements from Bogomil to Hus*, 3rd ed., London: Blackwell, 2002.

Lawrence, C. H. *The Friars: The Impact of the Early Mendicant Movement on Western Society*, London: Longman, 1994.

Little, Lester. *Religious Poverty and the Profit Economy in Medieval Europe*, Ithaca: Cornell University Press, 1978.

Moore, R. I. *The Origins of European Dissent*, London: Blackwell, 1977.

Moorman, J. R. H. *A History of the Franciscan Order*, Oxford: Oxford University Press, 1968.

Roach, Andrew P. *The Devil's World: Heresy and Society, 1100–1300*, New York: Pearson Education, 2005.

CHAPTER THIRTEEN

~

Religious Movements in the Middle Ages*

Herbert Grundmann

A volume on the religious culture of the Middle Ages cannot ignore the ground-breaking impact of Herbert Grundmann's Religious Movements in the Middle Ages. *Before the publication of the work in 1935, historians of medieval Christianity focused almost exclusively on doctrines and institutions. By focusing instead on religious culture, Grundmann believed he had found the key to understanding European Christianity in the twelfth and thirteenth centuries: whether mendicant or monastic, lay or clerical, heretic or orthodox, male or female, all the significant movements of the time shared a commitment to the apostolic life of poverty and preaching. While the details have been challenged, Grundmann's thesis continues to set the agenda for research today.* Religious Movements *was published in English in 1995. Each of the other selections in this section show a debt to Grundmann. In the following selection, Grundmann describes the development of heretical movements in the wake of the Gregorian Reform. Why did the heretical groups criticize the church? What makes them heretical? What role does doctrine play in the heretical movements? What are the "social origins" of the heretics?*

The special character of the heretical movement of the twelfth century and the importance which the ideas of the apostolic life and Christian poverty had within it can best be illustrated by two letters from the middle decades of the century. In one of them, Abbot Evervin of Steinfeld reported to Bernard

* © 1995 by the University of Notre Dame. Reprinted with permission of the University of Notre Dame Press. Herbert Grundmann, *Religious Movements in the Middle Ages*, trans. Steven Rowan, Notre Dame: University of Notre Dame Press, 1995, pp. 7–17.

137

of Clairvaux about heretics interrogated in Cologne in 1143. In the second, a monk named Heribert reports on heretics in the region of Perigueux under the leadership of a man named Poncius, otherwise unknown, probably around 1163. These two letters are an improvement on many other documents about heresy in the twelfth century because they do not repeat the usual fantasies of Manichaean doctrines derived from old polemics against heresy but rather describe heretics on the basis of their own knowledge—in the case of Heribert the monk, with superstitious exaggeration, but in Abbot Evervin's case with thoughtful openness. The abbot had attended the interrogation of the heretics discovered in Cologne, and he gives their testimony without hostility or literary prejudice, in fact providing an honest account which shows he was deeply impressed by the religious content of their testimony. Most of the heretics had returned to the Church and done penance, but the "heretic bishop" and his companions demanded a public disputation, under the presidency of the archbishop, in which learned representatives of their party were to participate. They declared themselves ready to give up their errors if disproved, but otherwise they intended to be faithful to their beliefs until death. The Cologne clergy did not submit to a disputation, preferring to attempt to convert them, but, as so often with heresy trials in the twelfth century, the mob intervened before matters were decided and dragged the heretics to the pyre. The heretics had sought to convince their judges by citing the gospels and the apostles to support their convictions. Because they were convinced they lived in keeping with the gospels and the example of the apostles, they claimed to represent the true Church, the true followers of Christ. Having no need for the goods of the world, like Christ's apostles they possessed neither house nor field nor cattle. In contrast to this, the Catholic clergy piled house upon house and field upon field, heaping up wealth. Even if the members of orders, monks and canons, did not have these goods as private property, still they held them in common. They, the heretics, were the "Poor of Christ" who moved restlessly and painfully from place to place like the apostles and martyrs, in the face of persecution, satisfied to have only enough to live on. The heretical words recorded by Abbot Evervin were filled with the unshakable certainty and security of faith:

> We hold this, that we are not of this world. You, who are lovers of this world, have the peace of this world, since you are of this world. You and your fathers have become pseudo-apostles, adulterating the word of Christ—we and our fathers, having become apostles, dwell in the grace of Christ, and shall remain in it unto the end of the age. To distinguish them, Christ tells us and you, 'By their fruits you shall know them!' Our fruit is the way of Christ.

The goal of these heretics is to follow Christ through an apostolic life in poverty and ceaseless religious activity, in keeping with the counsels of the gospels and the writings of the apostles.

Yet these thoughts are not peculiar to the heretics in Cologne. The monk Heribert portrays heresy in Perigord in Southern France with less understanding for their doctrine and way of life, but showing the same characteristics. They, too, assert they are living the apostolic life and they also believe they achieve this not simply by renouncing meat, by moderation in drinking wine, and by external compliance with other biblical counsels, but particularly through complete poverty, renouncing the use of money. Just as was the case with the heretics of Cologne, they judged ecclesiastical life strictly by the norms of the Bible, and they accepted only what Scripture demanded. They were thus intensely concerned with their own knowledge of Scripture, and they were ceaselessly occupied as preachers, undertaking their wanderings barefoot.

In Cologne as well as in Southern France, the idea of Christian poverty and apostolic life as a wandering preacher is essential to their stance as "heresy," and this idea indeed remains the main theme of heresy until the start of the thirteenth century, among Cathars as well as Waldensians. Leading the life of the apostles, being true followers of the apostles, is the heretics' basic claim, and their break with the Church followed from that. Hence, the heretics were called "Good Christians," or simply "Good People," by all those who came in contact with them. No impartial observer can doubt their genuine and passionate conviction that they were reviving and realizing true evangelical and apostolic Christianity in their lives. They demonstrated this through their readiness to suffer martyrdom for these convictions far too often for it to be considered a mere phrase. The first condition for understanding the religious movements of the Middle Ages is to take these convictions and claims seriously.

All the same, the Church combated these devotees of the apostolic life with all its might. There were three grounds for this. First of all, the idea that the counsels of the gospels and writings of the apostles were the uniquely binding measure for the Church as well as for every Christian generated a decisively negative critique of the doctrines and usages of the Church, leading to rejection not only of the sacraments in their Catholic form, but also of the veneration of saints, prayers for the dead, the doctrine of purgatory, and so on. Secondly, the heretics who asserted they were leading the apostolic life in poverty did not recognize the *ordo* of the hierarchical Church, placing the legitimacy of ecclesiastical ordination in question. On the basis of their consciousness of having been called to carry out the gospels, they brought into being a competing church of "good Christians" with "perfect" or "elect" as clergy, and their "faithful" as congregations in precise analogy to the Catholic Church, even developing a sort of episcopal organization. Thirdly and last, in the course of the twelfth century the idea of poverty and apostolic itinerant preaching had come to be combined with dualistic doctrines in many areas, especially in Southern France. Increasingly influenced by speculative ideas from the Greek East, it yielded a strange rebirth for much of Manichee cosmogony and mythology. After the end of the twelfth century, Catholic polemic against heresy placed the greatest emphasis on this third point, on dualistic speculation and its abuses, particularly because the Cathars at least tried to justify themselves with citations from the New Testament. This tactic has so influenced perception that dualism has been stressed as the foundation of heresy ever since, with everything else seen to derive from dualism. To tell the truth, before the end of the twelfth century it is not the speculative problem of dualism which constituted the central conflict between heretics and Catholicism, but rather the questions of religious life and the Church. So far as we know, at the time of the emergence of heresy in the West in the first half of the eleventh century, dualistic doctrine was nowhere to be found. To be sure, Catholic literature designated the heretics as Manichees from the very beginning. This often enticed ecclesiastical writers to read St. Augustine to discover what Manichees taught, then simply to ascribe their doctrines to the heretics of their own time. When this did not happen, when they unmistakably dealt with the convictions and doctrines of contemporary heretics (even in official ecclesiastical documents on heresy), dualistic speculation either leaves little trace, or it fades entirely into the background in comparison to the major question: whether the true Church of Christ resides with those who claim the apostolic succession, and thereby the full and exclusive right to ordain all Church offices, or whether it belonged to those who lived like the apostles as the gospel demanded. In the twelfth century, dualistic speculation provided the philosophic "superstructure" for heresy's religious and moral demands. Dualism tells people more clearly what has to be done—and this was the service dualism performed for the heretical movement in the twelfth century. For persons aroused by religious and ethical inclinations to think about the nature of the world, the Catholic doctrine of the world was infinitely harder to understand, much less comprehensible than the Manichaean doctrine. The Catholic world-picture, largely influenced both by Augustine's intellectual commitment against neo-Platonic monism on the one side and Manichaean dualism on the other, is neither monistic nor dualistic, since it recognized neither the unity and identity of all being with God nor the division of all being into the two principles of light and darkness, good and evil. Thus Augustine does not deny that evil exists, but he does deny it to be part of real existence: he interprets evil as a negation of the good. Neither of the two intellectual powers which had once struggled for the future of Christianity, monistic neo-Platonism and dualistic Manichaeism, disappeared from the scene. On the contrary, they have threateningly shadowed Christianity throughout the years. During the crisis of the hierarchical system which took place in the twelfth and thirteenth centuries, both of these threats returned to the Christian West from the Greek East. But that return was only possible because primitive religious movements with newly awakened spiritual needs were seeking speculative doctrinal systems and were capable of absorbing new religious and ethical drives.

In any case, dualistic speculation emerged more clearly after the end of the twelfth century. As a result, the religious movement split. In contrast to the Cathars, who followed Manichaean dualism and in turn were repeatedly divided by speculative sectarian disputes, there stood groups within the movement for religious poverty and apostolic itinerant preaching who not only did not follow the transition to dualism, but in fact combated it. Yet the old concept of a singular religious movement continued to pursue them, and the Church continued to persecute them, not as dualists, but for their "apostolic" claims. Even before this division over speculative problems took place, the major concerns of the religious movement were not dogma but questions of the proper religious life and the true Church. To overlook this is to misunderstand the coherence the religious movement had in this period. The driving idea of the heretical movement of the twelfth century was to live according to the model of the apostles, to renounce all the goods of this world in voluntary poverty, to renew Christian life and pursue Christian doctrine by ceaseless wandering and preaching. This also entailed attacking the hierarchical Church and Catholic clergy as illegitimate successors to the apostles, insofar as they did not live in a truly Christian, evangelical and apostolic manner. All detailed criticisms of ecclesiastical institutions, of the sacraments (particularly marriage as a sacrament, the baptism of children, and the sacrament of the altar in the form of the Catholic mass), of purgatory, and the veneration of saints, arose from this basic idea of the heretics. Everything the heretics themselves used to replace the ceremonies of the Church (particularly the *consolamentum*, the laying on of hands according to the model of Paul, which communicates the Holy Spirit and has the claim to be legitimate ordination) also arises from that basic principle.

Some further remarks are needed in order to clarify the social foundations of the twelfth-century heretical movement. According to an assertion constantly repeated and seldom disputed or doubted, heresy, including the Cathar movement in the twelfth century, spread primarily within the lowest social strata, particularly among "craftsmen." As a result of this perception, since the end of the nineteenth century, historical research has tended to see heretical movements and associated phenomena as a sort of "proletarian movement." But such an assertion is false, applying in no sense to the religious movements of the twelfth century, and only marginally to the thirteenth.

Two things have caused people to believe that heresy spread primarily in the lowest social classes, particularly among artisans. The first is that Catholic writers often described heretics as *rusticani* or *rustici*, or as *idiotæ et illiterati*. The second is the frequent description of Cathars as *texterants*, weavers.

If the heretics are called *rusticani* or *rustici*, that does not mean they were peasants, but rather that they did not have academic training. The term *idiotæ et illiterati* means exactly the same thing. It really says nothing about the social origins of the persons designated, nothing more than that they were not trained clerics. *Rusticanus* and *rusticus* are antonyms of *doctus* or *sapiens*. Clerical writers all denigrated the fact that people without academic, literary training dared to assert they knew better than a theologically trained clergy, which is why they stressed that the heretics were *rusticani* or *idiotæ et illiterati*. They did not stop to consider that the apostles themselves, the heretics' supreme model, had once been called *idiotæ et sine literis* by the priests and scribes. When Francis, the son of a wealthy merchant, called himself an *idiota* and even a *pazzus*, citing the model of the apostles, he silenced learned mockery of pious simplicity for a time—at least until learned theologians from his own order took the field against heretics they called *idiotæ et illiterati*.

Even if the titles of *rusticani*, *rustici*, *idiotæ*, and *illiterati* tell us nothing at all about the social position of the heretics, still the French term for the heretics, *texterants*, weavers, would seem to indicate a social level where heresy was at home. The notion that heresy spread extensively among weavers was never asserted in sources of the twelfth century; rather, the term "weavers," *texterants*, *textores*, was simply the proper name for heretics in the French-speaking area, equivalent to different names used in other areas: Cathars in Germany, Arians in Provence, Patarenes in Italy. Just as was later the case, these names, along with those of "Waldensians" or *pauperes de Lugduno*, described only the "perfect," the actual preachers of heresy, who wandered through the world in keeping with the example of the apostles. These words were never used for their adherents, their congregations, the *credentes* or *fautores*. The question then, is why these wanderers traveling as preachers in the apostolic model were called "weavers." "From the practice of weavers," Eckbert of Schönau responds, "since they say that the true faith of Christ and the true worship of Christ does not exist save in their gatherings, which they hold in cellars and weaving-sheds and in underground dwellings of this sort." Why did these heretical wandering preachers come to be weavers? Because they were already weavers by profession and origin? Stephan of Bourbon tells about a priest in the bishopric of Toul who had been seduced by the heretics and set out for Milan together with forty members of his parish to have themselves completely trained in heresy. There he surrendered his priestly status and took up weaving. In this case a weaver was not made into a heretic, but rather a heretic became a weaver. There is nothing against the assumption that most heretical "weavers" had similar origins—and the precedent of Saint Paul, who supported himself on his journeys as a rug-weaver, might have played a role as well. It was part of the heretics' apostolic ideal to live from the work of their own hands, without earning more than was needed to satisfy the basic needs of life. Weaving, the very craft which was the first to develop into an industry demanding labor in exchange for subsistence wages, was obviously the "chosen profession" most suited to heretic preachers, who seldom stayed in one place for long. In the chief region for heresy, in Southern France and Provence, this heretic's craft grew by the end of the twelfth century to become a true "heretic industry," with its own enterprises for the preparation of wool and the making of broadcloth, and its own merchandising. In this manner the activities of members and adherents (including female) were organized, economic links were created, and support assured for the wandering preachers. All of this clearly indicates that the designation of heretics as "weavers" had nothing to do with origins among artisans, nor with any particularly strong participation of the lowest social groups in heresy. Weavers and artisans did not become heretics, heretics became weavers. It became the occupation of choice in which they could most conveniently unite their religious activities with their economic needs.

If general terms for the heretics give us no information about the connection of heresy to particular social levels, it is necessary to collect and sift individual reports in the sources concerning the social origin of particular heretics. This produces an entirely different picture. Guibert of Nogent names one of the two heretics condemned in 1114 as a mere *rusticus*, uneducated, but the other, *frater* Ebrardus, was probably a monk. Under Archbishop Bruno of Trier (1102/24) two clerics and two laymen were arrested as heretics at Iwers in the Ardennes. The monk Heribert writes on heresy in Perigord: "In this seduction were many, including not only nobles who abandoned their property, but clerics, priests, monks and nuns also joined in."

Bernard's secretary Gaufred relates that, not long before Bernard's arrival in Toulouse (1145), the heretics "seduced one of the judges of the city together with his wife, so that they left their property and resettled in a village which was full of heretics, and none of their neighbors could convince them to return." Bernard himself says: "Clergy and priests are to be found among them, untonsured and bearded, having abandoned their ecclesiastical flocks." According to Evervin's account, the heretics of Cologne in 1143 asserted that "many of our clerics and monks" (*plures ex nostris clericis et monachis*) belonged to them. Archbishop Hugh of Rouen (died 1164) directed his writing *Contra hereticos* particularly against all those "who left the clergy and went over to heresy." In 1172 a cleric Robert, "rather subtly literate, but to no use" (*subtiliter quidem, sed inutiliter litteratus*) was burned in Arras because he was unable to purge himself through the ordeal of the hot iron against the accusation "that he not only was a heretic, but that he also favored and defended heretics." According to the Annals of the Monastery of Anchin, "Nobles, non-nobles, clerics, knights, rustics, virgins, widows and married women" were accused of heresy at the Council in Arras in 1183. In 1206 Bishop Diego disputed in Servian (between Montpellier and Beziers) with an Albigensian Theoderich, who had earlier been named William and had been a canon of the church in Nevers, but who had been seduced into heresy by his uncle, the knight Evrard of Châteuneuf. After his uncle's condemnation in Paris in 1201 he had gone to Provence and there played a large role among the heretics. A *miles* answered the question posed by Bishop Fulko of Toulouse why he and his like did not drive the heretics out of the region: "we cannot, since we were raised with them, and we can see many relatives living decently among them."

In each of these cases, it was not a question of adherents or friends of heretics, of *credentes* or *fautores*, but of "heretics" themselves, preachers wandering in apostolic poverty. And these witnesses are not selected by any special criteria, since hardly any sources have been found saying anything more about the social origins of heretics among the documents until the start of the thirteenth century. These documents tell us heresy did not recruit primarily out of the lowest social levels, the "proletariat." Rather, wealthy townsmen, priests, and monks often joined the ranks of wandering heretic preachers; it was this participation of clergymen as well as prominent and wealthy persons in the heretical movement which was remarkable to contemporaries. It was already noted that women, in keeping with the apostolic model, were at work among the heretics as well, for they believed they could say with Paul: "Don't we have the power to bring along a sister, as do other apostles?"

If the social composition of adherents to heresy is examined, there is just as little evidence the lower classes were inclined to heresy, either exclusively or even predominantly. This is clearest in Southern France. When Bernard of Clairvaux tried to preach against heresy in Verfeil in 1145, the members of the higher classes (*qui majores erant*) left the church, and the rest of the people soon joined them. Bernard followed them outside to preach in the street, but the wealthy went into their houses, leaving only the commoners (*plebecula*) to listen, but these could hardly understand a word, since the *majores* sought to drown him out with their own noise. Bernard confirmed that it was the upper strata of the townsmen and the nobility which sympathized with the heretics in other towns as well. One chronicler expressly notes that heresy in the County of Toulouse about 1177 had not only blinded the simple folk, but also the clergy and the secular grandees, and that it only took one look at the situation in Southern France to see that it was precisely the leading classes and a great portion of the nobility which sided with heresy against the ecclesiastical hierarchy. Bernard of Clairvaux already asserted what has often been repeated ever since, that the upper classes in general and the nobility in particular promoted and protected the heretical doctrine of religious poverty out of greed, a lust for money and land, not for religious reasons. They desired to enrich themselves at the expense of the goods of the Church. Such motivations might have actually played a role with many of the politically interested lords of Provence, but it could not have led to the participation of virtually the entire nobility, the close attachment of the wives of nobles to heretical preachers, and the conversion of many wealthy nobles into voluntarily poor wandering preachers. Religious ideas and demands were always decisive, and insofar as our sources can answer the question of the impact of these ideas on various social levels, it is certain that many clerics, nobles, and wealthy burghers adhered to heresy. There is not the slightest trace of a "proletarian" membership.

~

CHAPTER FOURTEEN

Religious Poverty and the Profit Economy in Medieval Europe*

Lester K. Little

The two main attributes of the apostolic life were voluntary poverty and itinerant preaching. Vows of voluntary poverty were not controversial in themselves. Since Roman times, hermits and monks had taken vows of voluntary poverty. The difference lay in how those following the apostolic life reinterpreted the very idea of poverty. For a traditional monk poverty meant the renunciation of personal possessions. Along with the vow of celibacy, monastic poverty entailed a renunciation of power. By renouncing the right to own land and produce children to inherit and form alliances through marriage, a nobleman cut himself off from the prime sources of political power in his culture. Depending on the community he joined, however, he might well continue to lead a materially privileged life. New urban Christians viewed poverty differently. Individual merchants and craftsmen rarely had land or power to renounce. They had money, and for them voluntary poverty meant the renunciation of that money and the lifestyle it enabled. The tension inherent in integrating this view of poverty into the wealthiest institution in Europe would be a major source of both the vibrancy and conflict in medieval Christianity until the Reformation. The second attribute, itinerant preaching, also challenged traditional religious culture. In this selection, Lester Little connects mendicant preaching to the new urban spirituality. According to Little, although the friars renounced monetary wealth, the content and style of their preaching reflected the commercial activity of urban society. In what ways did mendicant preaching "fit" the new urban

---

* © 1978 Lester K. Little. Reprinted with the permission of Lester K. Little. Lester K. Little, *Religious Poverty and the Profit Economy in Medieval Europe*, Ithaca: Cornell University Press, 1978, pp. 197–203.

spirituality? Why does Little compare and contrast Benedictine monasticism and mendicant spirituality? What were some criticisms of the friars?

The social significance of the friars' programme emerges from an analysis of its message, or content, which included discussion of property, interest, credit, insurance, and moneylending. That same social significance is further clarified by an analysis of the medium used to transmit the friars' message. Preaching and the administration of penance were the principal means of expression used; but why, it must now be asked, were these means considered appropriate and therefore selected?

The dominant members of the urban sector of society were merchants, bankers, lawyers, notaries, school masters, and certain of the landlords who organized production on their lands for the market. They did not make their living by praying, or by fighting, or by "working," not, at least, by working with their hands. They talked; they argued; they negotiated; they wrote; they entertained; above all, they tried to persuade other people. Such were the defining or characteristic activities of those who prospered in the urban environment.

In order to see how a spirituality, both in its message and in the means used to propagate that message, can be related to the activities of the dominant class of a society, one can refer back to the first feudal age, where society was dominated by those who fought and the leading form of spirituality was that of the black monks. Their characteristic medium of expression was praying, the *opus Dei*. Praying had been part of the Benedictine programme from as far back as the sixth century, but it had changed significantly, coming to occupy a much larger proportion of the monks' waking hours, and developing into an intensely aggressive war carried on by the monks against the devil, a war in which the souls of the Christian faithful were at stake. Further examination of this war has shown that the monks themselves came from the class of fighters and also that their outside support came from that same group. The special virtue cultivated by the monks was patience, which was one of the main forms of humility, in turn defined as poverty, meaning poverty in spirit. The monks had to be able to bear affliction but at the same time inflict no harm upon anyone else. The ideal they sought to impose upon the laity was of the Christian knight who was strong, who protected the poor (including, among others, the monks themselves), but who, at the same time, did not shed blood. This ideal became a concrete programme in the Peace Movement, where armed strength found its justification in the maintenance of a peaceful order, and ultimately in the crusades. Such was the message of monastic spirituality. The medium of this spirituality was a symbolic war, ritual aggression in the form of liturgy, fought figuratively by spiritual soldiers.

The medium was a form of the very activity against which the monastic message was directed. The medium was fighting (a point noted by their enemies), but not reckless, physically violent fighting in which people got injured and killed; instead it was a kind of aggression that was carefully controlled and made predictable by ritual. The monks in this way confronted the great social problem of their day, namely violence. In the first instance they renounced it utterly for themselves as individuals; secondly they engaged in the same activity but transformed it so as to remove from it the harmful, objectionable elements; and thirdly they elaborated an ethic for the dominant members of society that permitted them to continue in their usual activities but in limited, unharmful, spiritually constructive ways. The connection between monastic spirituality and feudal society is explicable; both the monastic ideal, however traditional, and the monastic means of expression (again, no matter how traditional) were shaped by feudal society, and they in turn had a profound impact (for the very reason that they had been so responsive) upon that same society.

The Benedictines meanwhile did not cultivate talk. While they did not live under a strict rule of silence, they discouraged conversation and set prescribed periods for silence, including those reserved for spiritual reading; after all, they had brought about a major alteration of human behaviour in the West with their invention of silent reading. Neither did the Benedictines cultivate contentiousness; indeed the rule specifically admonishes against it. Nor did they cultivate entertainment; a good sense of humour can be found at nearly every turn in their history, but the rule frowns on levity. Nor did the monks specialize in persuasive discourse. They gave witness by their form of life to a truth they considered established. When they got drawn into the apostolate to the Germanic peoples they accomplished the task by their witness and by miraculous demonstration. Persuasive discourse would have been just as inappropriate for them to use as it would have been unsuited to their audience.

Urban audiences, on the other hand, wanted to hear speakers; they relished amusement and spectacle; they sought to be convinced and they demanded explanations. We must not exaggerate the new urban literacy, but neither can we deny or ignore its existence as a reality and as a factor in the changing abilities and desires of the laity. Urban society fostered a need for a spirituality that would express itself in speech. Yet at the same time the moral problems being raised in connection with the various urban professions focused upon this very means of expression. The masters, merchants, and lawyers all talked. While the masters lectured and disputed, the merchants hawked. Alan of Lille's model sermon directed to lawyers is entitled *Ad oratores, seu advocatos*; here the *oratores* are not the monks, not "those who pray," but the lawyers who plead in court. Who could be sure that these people who lived by talking were right or were telling the truth? Who can be sure of the truth when scholars are capable of arguing both sides of a question, when lawyers strive for justice in proportion to the amounts of money they are paid, and when prices that are said to be as low as possible one day are cut by one-third the next? Naturally enough people felt anxious about being manipulated by others. We should not be surprised by the *exemplum* in which a crafty lawyer gets his tongue pulled out, or the one that tells of a merchant who plies prospective customers with drinks. Less vivid (but more real) is the regulation of the town of Saint-Omer forbidding sellers in a certain market to attract the attention of potential buyers by coughing or sneezing.

But while the arts of persuasion lay under a cloud of doubt, the friars entered upon the scene talking: talking, preaching, or, as Thomas of Spalato said about Francis, "shouting." Francis engaged in a sort of street-corner or public-square hawking, a legacy from his pre-conversion days. Everywhere the friars went they talked, and where they encountered opposition they argued. They disputed the arguments of those they saw as heretics, especially in southern France and northern Italy, as well as the arguments of those clerics who saw the advent of the friars as an encroachment. The friars came forward with a new approach to confession and penance; they willingly entered into negotiation with the confessee to determine, through a series of questions and responses, the relative seriousness of the fault and hence the appropriate harshness of the penance. Federigo Visconti, the Archbishop of Pisa, described such an encounter as a battle of wits and words:

> O what a great battle takes place between the friar confessor and the penitent sinner. The sinner says, for instance, 'I will do everything that you wish, but I can in no way whatever give up such a one as my lover, or usury, or hatred, or the grudge I have against so-and-so.' Whence it is fitting that, as one knight fights another powerful, rebellious knight, the friar struggle and do battle with the spears of reason and persuasion against the sinner, that he may conquer him spiritually.

The disciplined contentiousness of the schools served the friars in administering penance as well as in preaching.

The friars were not staid in their public appearances. Francis himself willingly lived in the image of a jongleur, and the friars' use of the *exempla* was an open attempt to give sermons an immediacy, a recognizable quality, and a humour capable of holding an audience. There was nothing necessarily wrong with the work of the jongleur. How, indeed, had Waldes of Lyons been converted? But shouting and entertaining was not all there was to preaching; it was, as we have seen, a carefully developed art designed to gain a certain effect in listeners. The friars thus indulged in those very activities that were most characteristic of the new urban society, especially the urban elite—those very activities which, by the same token, were the nub of the argument of moral corruption in the new urban professions.

The friars further reflected the society they entered by their frequent use of a marketplace vocabulary, a practice that gained authority and impetus from that one-time cloth merchant, Francis of Assisi. Starting around 1240, the biographies of St. Dominic included a parody of legal practice and commercial language in the mention of a will he was purported to have made out to his followers: "Have charity," he is supposed to have told them, "keep humility, and possess voluntary poverty." There is an early Franciscan allegorical work on poverty entitled *The Holy Commerce* (*Sacrum Commerciun*), or, as a fourteenth-century writer once called it, *The Business of Poverty* (*Commercium Paupertatis*). The sermons of Anthony of Padua were laced with references to the types and places of work familiar to his hearers: pharmacists, shops in the square, usurers, mercenaries, metalworkers, and merchants. St. Bonaventure, too, occasionally used a commercial vocabulary, as when he argued for the usefulness of the friars, characterizing them as trustees for the Christian people, who are like debtors, and whose debt the friars try to pay off, or at least reduce.

In justifying the itinerancy of the preaching friars, Humbert of Romans cited the example of the Apostles but by passing first via a mercantile image. Worldly trade offered the example of those who, because they were eager to amass fortunes, never ceased to travel about in the world seeking profits. "And the Apostles also did thus, travelling through various provinces making a fortune in souls." Humbert still again used a variant of this same image where, in a long string of metaphors, he called preaching "a business that increases a householder's goods." Humbert proposed for preaching the standards usually applied to coinage:

In money, one takes into account the metal, the stamp, and the weight. The doctrine is the metal, the example of the Fathers that the preacher follows is the stamp, and humility is the weight. Whoever turns aside from duty is no longer precious metal, but only a worthless piece of clay; where formerly he had the sound of pure metal, now he produces no sound at all.

Another Dominican writer explained the system of indulgences, which came into more frequent use around 1230, as transactions with the church's Treasury of Merits. For a cash payment the penitent person could get credit against his penitential debt from the store of supplemental merit and good works on deposit there from the lives of Christ, Mary, and the saints. From such examples we can see that the friars employed an idiom that was unmistakably urban, just as their behaviour reflected, in a formal sense, the behaviour of the urban professions.

The friars would not have seen or described what they were doing as buying and selling and pleading and negotiating, but the point did not altogether elude their critics. Matthew Paris reported without comment some of the epithets applied to the friars in the university battle of the 1250s, such as "hypocrites," "false preachers," and "vagabonds." Matthew was less restrained in observing how, at the time when the Dominicans were building a comfortable home for themselves at Dunstable (1259), everyone was amazed to see these poor brothers, who professed voluntary poverty, spending so much money. Matthew was at his sharpest when he likened the friars' traffic in indulgences to the sale of sheep on the wool market. The cult of St. Francis grew in the thirteenth century, and it seemed to stimulate a proportionate growth of opposition. In 1289 a priest at Dieppe drew a sharp rebuke from the pope for something he had said and done during a sermon. The priest had apparently been preaching angrily against St. Francis; then from the pulpit he gestured irreverently at a representation of the saint in a window and denounced Francis as an avaricious merchant. And finally there was William of Saint-Amour, the friars' chief antagonist at Paris, who gave special emphasis to their facility of speech and their ability to seduce by means of swindling, double-dealing talk.

Like the Cluniacs who had once been insultingly called soldiers and described in military dress with their swords and lances and helmets, the Franciscans and Dominicans were correspondingly denounced for their avarice, their wealth, their merchandizing, their bargaining—in short, for their similarity to merchants. In a way that recalls the tie between the monks and feudal society, we have seen how the friars confronted the chief problem of the new society, namely moneymaking. In the first place, they rejected moneymaking for themselves, turning instead to the recently matured ideal of voluntary poverty. Secondly, however, they persisted in the linguistic and formal mode of the moneymakers, while avoiding the spiritually harmful aspects of such people's work. And thirdly, having themselves demonstrated part of the way, they provided for the leaders of urban society a revised moral theology that approved of moneymaking in certain, carefully defined circumstances.

The friars' spirituality was both determined by, and a determining factor within, the new urban society.

The case of the Benedictine monks and that of the Franciscan and Dominican friars are not merely two random cases chosen from two different historical periods. They are consecutive cases—one leads into the other. The experience of the monks was present as a factor during the formative period of the friars; the development of the friars' spirituality inevitably contained a more or less conscious reaction against that of the monks. Humbert of Romans, always an exceptionally astute and self-conscious observer, pictured the spirituality of preaching not only as a positive good (for numerous reasons, some of which have been cited above) but also as something better than a spirituality of liturgical intercession:

> Others consecrate themselves to the praises of God following assiduously in church the Divine Office, but the laity do not usually comprehend the words that are recited in the Office, whereas they do understand the language and instructions of the preacher. By preaching, too, God is extolled more manifestly and clearly than by these Offices . . .

Humbert's central criterion, we should note, is how well the message gets through to the laity. He emphasized that the sacraments are of no benefit to people who are not sufficiently informed and properly disposed to receive them; yet preaching can supply the information needed and can foster the right disposition. Since knowledge and good will can be obtained without the aid of the sacraments through preaching alone, preaching is to be thought preferable to the sacraments.

In a related argument, Humbert goes beyond the usual practice of citing apostolic authority for preaching to specify that that authority stands behind preaching more solidly than it does behind liturgy.

> The second reason that should lead us to prefer preaching is found in certain examples that recommend it. Jesus Christ, in the whole time He spent upon earth, celebrated mass but once, at the Last Supper; moreover, it is not said that He heard one confession. He administered the sacraments rarely and to a small number. He never devoted himself to the recitation of the canonical Office, and one can make the same observation about all the rest, except for preaching and prayer. It is also worthy of note that when He began to preach He spent more time in that than in prayer.

Humbert cites the example of St. Paul to the same effect, and then widens the focus.

Did the other Apostles and disciples of the Lord, throughout the world, devote themselves to any other task more than they did to preaching? 'They went forth,' says St. Mark, 'and preached everywhere' [Mark 16:201]. And so for our instruction there is the example of Our Lord, of St. Paul, and for all the Apostles and disciples of Jesus Christ.

A new, comprehensive approach to the spiritual life was being worked out by Humbert and Bonaventure and other leading friars in the middle of the thirteenth century. Many of the particular points of newness had made an appearance decades before, but when that had happened they had been unacceptable because they were perceived as too radically upsetting and threatening. By 1250, such changes could be looked at calmly, evaluated, accepted, justified, and—on the part of the friars and their most enthusiastic backers among the laity—truly assimilated.

Townspeople responded to the friars with material support. St. Francis had warned his followers, in the *Testament*, against having recourse to regular, wealthy patrons. The steady support that such patrons could supply would compromise the friars' vow of poverty and their self-imposed material instability. Still, Bonaventure figured that the margin of urban wealth in general was sufficient to support the friars, and he was apparently right. In other words, the sociological fact was that just by staying in cities the friars were fairly well assured of support. Stephen of Bourbon taught that while all alike shared an obligation to support the poor, this obligation fell particularly upon the rich. Moral considerations aside, Stephen was probably also right; the same point, moreover, confirms the aptness of the warning given by St. Francis.

~

CHAPTER FIFTEEN

Holy Anorexia*

Rudolf Bell

Most people would agree historians should not only describe the past, but also explain it to the present audience. When we are confronted with behaviors that strike us as odd, we want to know why people behaved as they did and what the behaviors meant to them and those around them. For the most part, medieval men and women did not leave us explanations. Even when they did, the language and conceptual framework of their explanations are opaque to us. Historians have tried to solve this problem in a variety of ways. One of the most popular is to apply the insights of modern social scientific method on individual or group behavior in past times. Explanations for the severe fasting of some thirteenth century women are a good example of this. There are several striking features to this phenomenon. First, the behavior was almost exclusively limited to women. Second, the behavior became prominent at the same time as the apostolic life movement; Clare of Assisi was famous for her fasting. Finally, the phenomenon was typical among urban women, the same women who would be most likely to respond to the apostolic life movement. In the following selection, Rudolf Bell applies modern psychoanalytical theory to the radical fasting of some prominent medieval women. Bell believes that modern medical theories concerning eating disorders provide the best model for explaining the fasting behavior. According to Bell, why did these women fast? What is the difference between anorexia nervosa and holy anorexia? Do you think it is appropriate to psychoanalyze someone from the past? Why or why not?

* © 1987 by The University of Chicago. Rudolf Bell, *Holy Anorexia*, Chicago: The University of Chicago Press, 1987, pp. 20–21, 114–117, 123–125.

In describing this behavior as "holy anorexia" I mean to draw attention to both the similarities and the differences between it and "anorexia nervosa." The modifier is the key; whether anorexia is holy or nervous depends on the culture in which a young woman strives to gain control of her life. In both instances anorexia begins as the girl fastens onto a highly valued societal goal (bodily health, thinness, self-control in the twentieth century/spiritual health, fasting, and self-denial in medieval Christendom). Her peers, and especially her parents, pursue this goal with only marginal success, more often than not honoring it only in the breach. She, by contrast, emerges from a frightened, insecure, psychic world superficially veiled by her outwardly pleasant disposition to become a champion in the race for (bodily/spiritual) perfection. Her newly won self-esteem and confidence initially receive the approbation of those she depends upon—parents, teachers, counselors— causing her to deepen her self-denial pattern until it takes over as the only source of her sense of self. Anorexia becomes her identity, and ultimately the self-starvation pattern continues beyond her conscious control. Insecurity (I am no one/I am a worthless, debased sinner) gives way to absolute certainty. The modern anorexic exhibits visual distortion and literally sees herself in the mirror as being heavier and wider than she is; she feels just fine and in fact accomplishes feats of considerable physical endurance. The holy anorexic sees Jesus' bridal ring on her finger and a place for herself in heaven; she feels God's love and energetically lives on the host alone. Each pursues her externally different but psychologically analogous, culturally approved objective with fanatical, compulsive devotion. Eventually, however, her self-destructive, life-threatening behavior commands the attention of family, friends, and professionals.

Our own world, imbued with a progressive spirit of scientific rationalism, defines anorexia as a nervous condition and sets out to "cure" its victims. While there is much dispute among medical experts about the most appropriate therapy, all agree that the anorexic must be helped to change her ways. Medieval people, on the other hand, were less sure of their power to control events and to shape the lives of others. Confronted with a young woman who fasted until her very life was at risk, they cautiously tried to determine whether this was the work of God or of the devil. Some of the holy anorexics to be considered in the chapters that follow actually underwent formal trials on charges of heresy and witchcraft, charges made at least in part because of suspicions about their eating habits. All of them, however, even those not formally tried, confronted a deeply skeptical male clerical hierarchy.

Among an unknowable total number of medieval anorexics probably only a small percentage managed to convince parents and then church officials that their strange behavior was inspired by God. Clearly it required enormous charisma and outward self-confidence (despite inner doubts that they never eradicated completely) to initiate and then to sustain such a lofty claim. The few who did so successfully quickly became objects of awe and reverence, people who seemed to exercise the power and might of carrying forth God's work and of knowing His will. Their anorexia came to be seen as part of a wider pattern of heroic, ascetic masochism amply justified in the literature of radical Christian religiosity. This public response, even when the "public" was limited to a small number of nuns and visiting confessors in a cloistered convent, reinforced the anorexic's sense of self, sometimes contributing to her "recovery," other times deepening her self-starvation pattern until it led to death. Either way, it was Christendom's patriarchy, not the girl herself, who had to define her anorexia as saintly rather than demonic or sick. We who seek to understand these women and to explore what that understanding may tell us about our own world can do so best if we keep in the foreground not only the psychological dimensions of self-starvation but also the cultural imperatives of medieval holiness, for it is the intersection of the two that results in holy anorexia.

Before tracing the historical development of holy anorexia from its beginnings in the early thirteenth century until its transformation during the Catholic Reformation, let us review briefly the psychological dimensions explored in the preceding three chapters. Whether anorexia leads to death, as in Catherine of Siena's case, or the girl recovers, as with Veronica Giuliani, or it is part of a later and perhaps more complex response, as with Umiliana de' Cerchi, Margaret of Cortona, and Angela of Foligno, certain traits are common to all holy anorexics. Their childhood, insofar as we are able to know it, provides them with a great capacity for faith. In their infancy doting parents, especially mothers, cue them to feel special, chosen above all others to be loved. The circumstances of early oral gratification in themselves are not that extraordinary—Veronica's mother's charity in wet nursing some neighboring child or Catherine's breastfeeding and weaning cycle probably served the mother's emotional needs more than her daughter's, and in any event were fairly commonplace—and so also the little girls' earliest religious impulses seem reasonable enough: a childish belief in the fanciful, magical, wondrous stories told of heroes past and present. They are of cheerful disposition, very outgoing, perhaps a bit boisterous and domineering in ways more usual for a little boy than a girl but still well within the bounds of acceptable and even endearing behavior, especially for a youngest or favored child. Among the 261 holy women under study we have reliable information about siblings for 120 of them; of these 120 fully 73 were the youngest child, and among these, 47 percent were well known for their compulsive fasting, whereas for the total population of female Italian saints since 1200 the corresponding figure is only 26 percent.

Holy anorexia in adolescence and adulthood, however, does not represent psychological regression to an infantile stage of oral contentment, a subliminal retreat to the safety of the womb as it were. There can be no retreat because that path invariably is blocked by painful experiences associated with the quest for autonomy, for a sense of self. Where such regression does ultimately occur, as we saw with Veronica Giuliani, it is part of a path toward recovery from the most self-destructive manifestations of holy anorexia. Often a death in the family seems to have been crucial. The pious and trusting little girl loses someone she loves deeply; her dependency is shattered and her faith is tested. Ultimately she passes the test and visualizes her dead mother, father, brother, or sister in heaven, or in purgatory and in need of human sacrifice and prayer. Yet the world of base physical urges and desires remains; it is her body, the girl decides with no small amount of pressure from catechism lessons only she takes literally and seriously, that brings death, that brought the death of her loved one. It is not any single zone—oral, anal, or genital—that she becomes fixated upon, but her entire body, all of which is hopelessly corrupt and impedes not only her own salvation but that of the people she loves.

The drive to destruction of her body—for the flesh cannot be tamed and therefore must be obliterated—is especially prominent among holy anorexics who have been married, but it is present in all of them. Since virgins and pious widows do not engage in sexual intercourse, food is the only thing that enters the bodies of these anorexics by their own volition, or because they are pressed to accede to the orders of their confessors. Over this invasion of their bodies these women retain but one choice—whether to bring a bowl to their lips or a fork to their mouths—and they choose to say no. Food is food, not an incorporated phallic symbol, but it is no less sexual for being food. It sustains the body, corrupt life on earth, and thereby kills the soul, life everlasting. Death, the enemy that stole her loved one and ominously threatens her, must be defeated, and the surest way to triumph over the fear of death is to die willingly. For some—Veronica Giuliani and Angela of Foligno are the clearest examples we have examined thus far—bodily desires eventually do die, and then a soul liberated from the flesh may nonetheless remain its temporal prisoner until nature runs its course, although not without setbacks and relapses of doubt. For others, such as Catherine of Siena and Umiliana de' Cerchi, the battle ends only with total annihilation of the flesh and death. Either way, autonomy demands freedom from the shackles of sexual desire, hunger, and weariness.

Early in her saintly career the holy anorexic fully commands the war against her body and therefore suffers deeply at every defeat, whether it is a plate of food she gobbles down or a disturbing flagellation by nude devils and wild beasts. Then with varying degrees of success the holy radical begins to feel victorious in her contest, and she surrenders active control over the battle to the depths of her psyche or to established conventional norms. Changes in hormonal balance, fueled by the psychic effect of sustained mental prayer, suppress the life-preserving needs for nourishment and rest. Lowered body temperature, insensitivity to external heat or cold, slowed pulse rate, general inanition, and unresponsiveness to pain all occur frequently in the hagiographical accounts; they portray the expected outcomes of extreme self-starvation.

Just as critical as the course of this war against bodily urges, wherein the quest for autonomy is purely internal, is the contest for freedom from the patriarchy that attempts to impose itself between the holy anorexic and her God. The authority figure may in fact be female, as for a time it was during Catherine of Siena's battle against her mother or when Veronica Giuliani fought her abbess, but always in the official church it is a male priest who dispenses the saving body of Christ. The holy anorexic rebels against passive, vicarious, dependent Christianity; her piety centers intensely and personally upon Jesus and his crucifixion, and she actively seeks an intimate, physical union with God. Once she convinces herself that her spiritual bridegroom communicates directly with her and she thereby achieves true autonomy, the commands of earthly men become trivial. Her total dependence upon God's will, ultimately hailed as heroically virtuous by the very patriarchy she is rebelling against, legitimizes her defiance and places her in a position of enormous strength. For in her actions on earth the "will of God" to which she yields is a force she alone interprets and arbitrates. The wedding ring that Jesus placed on Catherine of Siena's finger, and later her stigmata, could be seen only by Catherine, a circumstance that led her followers not to suspect a fake but to be all the more convinced of the truth of their "Mamma's" special relationship with God. Her will is to do God's will, an assertion not quickly or easily allowed by suspicious male clerics anxious to defend their powers against female interlopers. Only a very few women had the stamina and charisma to sustain such a claim, and even among these holy anorexics there is no reason to suggest that they intended in a careful and planned way to appropriate male prerogatives (a statement that would have to be modified were we to expand our scope to include anorexic heretics). Intentions aside, however, holy anorexics did in fact break out of the established boundaries within which a male hierarchy confined female piety, and thereby established newer and wider avenues for religious expression by women more generally. Although recovered anorexics usually led satisfying personal lives, it was more often their sisters who starved themselves to death without ever reaching psychological equilibrium and absolute certainty about their autonomy, who spearheaded advances in women's religiosity.

The reader who has stayed with me through the preceding chapters may have a number of questions that have not been addressed thus far. Are there male holy anorexics, and what about them? Are there anorexics before the thirteenth century, and what about the desert ascetics of early Christianity? What of the female saints who were not anorexic, maybe even pleasantly plump, such as Catherine of Bologna? In short, I have tried to set forth three psychological types, each illustrated by historical personages, but thus far I have not placed holy anorexia in its historical setting. With this task I now proceed.

The first major holy anorexic on the Italian scene we turn to is Clare of Assisi, companion of Saint Francis and founder of the Poor Clares, the Order which to our own time is present throughout the Catholic world. Testimony on her diet comes from the nuns who lived with her at San Damiano and appeared before Bishop Bartholomew of Spoleto in November, 1253, within three months of Clare's death, as he carried out an order from Pope Innocent IV to conduct an investigation of her life. Sister Pacifica of Guelfuccio, who had known Clare from their childhood days in Assisi and who may have joined her in running away from home forty years earlier, was the first to speak. She said that the putative saint for many years had eaten nothing at all on Mondays, Wednesdays, and Fridays. Even on other days she ate very little, so little that she became gravely ill. Then Saint Francis himself and the Bishop of Assisi ordered her to take at least an ounce and a half of bread each day. Sister Benvenuta of Perugia testified next, and when interrogated specifically about how she knew that Francis had ordered Clare to eat, said she had been present when he gave this command. The other sisters confirmed all this and added other details about her special austerities during Lent and the forty days before Christmas.

Our concern is with Francis's command. We know that he too was very abstemious, but it was he who ordered her to eat, not vice versa. That Clare might have ordered Francis to change his diet, or for that matter to alter any of his religious practices, was a cultural impossibility. It was Clare and her sisters who were enclosed in the convent walls of San Damiano that Francis had selected for them, while he and his brothers took to the highways to spread the message of Lady Poverty. At Francis's wish, he and his followers might visit the Poor Clares to serve their spiritual and temporal needs (until Gregory IX in 1230 forbade such visits unless licensed by him). In later years the Observant or Strict Clares maintained that Franciscan friars were obligated to serve their needs, but the plain meaning of Francis's practice won out—the men chose whether to visit and serve, and no obligation to the women existed. Thus even Saint Francis, quite properly known for his gentle ways and concern for the weak, qualities considered feminine and nurturing by his culture, could not transcend the male-dominant role in his relationship with Clare. If their caloric intake/body weight ratios had been identical, still she would have been the anorexic and he not. He too severely damaged his health with his self-punishing asceticism, but there was no one to order him to eat, and a whole world in which to express his drive for autonomy. For Clare and her sisters there was Francis to guide them, then a male prelacy to order them, and finally only their own bodies to conquer.

Clare ultimately recovered from the illness brought on by her not eating and, as with many other former anorexics, she exerted considerable talent and energy as a prioress. She too came to doubt the wisdom of severe austerity. In the rules she wrote for her order, Clare specified that Lenten restrictions were to be observed by the sisters every day of the year except Christmas. Exceptions were to be made, however, for the young, the weak, those serving outside monastery walls, and "in times of manifest necessity." The Lenten diet, it may be noted, was monotonous and sparse but not unhealthy. In a letter to Blessed Agnes of Prague, Clare even more explicitly backed away from her earlier excesses, displaying much the same experiential wisdom shown by present-day recovered anorexics.

> Since we do not have a body of bronze, nor is ours the strength of granite—indeed we are rather fragile and inclined toward every bodily infirmity—I pray you and beseech you in the name of the Lord, oh dearest one, to moderate with wise discretion the almost exaggerated and impossible austerity which I know you have embarked upon so that . . . your sacrifice always will be seasoned with the salt of prudence.

Clare's innovative, living model of self-abasing female piety riveted the attention of thirteenth-century Italian people, and many were the women who followed her path, beginning with members of her own family. Initially her relatives had used force to try to drag her bodily away from the Benedictine house of refuge where Francis had placed her after she had run away from home on the night of Palm Sunday in 1212 to meet him at nearby Porziuncola. There he had cut off her hair and vested her in a sackcloth, and it was in this penitential garb that her friends and relatives found her a day or two later. Unable to move her by verbal threats, nor by pulling at her as she clung to an altarcloth, they left empty-handed.

CHAPTER SIXTEEN

~

Women Mystics and Eucharistic Devotion in the Thirteenth Century*

Caroline Walker Bynum

At the same time that Bell was studying medieval women's fasting behavior using psychoanalytical theory, Caroline Walker Bynum approached the problem from a different direction. Bynum believed that it was inappropriate to analyze people from different eras and cultures using contemporary psychological theories. Instead, she explored how gender, fasting, and food fit into the religious culture of the time. Since women rarely had the right to renounce money or property and were not allowed to beg and preach, women fasted as a means to express the apostolic life. When combined with eucharistic devotion, fasting allowed women to express both the sacramental piety encouraged by the papacy and the voluntary poverty of the apostles. According to Bynum, why did women mystics fast? Why does she reject Bell's psychoanalytical interpretation? What roles do food and the body play in the piety of these women? How does extreme fasting express the apostolic life? Which interpretation do you think is more convincing, Bell's or Bynum's?

Eucharistic ecstasy was not, however, merely a response to the clericalization of the church, to a pattern of religiosity in which holy men were clerics and holy laypeople were women. Women's devotion to the body and blood of Christ was also a response to their social and psychological experience.

A few decades ago, female mysticism was frequently seen as an expression of psychological deprivation or of outright pathology. I have no interest in

* © 1984 by Caroline Walker Bynum. Reprinted with the permission of Caroline Walker Bynum. Caroline Walker Bynum, "Women Mystics and Eucharistic Devotion in the Thirteenth Century," *Women's Studies*, vol. II, 1984, pp. 196–206.

reducing the phenomena I have been describing to abnormal (or even normal) psychology. But one element must be mentioned, which is specifically relevant to eucharistic devotion. There are clearly, in some medieval women, behavior patterns which parallel what modern psychologists call "anorexia nervosa"—an inability to tolerate food, which leads to self-starvation (usually in adolescent girls) and which has in our own day been given powerful spiritual significance in the life and writings of Simone Weil. Anorexia nervosa typically involves insomnia, hyperactivity, grossly distorted sense perception and suppression of menstruation. Anorexics focus obsessively on food, which is, to them, a symbol both of physicality and of control. Obsession with food—either through binge eating or through intense fasting—is often triggered by the nagging awareness of corporality evidenced by the onset of menstruation. Refusal to eat is a way of asserting power over a body which appears to have slipped away from control into painful or embarrassing excretions, and over a family or a society which is rushing the girl headlong into an adult female role which she does not choose and which promises less freedom than did childhood. Although one should not say that medieval women suffered from "anorexia" (or, for that matter, from hysteria or depression—since any such syndrome must be part of a particular culture and should not per se be transferred across cultures), medieval women do show striking parallels to the modern syndrome—parallels which suggest psychological and social reasons for the fact that eating and not-eating are more central images in women's lives than in men's.

All medieval miracles of surviving on the eucharist alone are female miracles (with one exception). Most are told of adolescent girls. In addition, fasting is a more common practice among female ascetics, and visions and miracles having to do with food are also more common among women. Miracles in which special sensations (especially sweet taste) accompany the eucharist are almost exclusively female; so are miracles in which consecrated and unconsecrated hosts are distinguished. And there is no question that, in some female mystics, disgust at all non-eucharist food becomes an involuntary physiological reaction. The vomiting out of unconsecrated hosts, for example, was sometimes part of a general revulsion at food, especially meat. Moreover, refusal to eat ordinary food was often accompanied, as it is in modern anorexics, by frenetic attention to feeding others. Women saints, who fasted themselves, frequently multiplied loaves and fishes for their adherents.

Such reactions to food are found especially in religious women who experienced puberty in the world and whose conflict with family over vocation was intense. Mary of Oignies, married at fourteen, moved immediately to extreme fasting. The memory of having eaten a bit of meat after an illness precipitated the vision during which she cut off her own flesh with a knife. Ida of Louvain's adolescent conflict with her father led to bodily mortification and stigmata. Christina Mirabilis, a lay woman of origins so humble she had nothing to renounce for God except food, fled into the desert in adolescence to fast; but (says her biographer) "no matter how subtle her body," she still needed some nourishment, so God filled her "dry virgin breasts" with milk and she nursed herself. Juliana of Cornillon as a young child was forbidden by her nurse to fast as much as she liked; later in life she found it very difficult to eat and literally could not swallow what she chewed until after vespers. A century later, Catherine of Siena, after protracted conflict over vocation with her family, became unable to eat anything except the eucharist. Ordered by Christ to join her family at table and taste something, she afterwards rammed twigs down her throat to bring up the food she could not bear in her stomach.

For such cases it is easy to give psycho-social explanations. It is not surprising that women, who often could not control the disposition of their own bodies against wishes of family or religious advisers, voluntarily or involuntarily punished those bodies at moments of life-crisis. Nor is it surprising that, since women were usually not able to renounce property (either because, like Christina Mirabilis, they possessed none to renounce or because medieval mores did not permit even religious women to beg), they chose to renounce food, the one pleasure they not only fully controlled but were also chiefly responsible by role for preparing for all of society.

As in modern anorexia, "control" was a basic issue to medieval women who adopted relentless fasting as a kind of self-definition.

But if food was sometimes a symbol of self and of the world, invoked at moments of decision or conflict, the fasting and nausea of medieval women were not simply world rejection, nor were they simply control of self substituted for control of circumstances. Angela of Foligno, desiring to punish herself for hypocritical piety, wanted to parade through the streets with rotting fish and meat tied around her neck; she described herself as tempted by the devil to give up eating entirely. Later she came to see these reactions as pathological and found the eucharist to taste like especially delicious meat. Thus not-eating was complemented by holy eating. Food was filth; it was also God. The woman's revulsion at her own body, even when it took what appeared to her and her contemporaries to be bizarre forms, was given a theological significance more complex than dualism. The peasant saint Alpais did not, after all, die of anorexia. She survived for forty years on the eucharist and became a living proof of the efficacy of the sacrament. The point of even the oddest of these stories was ultimately not rejection of the physical and bodily but a finding of the truly physical, the truly nourishing, the truly fleshly, in the humanity of Christ, chewed and swallowed in the eucharist. Even here, physicality was not so much rooted out or suppressed as embraced and redeemed at that point where it intersected with the divine. So, in addition to the psychological and social explanations which I have just given, there are theological and religious reasons for women's spirituality.

If we look at the thirteenth-century theological context, it is clear that women's concern with matter, with physicality, with imitation of the human Christ, must be located against the background of the war against heresy. Controversy over the eucharist re-emerged after centuries of silence in the late eleventh century; and twelfth-century theologians themselves (for example, Hildegard of Bingen) saw denial of the eucharist as one of heresy's major threats. Modern scholars have frequently argued that the central theological purpose behind the proliferating eucharistic miracles was support for the doctrine of transubstantiation. Recent historians have also suggested that thirteenth-century eucharistic devotion was part of the general effort of theology and spirituality to propose an alternative to Cathar dualism. We can see such motives reflected, for example, in the writings of James of Vitry and Thomas of Cantimpre, who held up women saints with their concentration on Christ's body and blood as a counter to the Cathar view that the physical world is the creation of an evil God. The cardinal legate who helped Juliana of Cornillon propagate the feast of Corpus Christi supported it explicitly as a weapon against dualism. Furthermore, it seems clear that confessors urged women toward eucharistic piety in an effort to keep their devotional life not only orthodox but also firmly under ecclesiastical control. We must, however, look beyond any conscious effort to propagandize against the Cathars if we are to understand the extent to which thirteenth-century spirituality is a response to the threat of dualism. Indeed it is possible to argue that the theme of the positive religious significance of physicality runs throughout thirteenth-century theology. For example, the piety of the mendicants—the Church's army of preachers against dualist heresy— was permeated by attention to the fact of physicality, both in a newly intense asceticism and in an interpretation of all creation as the footprints of God. Moreover, one of the most important of thirteenth-century philosophical formulations, Thomas Aquinas's statement of the hylomorphic composition of the human person, is a new effort to come to terms with matter. Most fundamentally, that doctrine says that what the person is—the existing substance man—is form and matter, soul and body. To Aquinas, the person is his body, not just a soul using a body; and the resurrection of the body becomes, for the first time, not merely theologically but also philosophically necessary. Usually not directly in touch with abstract theological or philosophical speculation, women nonetheless evidenced in their visions this general anti-dualist stance. The author of the nuns' book of Unterlinden commented that *homo* (our humanness) really includes all creatures. Marguerite of Oingt saw Christ's humanity as a clear mirror in which is reflected all the beauty of creation. Gherardesca of Pisa worshipped God's glory in a piece of straw. Nlechtild of Hackeborn saw a vision of the celebrating priest in which his vestments were covered with every twig and hair of the flora and fauna of the universe. And as she looked in surprise she saw that the smallest details of creation are reflected in the Holy Trinity by means of the humanity of Christ, because it is from the same earth that produced them that Christ drew his humanity.

In fact, eucharistic practice as reflected in art and architecture underlines the extent to which reverence for the host was reverence for the divine in the material. Not only does the thirteenth century see the growth of the practice of reserving the host in pyxes or tabernacles; the eucharist was also sometimes reserved in a reliquary, mobile tabernacles were modelled on reliquaries, and pyxes were sometimes displayed alongside reliquaries. The practice of burning candles or lamps before the host was borrowed from the manner in which relics were revered. Thus the host was clearly treated as a relic of Christ; tabernacles were thrones or tombs for Christ's body. And it is interesting to note that our earliest evidence for visits to the reserved host seen as a relic of Christ, a fragment of his physicality, comes from an English rule for female recluses and from the life of Mary of Oignies.

Changes in the twelfth-century notion of *imitatio* also lie behind women's eucharistic devotion. Scholars have stressed that the twelfth-century search for the *vita apostolica* was a search for perfect poverty; somewhere in the course of the century (in a by no means unidirectional development), the apostolic life came to mean preaching. What scholars have failed to underline, however, is the extent to which imitation—of the martyrs, of the apostles, and of Christ—became more and more literal. Thus by the late twelfth century, *imitatio* had moved far beyond the Cistercian notion of affective meditation. Whereas Bernard of Clairvaux taught that we identify with Christ by extending our compassion to his humanity through pitying the suffering humanity of our neighbors, Francis and Mary of Oignies became Christ on the cross while a seraph looked on. Indeed some male descriptions of holy women stress explicitly that *imitatio* is fact, not memory or imagination. We are told, for example, that Margaret of Cortona and Lukardis of Oberweimar became one with the crucifixion rather than simply remembering or pitying Christ's suffering. Margaret of Ypres's extreme self-flagellation as a means of joining with Christ was called a *recordatio* (remembrance); but in such a passage the very meaning of the word "remember" has changed. Beatrice of Nazareth, more theologically sophisticated than many of her fellow women mystics, spoke of three grades of moving toward Christ: turning toward grace; growing in the memory of Christ's passion; and, finally, inhering in Jesus.

This sense of *imitatio* as becoming or being lies in the background of women's eucharistic devotion. The eucharist is an especially appropriate vehicle for the effort to become Christ because the eucharist is Christ. The fact of transubstantiation is crucial. One becomes Christ's crucified body in eating Christ's crucified body. Thus reception of the eucharist leads so naturally to stigmata, visibly or inwardly, that contemporaries hardly worried about how to account for their appearance. *Imitatio* is incorporation of flesh into flesh. Both priest and recipient are literally pregnant with Christ. The metaphor of the good soul as Christ's mother, which had a long lineage, became in the thirteenth century more than metaphor. Caesarius of Heisterbach described a priest who swelled up at the consecration pregnant with Christ. Ida of Louvain swelled with the eucharist. By the fourteenth century Dorothy of Montau repeatedly experienced mystical pregnancy and was almost required by her confessor to exhibit it as part of her preparation for communion.

Concern with the literal following of Jesus, with the problem and the opportunity of physicality, was thus a basic theme in thirteenth-century religiosity. But it was reflected and espoused especially intensely in women's lives and in women's writing. For this, there are specific theological reasons. To put it simply, the weight of the western tradition had long told women that physicality was particularly their problem. Some modern commentators have made much of the fact that certain patristic figures argued that woman qua woman was not created in God's image, although woman qua human being was. This is a complex point—and certainly in thirteenth-century legal and theological writing it was usually interpreted as referring to woman's social role (i.e., her subordination to man in the family), not to her anatomical nature or biological role. But in any case it was certainly not absorbed by late medieval women (even married women) as a prohibition of their approach to God, their imitation of Christ. Their writing is full of references to being created in God's image and likeness.

Women were also told that, allegorically speaking, woman was to man what matter is to spirit—i.e., that they symbolized the physical, lustful, material, appetitive part of human nature, whereas man symbolized the spiritual or mental. The roots of this idea were multiple, scientific as well as theological, and it did unquestionably influence women writers. The first great woman theologian, Hildegard of Bingen, knew the tradition, and indeed argued against some of its implications. Women do not, however, seem to have drawn from such teaching any notion of female incapacity. Most of the references to womanly weakness in thirteenth-century spiritual writing come from the pens of male biographers. These biographers occasionally compliment women saints on their "virility." But women writers by and large either ignore their own gender, using androgynous imagery for the self (as did Gertrude the Great and Hadewijch), or embrace their femaleness as a sign of closeness to Christ. If anything, women drew from the traditional notion of the female as physical a special emphasis on their own redemption by a Christ who was supremely physical because supremely human. They sometimes even extrapolated from this to the notion that, in Christ, divinity is to humanity as male is to female. Elisabeth of Schonau, in the twelfth century, had a vision of the humanity of Christ as a female virgin. And Hildegard of Bingen wrote in the *Liber divinorum operum* explicitly: "Man . . . signifies the divinity of the Son of God and woman his humanity."

This was not to imply that the human Christ was a body without a soul (a clearly heretical Christological position), nor was it to deny Christ's divinity. But as spirituality in general came more and more to stress Christ's humanity as manifested in his physicality, women—who were the special symbol of the physical—suggested that that physical, tangible humanity might be symbolized or understood as female. And the fact of the virgin birth contributed to this. One could argue that all of Christ's humanity had to come from Mary because Christ had no human father. So in some sense Mary could be seen as adding humanity to the Logos. This is in fact exactly what Hildegard of Bingen and Mechtild of Magdeburg do argue. Hildegard describes that which is redeemed by Christ—the physicality that comes from Mary—as feminine; and this is enhanced by her sense that Christ's body is also *ecclesia*, which is equally feminine. In a eucharistic vision, Hildegard saw woman (*muliebris imago*) receiving from Christ, hanging on the cross, a dowry of his blood, while a voice said: "Eat and drink the body and blood of my Son to abolish the prevarication of Eve and receive your true inheritance." Although the priesthood is, to Hildegard, both revered and essential, the priest enters this eucharistic vision only after Holy Church; and the image of both sinful and saved humanity is the image of woman. A century later, Mechtild of Magdeburg argued that the Incarnation joined the Logos (the pre-existent Son of God) with a pure humanity, created along with Adam but preserved as pure in Mary after the fall. Thus Mary became a kind of pre-existent humanity of Christ. Such a notion is reinforced even in iconography, where we find that Mary has a place of honor on eucharistic tabernacles. For Mary, source of

Christ's physicality and his humanity, is in some sense the reliquary or chest which houses Christ's body. To Hildegard of Bingen as to Marguerite of Oingt, she was explicitly the *tunica humanitatis*, the clothing of humanity which God put on in the Incarnation.

Mary was, of course, important in women's spirituality. Particularly in southern European saints' lives, the theme of *imitatio Mariae Virginis* is strong. The biographer of Douceline of Marseille, for example, actually sees Douceline as imitating the poverty of Mary whereas her beloved Francis imitated the poverty of Christ directly. But the reverence for Mary that we find in thirteenth-century women mystics is less a reverence for a "representative woman" than a reverence for the bearer and conduit of the Incarnation. The ultimate identification was with Christ as human. Some women saints swoon with Mary before the cross; all women saints swoon on the cross with Christ himself.

Thus women theologians took from the theological and scientific tradition a notion that male is to female as soul is to matter and elaborated it in their own way as an identification with the human Christ in his physicality. Modern claims that medieval women were alienated from a male Christ (i.e., a God not of their gender) quite miss the point; these women saw themselves less in terms of gender than in terms of matter. Modern claims that women were deprived of a sense of self worth or forced into denial of their sexuality by the traditional association of woman with the physical also miss the point; these women found physicality as they understood it redeemed and expressed by a human God. Contrary to what some recent interpretations have asserted, thirteenth-century women seem to have concluded from their physicality an intense conviction of their ability to imitate Christ without role or gender inversion. To soar toward Christ as lover and bride, to sink into the stench and torment of the crucifixion, to eat God, was for the woman only to give religious significance to what she already was. So female devotion to the eucharist—and to the dying or the infant or the bridegroom Christ— expresses a special confidence in the Incarnation. If the Incarnation meant that the whole human person was capable of redemption, then that which woman was seen as being—even in the most misogynist form of the Christian tradition—was caught up into God in Christ. And if the agony of the crucifixion was less sacrifice or victory than the redemption of that which is human (matter joined to form), then the crucifixion could be imaged as death or as eating or as orgasm (all especially human—bodily—experiences). Women mystics seem to have felt that they qua women were not only also but even especially saved in the Incarnation.

~

CHAPTER SEVENTEEN

The Devil's World: Heresy and Society, 1100–1300*

Andrew P. Roach

Historians have long debated the appearance of significant dissident and heretical groups in the twelfth and thirteenth centuries. The most prominent heretical group was the Cathars. Based in southern France and northern Italy, the Cathars rejected the Trinitarian monotheism of orthodox Christianity and constructed alternate religious institutions. Many scholars have taken the rise of the Cathars to be a sign of the failure of the medieval church to christianize Europe on a deep level. According to this point of view, the extent of obedience to the formal church hierarchy and the level of commitment to central doctrines should measure christianization. Others argue that the success of the Cathars was an unintended consequence of christianizing efforts. The following selection by Andrew P. Roach is a good example of this point of view. Roach does not dismiss the importance of doctrine. Both orthodox Christians and Cathars understood and endorsed the views of their respective leaders. According to Roach, however, people did not become Cathars because of their theology. Instead, he argues that medieval Europeans were sophisticated consumers who treated religious institutions as service providers. The medieval church had been very effective in impressing its ideas of holiness and Christian community onto the laity. Now it was compelled to compete with a new provider of holiness and religious community. What do you think of Roach's consumer model? What are its strengths? What are its weaknesses? According to this model, why were the Cathars so successful?

---

* © 2005 Pearson Education Limited. Andrew P. Roach, *The Devil's World: Heresy and Society 1100–1300*, New York: Pearson Education, pp. 114–120.

The real impact of Dominic and Francis was that they made it once again fashionable to be orthodox. Francis may have led the life of someone who thirty years before would have been considered a heretic, but he insisted on absolute obedience to the Church and to the papacy in particular. The Dominicans offered a dynamic intellectual alternative to heresy and moreover offered a career structure to bright young students and academics whereby they could use their skills, keep their principles and even advance up the career ladder.

The Cathars in southern France shared in some of the intellectual advances of the period, driven no doubt by the keen competition for new recruits, but they were stronger at providing the low-level pastoral care so much in demand in the early thirteenth century. People wanted two things from religious movements, first, men and women whose lives they could respect and, secondly, some sort of assurance as to their own salvation. At its height the Cathar movement delivered both with efficiency and conviction. There were appropriate "good Christians" to perform the vital *consolamentum* ceremony on the deathbed of a believer to secure the soul's place in heaven and in the meantime the "good men" preached, blessed and gave advice and help.

Conditions for the heretics were growing harder. One area of activity for the eager recruits for the Dominican friars in particular was the inquisitions which were organised against the Cathars in the 1230s and these, despite pauses and setbacks, became gradually more professional and wide-ranging by the early 1240s. Cathar "good men" proved difficult to catch, but the sect was vulnerable because of the crucial importance of the presence at a believer's deathbed of the "good man" or *perfectus*, as the inquisitors termed him. Through him, with the help of prayers and a copy of a gospel or New Testament placed on the head, the believer gained admission to the "Church of God." This Cathar *consolamentum* combined mechanistic ritual and a profound spiritual experience. While the adherence to exact formulae conveyed security of salvation to the believer, the ceremony was also usually the culmination of a lifetime's relationship with the Cathars in which there were responsibilities on both sides. When the *perfecti* arrived they had to ask about the attitude of the believer to the Cathar Church and indeed whether he was in debt to the Cathars, in which case it must be paid promptly if possible. In life, the responsibilities of the laity to the *perfecti* were not onerous, they had to greet them respectfully, with a bow and a request to be blessed. They had to provide meals, accommodation and occasionally a guide as they moved in pairs around the region. Raymond Carabassa and his companion stayed with a woman of Bram in Languedoc for four months in 1242, paying for their food. Two years later as he once again moved from village to village Raymond was given freshly baked bread and produce from a believer's vineyard. Other gifts to *perfecti* included fish, nuts, leeks, beans and strawberries.

Much of this pattern of unexpected guests for dinner, and lodgers staying for periods of one night to months on end, is part of the system of reciprocal favours recognisable to anyone who has lived in remote communities or a student house. It is a kind of "goodwill economy" which forms and binds communities. Other factors could also open the door and may have determined the extent of hospitality; *perfecti* were well aware of family connections such as when Lombarda of Villepinte stayed for three weeks in Fanjeaux in the home of her son-in-law's brother. Family ties succeeded where bribery failed in releasing *perfecti* captured at Mirepoix in 1243 because one of the "good men" was the uncle of his captor. Lordship was also important; the Niort family protected heretics in the 1220s and 1230s in their lands south of Carcassonne.

It was in death that believers paid their dues to the Cathar Church. In return for the *consolamentum* the *perfecti* expected a bequest. Esclarmonde, wife of Lord Assam, left the heretics a tunic, 22 pence, an embroidered linen cloth, a gold coin, a winnowing fan and a cloak. Two *perfecti* had to be fetched to her as she lay ill in a cowshed. Often the gifts were more portable such as cash or horses, although in the years before the Albigensian Crusade, even land was given. While the Cathars stressed that the believer should not be turned away if unable to pay, the lay consensus was that it was appropriate for *perfecti* to receive something for their efforts, so that after an unnamed sick woman had been consoled on her deathbed in Moissac, two *saumatae* of wine were collected from a number of people for the "good men."

Such arrangements required the *perfecti* to command widespread respect, for not only did the believers themselves have to have faith in the heretics, but their relatives had also to have at least enough regard for the heretics to hand over the bequest: it is here that the ties of blood and time paid their dividend or, as one knight put it: "We cannot [expel them and hunt them down], we were raised with them, we have relatives among them and we see them living lives of honour."

The "good men" never forgot that believers had a choice. In towns like Gourdon and Montauban, north of Toulouse, where there were Waldensians and Cathars, several believers gave money and food to both, despite their mutual antagonism. There was a practical element to visiting heretics. The Waldensians developed a speciality in medical care, relying both on their technical knowledge and their high spiritual prestige to bring about a cure. The laity clearly understood that there were differences between the two groups as formal disputes between them were common events, such as the one G. Ricart escorted the Cathar "good men" to one Easter Day. These were semi-public affairs taking place in people's homes.

Inquisition penances from the early 1240s reveal a world where previously people had made day-by-day decisions about which religious group to patronise. Sometimes there were family influences. One witness listened to Waldensian preaching, but gave more practical support to a group of Cathars, taking them from Toulouse to Montauban, because one of them was his sister. He respected them enough to make them a gift. There are hints that some people were working out their own individual theological views: a man disputed with the Cathars about the creation, another received a Cathar "good man" into his home only to tell him he preferred the Waldensians, yet another declared to the inquisitors his disbelief in all the Church's sacraments, and that it was a sin to swear, kill or lie with one's wife. He thought that only in the Cathar Church were all saved. Most were not so exclusive: there were plenty of lay people ready to share their table with both groups and declare them to be "good men."

Local ties often counted for more than wider allegiances. One known Cathar supporter from Castelnaudary, far from home on business in Narbonne, lay dying, so his companion fetched two local *perfecti*. Because the man could not be sure of these spiritual figures as he could of his local ones from Toulouse, he instead asked for the Cistercian monks of Boulbonne Abbey close to where he was born and so committed his body into their hands.

Given the movement's dependence on deathbed bequests, it is not surprising that so much effort went into gaining popular respect. The *perfecti* took on a range of pastoral responsibilities. Preaching and debating were important. According to one believer, speaking was one of the manifestations of the divine within corrupt human flesh:

> Lucifer had made Man and God said that he would make him speak. But Lucifer answered that he could not and so then God breathed into the bones of Man and Man spoke.

The Cathars seem to have been largely successful in imparting the basic doctrine of dualism, of creation being an unending war between God and the Devil, with the Devil responsible for the corrupt, visible things of this world, although whether evil was an independent force or originally part of the creation of a beneficent God was left uncertain. There were also the inevitable attacks on the Church, with marriage, baptism and the Eucharist receiving regular mockery, as well as the idea of the literal resurrection of bodies. Preaching and disputing with opponents from the Dominicans and Waldensians continued despite the deteriorating security situation until around 1230. After then such confrontations became more risky. A Cathar *perfectus* around 1241 was willing to visit the home of a Waldensian supporter to argue his case, but it was dangerous and unlikely to bring tangible benefits to the movement.

"Good men" often shared meals with believers and this was an important part of their contact. There was some ceremony to it with *perfecti* often blessing bread and then distributing it. The obvious parallels with communion or the Eucharist should be treated with caution. The bread was as important as the ceremony and could be kept. Bread baked by a *perfecta* on Christmas Day 1242 was carried to a household and then blessed by two "good men," but more often the household provided its own bread. In a similar fashion, people brought loaves of bread for Francis and there was a competitive aspect to the phenomenon.

> The perversity of heretics was shamed, the faith of the Church was extolled and, as believers rejoiced, heretics hid . . . [short paragraph praising Francis's devotion to the Church] . . . The people used to bring him loaves of bread to bless, which they kept for a long time, and, on tasting them, they were cured of various diseases.

In neither case is it clear what the bread was actually for. An Italian treatise on heretics, written in the late 1230s and attributed to the Franciscan James Capelli, attempted to analyse this difficult area.

> Some of them say that the purpose of the act is to ward off contamination from partaking, of food, for they believe foods to be evil. Certain others, however, say that this is done only in commemoration of the death of Christ.

Both the Cathars and Francis were trying to satisfy the laity's appetite for a graspable holiness. The Church eventually provided bread blessed by the priest for the laity, outside of the Mass. "Parishioners should find blessed bread (*panem benedictum*) with candles on any Sunday in every Christian church in the world," declared the reforming bishop of Salisbury in 1256.

In the days before persecution the Cathars looked after both the living and the dead. Through their network of local deacons acting within bishoprics, they could confer the *consolamentum* on dying believers and could then bury them in Cathar cemeteries. Rather than being exclusively a badge of allegiance, these most likely flourished in competition with crowded local

Catholic churchyards. Several Cathar believers still found their way into consecrated ground. Even more valuable to the heretics were the houses of Cathar men and women throughout Languedoc. These communities were small and informal: they took in children, especially young girls and women, particularly widows. There was little indication of permanence and indeed individuals seem to have been able to leave as their life circumstances changed. There are similarities with communities in Italy, such as the Humiliati. The loss of these institutions which cemented Catharism into the social fabric was a major effect of the Albigensian Crusade and forced the heretics to rethink their relationship with believers.

In the 1220s and 1230s there were still options open: Paubert Sicart rented land to some Cathar *perfecti* not far from Montauban, his wife received presents of wine. A community of "good men" established a weaving workshop at Cordes around 1225. These were the pathetic remnants of a once considerable Cathar infrastructure:

> They used to have fields, vineyards and their own houses, workshops, oxen, asses, mules and horses, as well as gold and silver and many earthly possessions in this world. They laboured day and night and they were great businessmen for earthly money.

Wrote their old adversary, Durand of Huesca, in the early 1220s, simultaneously gloating over the fall in Cathar fortunes and sneering at the hypocrisy of a group who professed to despise the things of this world. In truth, the Cathars faced a serious problem, for they were now more dependent than ever on lay supporters' goodwill and yet had far fewer resources with which to maintain it.

One solution to these losses was to fall back on the one major fixed asset which remained, the small castle of Montségur. This lay in the foothills of the Pyrenees, remote enough to be difficult to besiege, but still close enough to the road and river network for most of Languedoc to remain relatively accessible. The castle had been renovated just before the Albigensian Crusade and belonged to Raymond of Percille, a minor noble and Cathar sympathiser. Having already served as a refuge in the early days of the crusade, the fortress's role was consciously enhanced around 1232 by the veteran Cathar bishop of Toulouse, Guilhabert de Castres. As the decade wore on and inquisitors were introduced into southern France the castle became the home of most of the Cathar hierarchy, with both Guilhabert and, after his death around 1240, his successor, Bertrand Marty, staying there. *Perfecti* were able to use it as a base so that the Cathar network of pastoral care proved stubbornly durable. As for the castle, it became a religious community, a site of pilgrimage, a place for believers to die, and a chance to meet relatives who were *perfecti*. It also became a workshop and financial centre.

In 1244 Peire-Roger de Mirepoix took 50 doublets made in the castle, possibly by the *perfecti* themselves. A market emerged there where people came from the surrounding villages to sell foodstuffs to the heretics. The Cathars may well also have banked savings; one long-time supporter made discreet enquiries after the fall of the castle about what had become of the 300 *solidi* he had deposited with the heretics there. Such a move should not surprise us; there is evidence that the Templars performed similar functions in their castles. Nor was it the only benefit the *perfecti* could provide, in that there are records of them lending small sums of money to supporters, but this would be nowhere near as lucrative as acting as a *depositarius* for the heretics: collecting money left to the heretics and storing it until required. The heretics commonly dispensed their favour as "little gifts," shirts and shoes for a scribe, a cap for a barber in return for shaving them and sharing a jug of wine.

These profits lie in the shadowy area between a market and a goodwill economy. No transaction was without its spiritual dimension. When Peire de Corneliano and his uncle undertook to guide seven "good men" from the citadel at Roquafort to the church at Crassenx, a fee of ten *solidi* was agreed, but the heretics refused, or were unable to pay, so Peire ceased to even greet Cathars for the next thirty-four years. Peire's extreme reaction may indicate a deep sense of betrayal. One function of the Cathars was as a religious confraternity, an essential part of which was to provide a network of trust and credit in the wider market.

POPULAR RELIGION IN THE LATE MIDDLE AGES

POPULAR RELIGION IN THE LATE MIDDLE AGES

Historians usually distinguish between the high or central Middle Ages of the twelfth and thirteenth centuries and the late Middle Ages of the fourteenth and fifteenth centuries. This is not an objective or neutral distinction, but neither is it arbitrary. While the twelfth and thirteenth centuries are rightly described as a time of robust economic, political, and cultural development, events of the later Middle Ages point to a general reversal of those trends. Endemic hunger, disease, and violence are typical features of most traditional societies, but fourteenth- and fifteenth-century Europe saw more than the normal amount of these scourges. Climactic changes in the early part of the fourteenth century caused several years of poor agricultural yield that led to widespread famine. In the 1340s, bubonic plague swept Europe, killing up to one-third of the population. Technological, economic, and administrative innovations changed the nature of warfare. Relatively small armies of mounted knights, mustered seasonally and rarely committed to large-scale battles, were replaced by large standing armies of conscripts and mercenaries, equipped with artillery and, eventually, firearms. Incessant dynastic struggles devastated regions of England, France, Italy, and Germany. Unpaid (and often even well paid) mercenary bands preyed on the civilian population.

The tragic human toll of these events notwithstanding, many scholars have begun to reassess the late Middle Ages in more positive terms. While famine and plague reversed the demographic trend of the previous era, they did not derail the economic development that it had fostered. The European economy continued to grow, and the standard of living of survivors rose dramatically. The developments that allowed princes to wage war on an unprecedented scale were themselves part of the larger trend toward internally stable centralized governments begun in the previous era. In spite of the very real calamities of the late Middle Ages, there are also significant continuities from the twelfth to the fifteenth centuries.

The historiography of late medieval religious culture follows a pattern similar to that of the period in general. Both contemporary observers and modern scholars have painted a dismal picture of the religious culture of the time. Once the engine for reform and renewal in Western Christianity, the papacy was widely criticized for its corruption. Accusations of clerical abuse and incompetence become more common. The church and the laity seem to have cooperated in a mechanical and mercantile view of salvation. Yet critics often had powerful reasons to depict late medieval Christianity as flawed and corrupt. Much of the contemporary criticism of the late medieval church came from within the church itself. Mendicant friars criticized parish priests as both sides competed for the allegiance of the laity. Various types of reformers criticized the institutional church while being supported by church income. Lay people criticized the clergy while participating wholeheartedly in parish life. Modern scholarly criticism of late medieval Christianity should be taken with a grain of salt, as well. Protestant scholars often describe a decadent late medieval Christianity to justify the Reformation. Many Roman Catholic scholars contrast a golden age of Christianity in the thirteenth century with a degraded religious culture in the fourteenth and fifteenth centuries to show that the Protestant reformers were not reacting against true Christianity, and thus tragically overreacted.

Many of the issues and events that are cited as evidence of religious decline in the late Middle Ages can also be used to show the depth and strength of religious life in the period. Take for example the series of crises that confronted the papacy in the fourteenth and fifteenth centuries. During the thirteenth century, the pope was not only the unquestioned leader of the Western church, he was also the most powerful political figure in Europe. This power and prestige would not survive the fourteenth century. In 1303, agents of the King of France kidnapped Pope Boniface VIII. The elderly prelate died soon after as a result of the trauma. While shocking, the episode was part of a wider change in the relationship between the papacy and increasingly powerful European monarchs. By the end of the fifteenth century, the papacy had lost direct control of religious affairs in regions of Europe governed by strong royal dynasties, such as England, France, and Spain. The nobility of Bohemia successfully rejected papal authority outright. The papacy had become so vulnerable to political pressure that it moved from Rome to Avignon, a town in what is now southern France, to avoid being dominated by the central Italian nobility. The final insult to papal prestige came in 1378 when French cardinals in Avignon and Italian cardinals in Rome elected opposing popes. The so-called Great Schism lasted until 1415.

By the standards of the Gregorian Reform, the late Middle Ages were a disaster for the papacy, and thus, Christendom. Looked at from a different angle, however, the picture is not so bleak. First, it would be wrong to equate the papacy with Western Christianity in general. Second, it would also be wrong to equate the power and prestige of the papacy with the effectiveness of the institutional church. Late medieval popes may not have wielded the power of their thirteenth-century predecessors, but the network of local parishes, organized into dioceses administered by bishops, connected with the vast majority of Europeans at a level of intensity and consistency unprecedented in the history of any religion. While the Avignon popes were accused, often accurately, of massive corruption, they presided over the largest, most sophisticated, and most effective institution in Europe. We should not treat the conflict between the papacy and the political rulers as a struggle between church and state. Events in the Iberian Peninsula and Bohemia attest to this. While denying the right of the papacy to interfere in their domestic policies, the Spanish monarchy and nobility defined themselves primarily in terms of the Christian culture encouraged by the Roman church. Muslims and Jews had to convert to Christianity to remain on the Iberian Peninsula. The Spanish church was at the forefront of the Catholic response to the Protestant Reformation. Spanish troops and mercenaries paid with Spanish gold played crucial roles in the many military conflicts with Northern European Protestant armies. Spanish missionaries were the primary exporters of Roman Catholicism to Asia and the Americas in the sixteenth century. The Bohemian nobility on the other hand, rejected both the pope's right to interfere in domesticate affairs and his doctrinal authority, in favor of the ideas of Czech theologian Jan Hus. The Hussites, however, did not reject Western Christian culture in general. Indeed, they believed that Hus' vision was more Christian than that of the papal church.

In the last several decades, two important trends have caused scholars to reevaluate late medieval religious culture. First, scholars have begun the task of exploring late medieval religious culture on its own terms. Recall that in section one, we introduced some of the problems inherent in evaluating the depth and quality of Christian culture. Both Protestant and many Roman Catholic historians have dismissed late medieval Christianity for theological reasons. To these scholars, most late medieval Christians held erroneous theological views and behaved more like pagans than Christians. While these are important and legitimate issues for theologians to take up, historians have a more basic question to answer: What did late medieval Europeans believe and how did they experience their religion? This leads to the second important development. Most traditional accounts of late medieval Christianity took a "top down" view, focusing on the papacy, theologians, and learned supporters and critics of the church. More recent accounts have taken a "bottom up" approach, which has served to resolve some of the perplexing issues confronting those studying the period. This section includes excerpts from some of the most important works using this approach. Before examining them, it will help to have a sense of late medieval popular religion in general.

In spite of demographic calamities and ecclesiastical crises, late medieval Christianity represented the culmination of many of the trends that we examined in previous chapters. Economic and political structures continued to become more sophisticated, resulting in a continued increase in literacy. Not only was the urban middle class growing, but the nobility, having lost their monopoly on military careers, were taking a keener interest in the opportunities open to the educated. Thus, the literate spirituality of the *vita apostolica*, which emphasized voluntary poverty and preaching, continued to grow in influence. Mendicant orders such as the Franciscans and Dominicans were popular preachers throughout Western Europe and achieved significant influence by serving as university professors, advisors to powerful princes, and high-level officials within the institutional church. Nevertheless, even the mendicants could not meet the demand for preaching or Christ-like living. Wealthy urban leaders began to endow preachers in many cities. In Northern Europe, a movement known as the *devotio moderna* provided a means for both those who wished to live a cloistered life and those who wished to live in traditional family units to organize their lives around a devotion practice focused on the imitation of Christ.

While the imitation of Christ was central to literate devotion in both the central and late Middle Ages, there are significant differences between the two periods. In the twelfth and thirteenth centuries, devotees of the *vita apostolica* focused primarily on imitating the ministry of Christ. In the subsequent two centuries, the focus shifted to Christ's Passion—his torture and death. We should be careful to not draw too sharp of a distinction. The Passion of Christ was important in the early *vita apostolica*. It was believed that Francis of Assisi received the *stigmata* (wounds of the hands, feet, and side identical to those inflicted on Jesus) as a sign of his authority. Nevertheless, the later Middle Ages witnessed widespread fascination and devotion to the suffering Christ. Many scholars have tried to explain this trend in light of the calamities of the period. This may be so, but for our purposes it is more important to see how a focus on the suffering Christ by literate Christians fit into late medieval popular religion in general.

While a Gregorian reformer would have been galled by the situation of the papacy in the late Middle Ages, he could not help but be impressed by the vigor and tone of religious life on the local level. In spite of widespread criticism of the clergy, the parish, especially the sacramental rituals performed by the parish priest, formed the basis for late medieval Christianity. According to the doctrine of the time, a person could only get to heaven if he or she received God's grace through the sacraments: baptism, confirmation, penance, communion, ordination, marriage, and last rites. The most important of these were baptism, which washed away original sin; penance, which absolved sins committed after baptism; and communion, which conveyed God's saving grace through bread and wine transformed into Christ's body and blood. Only a priest could offer the sacraments. The Mass, the name for the liturgical ceremony in which bread and wine become the body and blood of Christ through the invocation of the priest, was the center of medieval piety. Its power came from reenacting the sacrifice of Christ. Even in the most lethargic parishes, the vast majority of parishioners attended Mass once a week. Many of the devout attended Mass several times a week. Devotional practices developed around the Mass. The consecrated Host (the body and blood of Christ) was worshiped during and after the Mass. One of the most popular religious festivals, the Corpus Christi procession, was essentially a parade led by the consecrated Host, which was adored by those participating in and watching the procession. Because of the centrality of the Mass, three of the five selections in this section examine the Mass as a key to interpreting late medieval religious culture. Penance was the second focus of late medieval piety, because a Christian could only receive communion, and thus God's saving grace, if his or her sins had already been forgiven through confession and the performance of penitential acts. Parish priests and mendicants became specialists in hearing confessions. The devotional life of late medieval Christians revolved around the performance of penitential acts. Late medieval Christians, from royalty to peasant, participated in a religious economy that focused on the value of suffering and sacrifice for salvation. Acts of penance included some of the most dramatic expressions of late medieval piety, such as going on pilgrimages, or huge financial donations. Everyday behaviors such as repeated recitals of the Lord's Prayer and the Ave Maria, fasting and abstaining from sex during Lent and Advent, and small donations of money or time to the local parish were also part of penitential devotion.

For us, living in a society that values individual fulfillment and quality of life, this may seem like an oppressive religious culture. Certainly for some sensitive souls, like Martin Luther, it was. For the most part, however, this was indeed a popular religious culture. Late medieval Christians gave generously of their time and financial resources. The papacy and clergy were criticized for being immoral, not for being too rigorous or puritanical. Clearly, late medieval Europeans were very different from us. Each of the five selections in this section attempts to bridge this deep divide. Our first selection is one of the early challenges to the traditional view of late medieval Christianity. Rather than seeing a weakening of Christian culture, Bernd Moeller claims that there is no distinction between religious culture and society in the late Middle Ages. The vast majority of late medieval Christians not only assented to the teaching of the church, but also enthusiastically participated in the religious life afforded by traditional institutions. The next two selections explore this claim in depth. Eamon Duffy reaffirms Moeller's thesis, while Keith Thomas sees a barely christianized society. The final two demonstrate how a bottom up approach has shed welcome new light on late medieval religion by including new kinds of sources. Parish records reveal the extent of women's participation in local religious life. Studying popular songs from fifteenth-century Germany and Bohemia allows us to approach the everyday beliefs of both Hussites and their opponents.

Further Reading

Bossy, John. *Christianity in the West: 1400–1700*, New York: Oxford University Press, 1985.

Brown, Andrew. *Church and Society in England, 1000–1500*, New York: Palgrave Macmillan, 2003.

Cameron, Euan. *The Reformation of the Heretics: The Waldenses of the Alps, 1480–1580*, Oxford: Oxford University Press, 1984.

Duffy, Eamon. *The Stripping of the Altars: Traditional Religion in England, c. 1400–c. 1580*, New Haven: Yale University Press, 1992.

French, Katherine L. *The People of the Parish: Community Life in a Late Medieval Diocese*, Philadelphia: University of Pennsylvania Press, 2000.

Fudge, Thomas A. *The Magnificent Ride: The First Reformation in Hussite Bohemia*, Brookfield, VT: Ashgate Publishing, 1998.

Kaminsky, Howard. *A History of the Hussite Revolution*, Berkeley and Los Angeles: University of California Press, 1967.

Lerner, Robert E. *The Heresy of the Free Spirit in the Latter Middle Ages*, Berkeley and Los Angeles: University of California Press, 1972.

Oakley, Francis. *The Western Church in the Later Middle Ages*, Ithaca: Cornell University Press, 1979.

Rubin, Miri. *Corpus Christi: The Eucharist in Late Medieval Culture*, Cambridge: Cambridge University Press, 1991.

Swanson, R. N. *Religion and Devotion in Europe, c. 1215–c. 1515*, Cambridge: Cambridge University Press, 1995.

Thomas, Keith. *Religion and the Decline of Magic*, New York: Oxford University Press, 1971.

Thomson, John A. F. *Popes and Princes, 1117–1517: Politics and Polity in the Late Medieval Church*, London: Unwin Hyman, 1980.

~

CHAPTER EIGHTEEN

Religious Life in Germany on the Eve of the Reformation*

Bernd Moeller

Coming to grips with late medieval Christianity is especially important for scholars of medieval and early modern Germany. As the birthplace of the Protestant Reformation, late medieval German religious culture has been the subject of intense study and debate since the sixteenth century. For the most part, however, scholars defending a particular confessional standpoint usually undertook historical inquiry into the period for polemical reasons. Both Protestant and Roman Catholics were inclined to see late medieval German Christianity as corrupt and inauthentic. Protestants obviously wished to justify the actions of the reformers. Roman Catholics argued that the degraded Christianity that the reformers condemned was a local aberration and the reformers were wrong to reject traditional Christianity in toto. In the second half of the twentieth century, historians began to re-examine the period, for its own sake. One of the leaders in this trend was German historian Bernd Moeller. While not ignoring theological factors, Moeller was deeply interested in the social context of religious beliefs and practices. His seminal work, Reichstadt und Reformation (The Cities and the Reformation), is still a standard in the field over forty years later. Following its publication in 1962, Moeller turned his attention to the century preceding the Reformation. Contrary to the accepted wisdom of the time, Moeller claimed that fifteenth-century Germany nourished a vibrant and complex Christian culture. According to Moeller, the defining feature of late medieval German Christianity was "churchliness" (Kirchlichkeit). While

* © Bernd Moeller, "Religious Life in Germany on the Eve of the Reformation," *Pre-Reformation Germany*, ed. Gerald Strauss, New York: Harper and Row, 1972, pp. 14–20, 24–30.

the clergy may have been worthy of criticism, Moeller argues that there was no distinction between secular and religious in fifteenth-century Germany, that late medieval Germany was a religious culture. What evidence does Moeller present to defend his thesis? In your own words, define what Moeller means by Kirchlichkeit.

One decisive feature, in particular, of the religious spirit of this era has not yet been grasped with sufficient clarity: its containment within the ecclesiastical organization (*Kirchlichkeit*). A look at the religious life in Germany in the second half of the fifteenth century makes it impossible to speak of dissolution of the medieval world. On the contrary, it would be nearer the truth to say that there was hardly a period in the second millennium of ecclesiastical history which accepted with less resistance the Catholic Church's absolutist claims in matters of dogma.

It will be necessary in the course of this study to make this assertion somewhat more concrete and precise. Nonetheless, it is quite simple to show that its opposite is most certainly not true, since it was during these decades that heresy—meaning the fundamental rejection of the medieval church—lost its impetus and became as good as extinct. It is true that a few scattered groups of Waldensians appear to have held out in remote mountain areas of central Germany down to the sixteenth century, but these remained underground. As far as we know, the last heresy trials of Waldensians or Hussites on German territory took place—with one isolated exception—before 1470. After that date the only cases that came before the Inquisition were more or less harmless agitators, blasphemers and the like, or else religious zealots like those Augsburg sectarians who caused a stir in 1480 for wanting to receive the sacrament daily, or several times a day. The principal business of the Inquisition courts was now with witchcraft. The disappearance of the heretics was, moreover, not brought about by violent suppression. There is a good deal of symbolical significance in the resigned confession of the German Hussite, Friedrich Reiser, who said in 1456: "Our cause is like a fire going out." The great heretical movement which had, ever since the twelfth century, caused the church such lasting anxiety even in Germany petered out in the latter half of the fifteenth century. All its energy and missionary zeal had collapsed: heretical ideas no longer inflamed men's minds.

But this most certainly does not mean that religious fervor and emotion had declined. On the contrary, there is a great deal to suggest that piety in fact increased considerably in intensity during these years. Perhaps the most impressive piece of evidence of this is Karl Eder's demonstration that in the region investigated by him, Upper Austria, the number of Mass-endowments continually grew between 1450 and 1480 to an extent hitherto unknown, and reached its peak in 1517, only to start falling drastically from 1518 on and soon to cease altogether: this area remained Protestant for a long time. The same tendency emerges from Arnold Oskar Meyer's—admittedly incomplete—list of Silesian endowments in honor of St. Anne during the Middle Ages, while for north Germany it has been shown that the city of Hamburg boasted no fewer than ninety-nine confraternities at the beginning of the Reformation, of which the majority had been set up after 1450. It might be added that no other period saw so many feast days, and processions, and, even more interesting, that from Alsace and Upper Austria right up to Holland and the Baltic there occurred a "new spring" in church building, which resulted in the last, most fragile, blossoming of "late Gothic." These facts would seem to suggest that the picture was essentially the same throughout the German-speaking territories.

It should not, of course, be overlooked that these phenomena can be partly explained by external factors. The growth of the veneration of St. Anne, for instance, was very much a matter of fashion and was not restricted to Germany. Enthusiasm for endowments was doubtless prompted to a large extent by the desire of the burgher class for maintaining its visible status, a wish that was able to find new forms of expression in the age of early capitalism, of great merchant companies and the accumulation of new wealth. One endowment tended to prepare the way for the next, and it is surely significant that altars came increasingly to be named after the family that had presented one rather than after the saint. It is, of course, obvious that external factors such as these do not account for the phenomena as such. For confirmation we need only turn to the charters of endowment which time and time again speak of the motives of donors: Endowments are made for the "obtaining of external salvation"; membership in a confraternity is to ensure "all good things and the salvation of body and soul." Ecclesiastical and religious life was intimately and inseparably fused with secular life, and the willingness, indeed the longing, to sanctify one's secular existence within the framework of ecclesiastical discipline and with the aid of the treasury of grace made available by the church were at no time more widespread than in the late fifteenth century. In no other age did they receive such tangible expression.

When examined more closely, however, expressions of piety and ecclesiastical religion during this period turn out to be varied and differentiated. We must recognize above all two fundamental moods and trends which were in many ways mutually opposed. There prevailed on the one hand an inclination to mass movements; that is to say, a tendency toward hysteria ending often enough in violence, and a habit of oversimplifying and vulgarizing sacred things. On the other hand, the age witnessed a tender individualism and a bent for tranquil spirituality and religious modesty.

The former tendency was certainly not peculiar to this period. It had been characteristic of the later Middle Ages ever since the mid-fourteenth century. We may account for it in part by shifts in the social structure of Western Europe—the rise of urbanism and burgherdom; in part by such shattering collective experiences as the plague epidemics. It was an age in which "people" were not just passive participants in religious and ecclesiastical life, but instead played an active part in shaping this life.

Mass pilgrimages, for example, could flare up like a psychosis from one day to the next, and they could cease again just as suddenly. In some cases the occasion was a notable miracle—a host miracle generally—in others, as for instance in Sternberg (Mecklenburg) in 1492, where a priest was burned for selling a consecrated host to a Jew, the motive seems inappropriate and entirely without sense. In still other cases—for example, the strange children's pilgrimage of 1457 to Mont St. Michel in Normandy, which drew its pilgrim mainly from south Germany, the occasion cannot even be discerned now. But in addition to such religious mass movements, the period produced ugly mass excesses such as the systematic witch-hunting which first appeared in south Germany in the 1480s as a result of the agitation of the Dominican Inquisitor Heinrich Institoris. Although these excesses met at first with opposition from the authorities and did not yet enjoy much popular support, they form as much a part of the general picture of the period as the local persecutions of Jews which became increasingly frequent in this age of rising capitalism.

The supernatural world was still very real and very close to the men and women of this age, and the panic aroused by the terrors and calamities of the time (though these were, comparatively speaking, not particularly serious) increased their sense of dependence on, and their longing for harmony with, the powers of heaven. Miracle sites multiplied rapidly and were to be found in every corner of the empire. Often enough these miracles were manifest frauds; occasionally they culminated in dreadful scandals, like the notorious Jetzer case in Bern in 1509, where four Dominicans were burned at the stake because, maliciously or because they had been duped, they had used the novice Johann Jetzer to perpetrate a spurious miracle of the virgin directed against Franciscan doctrines concerning the immaculate conception of Our Lady, and had come to grief with it.

It was probably about this time, too, that the veneration of saints reached its peak and at the same time took on new outward manifestations. Saints tended to be brought more and more closely into the everyday life of average people. In paintings they emerged from their gilt background, became individualized, and were brought up to date in both dress and facial expression. In the cults associated with them, especially in the intimate atmosphere of confraternities, saints were treated with confidence and, one might even say, intimacy—an attitude productive of such quaint and touching practices as the action of the Confraternity of Our Lady at Den Bosch in Holland in 1456 in giving a dead brother a letter to St. Peter containing a pledge of the brethren's good works to help him speed through the Gate of Heaven. Another aspect of this trend is the full development of the system of patronage, which established certain saints for particular sections of the population or for particular emergencies, dividing up the heavenly court to correspond exactly to the structure of human society and human lives. It was at this time, finally, that it became a general practice to name children after saints, with the result that the old Germanic names pretty well vanished altogether.

Behind all this longing for salvation doubtless there lay an insecurity concerning salvation, an endeavor to bring the mediators between God and man to one's own side as it were, and to procure a guarantee of salvation. At no other time was death conceived with such realism, or feared with quite such anguish. We may see examples of this in the strenuous exertions, very moving in their way, of the well-to-do to utilize every possible advantage offered by the late medieval church in return for good works. We think in this connection of those monster collections of relics made especially at the beginning of the sixteenth century, the decisive motive for which was in each case to receive a correspondingly immense period of indulgence. Cardinal Albrecht of Brandenburg managed to reach 39,245,120 years according to his own estimate. At all events, the general boom in indulgences from the time of Sixtus IV's pontificate on is sure to have been motivated to a considerable extent by the wishes and needs of the faithful and not merely, as earlier critics of the papacy used to maintain, by the financial interests of the church. No less grotesque and no less revealing appear some of the testaments drawn up at this time. Count Werner von Zimmern had a thousand Requiem Masses said for his soul in 1483, and Duke Adolf von Geldern, on the death of his wife in 1569, ordered the bells of all the churches in Arnheim to be rung for three days and caused the Office of the Dead to be celebrated and private Masses to be said by all the priests in his lands.

These were the anxious gestures of people in distress and in need of help. Earlier times had not known their like in such cumulative intensity. They form a strange, though by no means fortuitous, contrast with the many expressions of vigorous, even "earthy" worldliness to be found at all levels of society. And yet they show that people took the church's competence and effectiveness in matters of salvation just as much for granted as they did the efficacy of good works. And their reliance on the quantity rather than the quality of such works was thoroughly characteristic of the Middle Ages. Moreover, the greatest hopes of strength and consolation continued to be the Mass and the eucharist, the central mystery of the church. A timid sense of reverential distance from the sacrament tended to develop, as revealed by the fact that, although people thrust forward enthusiastically to catch sight of the host, there was no increase in the number of communions, despite many efforts on the part of the church.

If the basic outlines sketched here are correct (and in a general survey of this kind it is impossible to do justice to all the differentiations and nuances), then a coherent and, in some sense, self-contained picture emerges. The religious agitation, in many instances convulsion, to be found throughout society, that *"mobilitas setu mutabilitas animarm et inconstantia mentis nunc in hominibus"* {restlessness of men's souls and agitation of their minds, ed.} discerned by an Erfurt theologian in 1466, sought peace and certitude in what was traditional, time-proven, and holy; it found rest and composure in the laws of the church. One may, it seems to me, say that the late fifteenth century in Germany was marked by greater fidelity to the church than in any other medieval epoch.

The search was, of course, not for the church as such, but rather for its treasury of salvation. In their intense and subjective preoccupation with eternal bliss, men seized upon the church's conventions and prescribed rituals and, in performing them with a new zeal and entirely of their own accord, they filled them with new content. And this was not merely a matter of exaggeration or excess. In fact, the laity came increasingly to consider itself responsible for the church's constitution and performance. This was an impulse which had long been at work, principally in the cities. Territorial princes and city magistrates, even individual citizens, took energetic action in matters of monastic reform, and toward the turn of the century it became customary to endow preaching benefices for the purpose of guaranteeing regular sermons of high quality (as is proved by the frequent stipulation that incumbents should hold a university degree), as a result of which many regions, especially in southwest Germany, had at least one endowed preacher in almost every city.

There can be no mistaking the fact that these and similar measures occasionally had an element of self-help about them. The widespread ecclesiastical devotion of the later years of the fifteenth century did not necessarily imply an uncritical acceptance of the claims to superiority and leadership put forward by the dignitaries of the church. It is true that, on the whole (and in comparison with the preceding age of reform), explicit criticism of the church was only sporadic and relatively modest in nature. Earlier historians, it seems to me, gave excessive importance to these criticisms, both as to their substance and their significance.

We have, for example, the *Grievances of the German Nation*, directed against particular abuses, mainly financial; also a few pamphlets demanding extensive church reform, such as the *Reformatio Sigismundi*, which had originated as early as 1439 in connection with the Council of Basel and gained some currency later on in the century, or the rabid pamphlet of the so-called "Upper Rhenish Revolutionary," though this remained as good as unknown.

The most important fifteenth-century critics of the church in the territories of the Holy Roman Empire were three theologians more or less closely connected with the *Devotio Moderna*: the two Dutchmen, Johann Pupper von Goch (d. 1475), and Wessel Gansfort (d. 1489), and the Rhinelander Johann Ruchrath von Oberwesel (d. after 1479). They are conspicuous principally for the fact that they were the first to give some evidence of independent religious thinking and reforming tendencies in the world of German scholasticism, which was otherwise "completely colorless, both in matters of theology and in ecclesiastical politics," to quote Gerhard Ritter, and moved firmly along the traditional lines of the schools. Nevertheless, both the influence and the reforming zeal of these theologians remained limited and faint. Though they resolutely emphasized the scriptural principle, even using it to contradict conventional exegesis, and raised repeated objections to such institutions of the church as indulgences and the meritoriousness of religious vows, and even, as in the case of Gansfort, championed Occam's view of the church as the invisible community of the righteous, very few people learned of these opinions, and fewer still took any interest or were carried along by them.

Only the humanists gave such ideas a certain echo. Though at this time still few in number and membership, humanist circles provided for the first and, in effect, only time in the fifteenth century, a forum for a general transformation in matters of religion and philosophy. In the case of some humanists—Celtis, for one—we can sense an alienation resting on fundamental principles, the emergence of a feeling for life akin to (and to some extent influenced by) that of the Italian Renaissance, and also a new optimism in regard to human existence. But even in this instance one must guard against the danger of making false assessments.

Though the German humanists were to play a significant role in the triumph of the Reformation, around 1500 they showed scarcely any signs of a deliberate rejection of traditional religion within the church. Rudolf Agricola wished to be buried in a monk's cowl in 1485, not a few of the humanists contributed their talents as poets and authors to the service of popular religiosity, and a number of them, such as the Basel preacher Surgant, used their new ideals in an attempt to make the influence of the church more effective, just as Reuchlin and Erasmus were to do later. Inasmuch as humanism was to exercise considerable historical influence in later years, and its advocates were always inclined to draw more attention to themselves than was their due, historians are inclined to attach too much importance to the movement at this early stage. Humanists were not representative of German religious life in the latter years of the fifteenth century.

Criticism of the church in humanist and popular literature, and the movement to extend lay influence in the church, may have been limited in scope and significance, but they provide a component which it would be a mistake to leave out of our picture. Along with the subjectivism of religious attitudes, the emancipation from religious tutelage implied in a man's choice of his own means of salvation, we witness a sense of disillusionment with the clergy's failure to live up to the demands and expectations of the devout. Criticism of the ignorance and immorality of the secular and regular clergy, and the efforts on the part of the laity to counteract abuses with the means at their disposal, might well be described as acts of self-defense. The fact that these things were done suggests that men were seeking salvation and wished to find it with the help of the church.

To what extent were disillusionment, criticism, and self-help justified? An attempt will be made here to sum up the conclusions reached by historians in regard to that old and still controversial problem of the moral and intellectual condition of the hierarchy on the eve of the Reformation.

As regards intellectual standards it has been shown that, in south Germany at least, between a third and half of all clerics had attended a university where they had at least studied the liberal arts. In north Germany the percentage of university-educated priests is sure to have been lower, and in any case it should be remembered that only a very small proportion of these men had actually studied theology. Not until after the Reformation did it become accepted as a principle that the study of theology should be an indispensable qualification for the clerical calling. Furthermore, the diocesan examinations for which prospective clergymen had to present themselves were extremely modest in their requirements.

In matters of clerical morality the situation in 1500 was not completely catastrophic either. Exact and reliable figures are unobtainable in this regard, although Oskar Vasella, the expert on these problems, is undoubtedly near the truth with the dark picture he has recently drawn of conditions in Switzerland. It is certain that the number of clerics living in concubinage was extraordinarily high; though these relationships were often marital in character, and there are signs of attempts to legalize these unions and thus bring them to some extent within the sphere of morality.

Concerning pastoral activity and care of the soul, finally, we may observe that the majority of clerics confined themselves to the reading of Masses. In the many parishes served only by a vicar on behalf of a nonresident parish priest, preaching and spiritual guidance were often neglected altogether, and there is evidence that even the activities of responsible and conscientious priests were largely confined to a perfunctory administration of the sacraments and devotions to the saints. All the same, a great deal of preaching went on, done by mendicant friars and by appointed preachers and even by parish priests; in fact, there is possibly a good deal to be said for the view that there was too much rather than too little preaching, especially since the standard of these sermons, so far as can be judged from extant drafts and copies (which would obviously be of particularly highly prized examples) was in keeping with the temper of the age and was often astonishingly, occasionally unbelievably, low.

The abuses among the late medieval clergy and the affront which these abuses presented to religious attitudes around 1500 make a complex set of phenomena. One contributory factor was the steep rise in the number of clerics, the product of that same pious zeal which endowed all those Masses and benefices, which introduced an element of assembly line production into their ministrations and diminished their quality. In pre-Reformation Worms about 10 per cent of the population consisted of secular or religious clerics. The church had reached the point where it was unable to do anything more than react to stimuli given by others. Its theology and its spiritual life lacked the genuine inner impulse to find its way out of the maze into which its own historical development had brought it. It produced no relevant, helpful response to the yearnings and explosive passions of men who submitted themselves to the church for guidance. The most characteristic symptom of this lack of response is the fatal importance given in this age to indulgence preaching, with its vulgar materialism and its preaching which was of its very nature so open to misunderstandings.

It would appear, therefore, that the revitalization and deepening of religious life in the second half of the fifteenth century aroused virtually no echo within the clergy. There are, in fact, indications that the condition of the clergy simply went on deteriorating right up to the brink of the Reformation. The role of leadership which had been accorded to the clergy ever since the early Middle Ages was still being claimed and was scarcely disputed anywhere; but the clergy were hardly capable of fulfilling this role. With their benefice-oriented mentality they remained essentially feudal. They were, moreover, long accustomed to forming a caste set apart from the laity, a state of affairs justified on the grounds of their sacramental functions, the *opus operatum*. Confronted now for the first time in the Middle Ages with intellectual and religious demands of an exacting and subtle nature, they had their power taken away, while the deterioration of their intellectual and moral standards would inevitably be found more and more intolerable as the level of the laity rose, particularly in Germany, for at the beginning of the sixteenth century the center of European spiritual and religious life began for the first time in history to shift north of the Alps.

There can be no doubt that the points discussed here, if not actually "causes" of the Reformation, were at least "prerequisites" of the great change. There is no room to go any further into the problems touched on—a brief indication must suffice. Nikolaus Glassberger, a Franciscan chronicler of Franconia during the later fifteenth century, once raised a troubled lament at the sorry condition of the church in contemporary France, the collapse of worship and the godlessness of the people, contrasting this with the flourishing religious life of Germany, where the divine service was celebrated with all solemnity and the people were devout and faithful to the church. What he saw may well have been true. In the late Middle Ages Germany was "a particularly medieval country," and this was evidently true right up to the Reformation. Luther's triumph in Germany—in other words, his power to carry men along with him—will clearly be misunderstood if we do not realize that one of its prerequisites was the extreme acceleration of medieval ecclesiastical religiosity. That the Reformation broke out, not in France, but in traditional, slow-moving medieval Germany, a land noted for its respectful attitude toward the powers that be, is a fact which should be carefully considered; it was certainly not a matter of chance.

CHAPTER NINETEEN

~

The Stripping of the Altars: Traditional Religion in England, ca. 1400–1580*

Eamon Duffy

Because a larger number of people were literate and a larger percentage of docu-
ments survive, we know a great deal more about late medieval popular religion than
we do of earlier periods. Yet there are still several obstacles in our way. Reading and
writing remained an elite activity. Moreover, for both the learned and unlearned,
Christianity was primarily a social and performative religion. While clerical and ed-
ucated lay elites pursued private devotional and meditative practices, we should not
assume that these activities replaced social and ritual practices. The challenge for
the historian is to uncover the meaning of these activities to the average Christian.
The Mass played a central role in late medieval piety. Here, according to official
doctrine, the bread (Host) is transformed into the body of Christ through the invo-
cation of the priest. In the Mass, medieval Christians found themselves, quite liter-
ally, in the presence of God. Older accounts of late medieval religion described the
lay congregation at Mass as mere observers of obscure and elaborate rituals being
performed by the priest. Since the typical lay Christian could neither understand
Latin, the language of the ritual, nor the technical theology underlying the Mass,
historians assumed that most Christians were ignorant spectators. In the following
selection from his highly influential book, The Stripping of the Altars, *Eamon*
Duffy argues that the Mass was rich in various meanings to the laity. As the focal
point of lay piety, the Mass was experienced on several levels. According to Duffy,
those who attended Mass were participants, not mere spectators. In what ways

* © 1992 Yale University Press. Eamon Duffy, *The Stripping of the Altars: Traditional Religion in Eng-*
land, c. 1400–c. 1580, New Haven: Yale University Press, 1992, pp. 112–120.

could lay people participate in the Mass? How does Duffy use the architecture and interior arrangement of churches to bolster his argument?

The prestige of the Sacrament as the centre and source of the whole symbolic system of late medieval Catholicism implied an enormously high doctrine of priesthood. The priest had access to mysteries forbidden to others: only he might utter the words which transformed bread and wine into the flesh and blood of God incarnate, those *"fyue wordes / withouten drede / that no mon but a prest schulde rede."* No layman or woman might even touch the sacred vessels with their bare hands. When the laity drank the draught of unconsecrated wine which they were given after communion to wash down the Host and ensure they had swallowed it, they had to cover their hands with the houseling-cloth, for the virtue of the Host and blood affected even the dead metal of the chalice. Power "leaked" from the Host and the blood: whooping cough could be cured by getting a priest to give one a threefold draught of water or wine from his chalice after Mass.

The mystery that surrounded the central sanctities of the Mass were reflected in the language in which, like the rest of the liturgy, it was celebrated. The combination of the decent obscurity of a learned language on one hand, and clerical monopoly—or at least primacy—in the control and ordering of the liturgy on the other, has led to the view that the worship of late medieval England was non-participatory. The fact that in most churches the high altar was divided from the nave by a Rood-screen has lent support to this notion. Bernard Manning, in what remains one of the most suggestive and sympathetic accounts of late medieval religion, nevertheless wrote of a tendency "to leave the service more and more to the clerks alone," and a more modern commentator has even talked of a "lay society separated by rood screens and philosophical abstractions from the 'alienated liturgy' of the altar." Enough has been said in the first chapter about lay assimilation of liturgical themes to make any such notion of general lay alienation from the liturgy untenable. But what of the specific case of the Mass: to what extent was lay involvement with this most sacred and central of the rites of Christendom passive or alienating?

Any attempt to tackle this question must start from the recognition that lay people experienced the Mass in a variety of ways and in a range of settings. The parish Mass was indeed celebrated at the high altar, and that altar was often physically distanced even from the nearest members of the congregation, and partially obscured by the screen. In some of the great parish churches, like St Margaret's, Lynn, or Walpole St Peter, parishioners would have been well out of earshot of anything said, as opposed to sung, at the altar. During Lent, moreover, a huge veil was suspended within the sanctuary area, to within a foot or so of the ground, on weekdays completely blocking the laity's view of the celebrant and the sacring. However, we need to grasp that both screen and veil were manifestations of a complex and dynamic understanding of the role of both distance and proximity, concealment and exposure within the experience of the liturgy. Both screen and veil were barriers, marking boundaries between the people's part of the church and the holy of holies, the sacred space within which the miracle of transubstantiation was effected, or, in the case of the veil, between different types of time, festive and penitential. The veil was there precisely to function as a temporary ritual deprivation of the sight of the sacring. Its symbolic effectiveness derived from the fact that it obscured for a time something which was normally accessible; in the process it heightened the value of the spectacle it temporarily concealed.

The screen itself was both a barrier and no barrier. It was not a wall but rather a set of windows, a frame for the liturgical drama, solid only to waist-height, pierced by a door wide enough for ministers and choir to pass through and which the laity themselves might penetrate on certain occasions, for example, when, as at Eye on festivals, they gathered with torches to honour the sacrament, and in processions like the Candlemas one and the ceremonies and watching associated with the Easter sepulchre. Even the screen's most solid section, the dado, might itself be pierced with elevation squints, to allow the laity to pass visually into the sanctuary at the sacring. This penetration was a two-way process: if the laity sometimes passed through the screen to the mystery, the mystery sometimes moved out to meet them. Each Mass was framed within a series of ritual moments at which the ministers, often carrying sacred objects, such as the Host itself at Easter, or, on ordinary Sundays, Gospel texts, the paxbred, or sacramentals like holy water or holy bread, passed out of the sanctuary into the body of the church. We shall explore some of these moments shortly.

But in any case, it is vital to remember that the parish Mass, important as it was for lay experience of the liturgy, was by no means the only or perhaps even the most common lay experience of the Mass. Many lay people, perhaps even most of them, attended Mass on some weekdays. These weekday masses were not usually the elaborate ritual affairs, with a procession, the blessing of holy water and holy bread, and some singing, which most parishes could have mustered on Sundays. The daily Masses to which the laity resorted to "see my Maker" were "low" Masses, short ceremonies celebrated at altars which, far from being concealed behind screens and out of earshot of the worshippers, were often within arm's reach. In his version of the *Doctrinal of Sapyence*, a treatise aimed at instructing "*symple prestes . . . and symple peple*," Caxton complained that far from standing well back in awe and reverence at Mass, "*moche peple . . . go nyghe and about the aulter and stolid so nyghe the aulter that they trouble oftimes the preest for the dissolutions that they doo in spekyng in lawhing and many other mailers and not only the laye men and women but also the clerkes by whom the other ought to be governed and taken ensample.*"

The surviving evidence of the ritual arrangements of countless English churches confirms this picture of the accessibility of the daily celebration to the laity. Great churches, of course, had many altars, in side chapels, in chantries divided from the body of the church by parclosing or wainscot, or against pillars. But even small churches had their quota of altars for the celebration of gild and chantry Masses, all crammed into the nave. Often these altars made use of the Rood-screen, not as a barrier against contact with the Mass, but as the backdrop for it. At Ranworth in Norfolk these altar arrangements survive intact, with two altars flanking the central portion of the screen, using the paintings on its extreme northern and southern sections as *reredos*. An identical arrangement operated at Bromfield in Suffolk, where the elaborate *piscina* to the south of the screen reveals the presence of an altar of some importance. Even the tiny church of Wellingham, only sixteen feet wide, had an altar pushed up against the south screen, while at South Burlingham the mark of an even more substantial altar against the north screen is still visible. The altars at Wellingham and South Burlingham must have crowded the east end of the nave, and awkwardly interrupted the decorative schemes of the screens against which they were placed. But many of these nave altars were much more carefully integrated into the planning of the screen, as at Ranworth, Bromfield, and, even more spectacularly, at Attleburgh. They were clearly among the most important focuses of ritual activity in the building. This prominence given to nave altars was no merely regional phenomenon. Jesus altars in many parishes attracted multiple benefactions for the maintenance of the worship of the Holy Name, and the Jesus altars in cathedrals like Durham, in great town churches like St Lawrence, Reading, and smaller buildings like All Saints, Bristol, were prominently placed in the people's part of the church, and had elaborate sung services endowed at them. The Jesus Mass at All Saints, Bristol, was celebrated several times a week, had a choir of its own and a set of organs; in addition to the Mass the priest and singers performed the "*Salve*" anthem at night.

The laity controlled, often indeed owned these altars. They provided the draperies in which they were covered, the images and ornaments and lights which encoded the dedication and functions of the altar and its worship. They specified the times and seasons at which the appearance and worship of the altar was to be varied. Their wills show an intense awareness of varying season and occasion—particular frontals or curtains for "good days," sombre array for requiems and year's minds, velvet or silk coats and bonnets and silver shoes to dress the altar images on festivals, and so on. The liturgy celebrated at these altars reflected the greater degree of lay involvement possible at them. The parish liturgy was fixed, following the order specified in calendar, missal, breviary, or processional. But most of the Masses said at the nave altars were votive or requiem ones, or Masses in honour of Our Lady or some favourite saint. As a consequence, the laity who paid for these celebrations could have a direct control over the prayers and readings used at them. It was standard practice for testators, whether founding a long-term chantry or less elaborately laying out a fiver on endowing an "annualer," to specify the use of particular collects, secrets, and post-communion prayers, or the celebration of a specific Mass or sequence of Masses on particular days of the week, or to stipulate the use of variant or even additional Gospels within the structure of a particular Mass. These extra Gospels were inserted at the end of Mass, just before the reading of the first chapter of St John's Gospel, with which every Mass concluded. And since this was a culture in which specific prayers or Gospel passages were believed to be especially powerful, to bring particular blessings or protection from certain evils, even the unlettered laity noticed, and valued, such variations. In many cases, perhaps in most, these variant liturgical prescriptions would have been arrived at in consultation with clerical advisers, "my ghostly father." But the fact remained that it was lay men and women who hired, and who could often fire, the clergy who carried out their instructions. It makes no sense to talk here about an "alienated liturgy of the altar." This was Eucharistic worship in which lay people called the shots.

The proprietary control of individuals, families, or larger groups like gilds over the liturgy of the nave altars raises another difference between the Masses said there and at the parish altar. Among the furnishings of these nave altars were their own "*paxes*," with their attendant peace rituals. Consequently, they represented a different ordering of community from that expressed or imposed by the Sunday Mass. Some of the implications of this can be teased out by considering the arrangements made in many places for the pro vision of a Jesus Mass at a nave altar.

The Mass in honour of the Holy Name of Jesus was, throughout the fifteenth century, one of the most popular of all votive Masses. From the 1470s onwards, Jesus brotherhoods proliferated throughout England, dedicated to the maintenance of a regular celebration of the Mass of the Holy Name, often on a Friday, at an altar over which there might be its own Jesus image, distinct from the Crucifix. These Masses often began as the specific devotion of a small group, or as an individual benefaction, but invariably generated other donations and bequests, large and small, "to the sustentation of the Mass of Jesus." Wherever it occurs, the Jesus Mass has all the hallmarks of a genuinely popular devotion. Yet the Mass of Jesus was also emphatically an observance seized on by elites in every community as a convenient expression, and perhaps an instrument, of their social dominance. From its beginnings in England the cult of the Holy Name had aristocratic backing, and achieved status as a feast in the 1480s under the patronage of Lady Margaret Beaufort, whose domestic clergy composed the Office. In many towns, the well-to-do and powerful emulated the court's patronage of the cult. At Reading, the Jesus Mass at the church of St Lawrence began on the initiative of one of the town's wealthier clothiers, Henry Kelsall, *"fyrst mynder, sustayner and mayntaync of the devocyon of the Masse of Jhu."* The Jesus altar dominates the nave at St Lawrence's, and the Mass itself was funded and controlled by an exclusive gild of ten wealthy men and their wives. The gild acquired considerable land in the area, and was responsible for paying the sexton's wages, in return for his care of the gear of the altar and gild. The importance of this group in the life of the parish can be gauged from a town ordinance of 1547, which stipulated that the wives of former members of the Jesus gild *"shall from henseforth sits & have the highest seats or pewes next unto a Mayors wifs seate towardes the pulpitt."*

The Jesus Mass at the town church of All Saints, Bristol, was similarly sustained by the benefactions of the wealthy, and celebrated at the former Lady altar (increasingly in the late fifteenth and early sixteenth century called the Jesus altar) in what was effectively the private chantry chapel of Thomas Halleway, a former mayor of Bristol, who had installed fixed pews with doors for himself and his family directly in front of the Jesus altar. On the other side of England, the Jesus Mass at Long Melford was celebrated at an altar in "my aisle, called Jesus aisle," as Roger Martin wrote. The aisle was the burial chapel of the Martin family, and when iconoclasm reached Long Melford in Edward's reign Martin took the *reredos* of the Jesus altar to his home, as much a manifestation of proprietary rights as of his undoubted traditionalist piety. As elsewhere, the wealthy of Long Melford were conspicuous in their bequests to the ornaments and maintenance of the Jesus Mass.

That the parishioners of St Lawrence, Reading, All Saints, Bristol, or Holy Trinity, Long Melford, came in numbers to the Jesus Masses is not to be doubted, and the existence of bequests to these masses and to hundreds like them up and down the country leaves no doubt that they felt that, whoever had begun it, the Mass was now the possession of the community at large. But the altars, vestments, vessels, and clergy belonged not to the community at large, but to Henry Kelsall and his gild brethren, to Thomas Halleway, to the Martin family. The *pax* kissed at those masses was not the property of the parish, but the possession of the gilds, families or individuals who had established the devotion. The Mass belonged more to some than to others.

This is not to suggest that the liturgy at these altars was in any simple sense an instrument of social hegemony or, worse, social control. The founders and donors of such masses saw themselves, and were seen by others, as benefactors bestowing a spiritual amenity on their parish, and such benefactions earned one an honoured place in the parish bede-roll. But the implications for the perception of the religious dimensions of community in towns and villages at such masses were clearly more narrowly defined and more problematic than that at the parish altar on Sundays. We shall explore further dimensions of the complexities of the notion of communality in a late medieval religious community in a later chapter. Here it is sufficient to notice that in this respect, as in others, it is impossible to talk of a single type of experience of the Mass.

CHAPTER TWENTY

~

Religion and the
Decline of Magic*
Keith Thomas

The efforts of scholars such as Duffy to depict the Mass and other rituals as positive examples of medieval piety is part of an effort to overcome the traditional assumption that late medieval religious practices evidenced a degraded form of Christianity. Even after polemical, confessional treatments of the period were banished from the scholarly mainstream, this criticism of late medieval Christianity has survived. Keith Thomas in his book Religion and the Decline of Magic *most cogently articulates the newer version of this thesis. Although approaching the subject from a modern, secular point of view, Thomas essentially agrees with the sixteenth century reformers that late medieval popular religion was an incoherent amalgam of sub-Christian superstitions. Thus, the Reformation served to eliminate the magical aspects of Western Christianity. According to Thomas, most medieval Christians saw the sacraments as sources of magical power, which they could manipulate for a variety of situations having nothing to do with their theological purposes. Indeed, Thomas challenges the claim that Western Europe was ever christianized on the popular level. How do you think Duffy would respond to Thomas? What would Duffy do with Thomas's examples? What would Thomas do with Duffy's examples? Do Karen Louise Jolly's theories (see section one) on popular religion and christianization help resolve this conflict?*

The medieval Church thus acted as a repository of supernatural power which could be dispensed to the faithful to help them in their daily problems. It was

* © Reprinted with the permission of Weidenfeld & Nicholson, a division of The Orion Publishing Group. Keith Thomas, *Religion and the Decline of Magic*, New York: Oxford University Press, 1971, pp. 32–40, 45–46.

inevitable that the priests, set apart from the rest of the community by their celibacy and ritual consecration, should have derived an extra cachet from their position as mediators between man and God. It was also inevitable that around the Church, the clergy and their holy apparatus there clustered a horde of popular superstitions, which endowed religious objects with a magical power to which theologians themselves had never laid claim. A scapular, or friar's coat, for example, was a coveted object to be worn as a preservative against pestilence or the ague, and even to be buried in as a short cut to salvation: Bishop Hugh Latimer confessed that he used to think that if he became a friar it would be impossible for him to be damned. The church and churchyard also enjoyed a special power in popular estimation, primarily because of the ritual consecration of the site with salt and water. The key of the church door was said to be an efficacious remedy against a mad dog; the soil from the churchyard was credited with special magical power; and any crime committed on holy ground became an altogether more heinous affair, simply because of the place where it had occurred. This was recognised by a statute of the reign of Edward VI imposing special penalties for such offences; if the consecrated area were polluted by some crime of violence a special act of reconciliation was necessary before it could be used again for religious purposes. Even the coins in the offertory were accredited with magical value; there were numerous popular superstitions about the magical value of communion silver as a cure for illness or a lucky charm against danger.

But it was above all in connection with the sacraments of the Church that such beliefs arose. The Mass, in particular, was associated with magical power and for this, it must be said, the teaching of the Church was at least indirectly responsible. During the long history of the Christian Church the sacrament of the altar had undergone a process of theological re-interpretation. By the later Middle Ages the general effect had been to shift the emphasis away from the communion of the faithful, and to place it upon the formal consecration of the elements by the priest. The ceremony thus acquired in the popular mind a mechanical efficacy in which the operative factor was not the participation of the congregation, who had become virtual spectators, but the special power of the priest. Hence the doctrine that the laity could benefit from being present at the celebration even though they could not understand the proceedings. If too ignorant to follow a private mass book, they were encouraged to recite whatever prayers they knew; so that during the Mass the priest and people in fact pursued different modes of devotion. The ritual was said, in a notorious phrase, to work "like a charm upon an adder." In the actual miracle of transubstantiation the "instrumental cause" was the formula of consecration. Theologians refined this doctrine considerably, but their subtleties were too complicated to be understood by ordinary men. What stood out was the magical notion that the mere pronunciation of words in a ritual manner could effect a change in the character of material objects.

The reservation of the sacrament at the altar as an object of devotion had become customary in England by the thirteenth century and the element of mystery attaching to it was enhanced by the construction in the later Middle Ages of enclosed sanctuaries to protect the elements from the gaze of the public. Literalism generated anecdotes of how the Host had turned into flesh and blood, even into a child. The notion spread that temporal benefits might be expected from its mere contemplation, and the belief was enhanced by the readiness of the Church to multiply the secular occasions for which masses might be performed as a means of propitiation. There were masses for the sick and for women in labour, masses for good weather and for safe journeys, masses against the plague and other epidemics. The *Sarum Missal* of 1532 contained a special mass for the avoidance of sudden death. In 1516 the Priory of Holy Cross at Colchester received a grant of land, in return for the celebration of a solemn mass "for the further prosperity of the town." It was common to attach special value to the performance of a certain number of masses in succession—five, seven, nine or thirty (a *trental*). The ceremony could even be perverted into a maleficent act by causing masses for the dead to be celebrated for persons still alive, in order to hasten their demise. The fifteenth-century treatise *Dives and Pauper* inveighed against those

> that for hate or wrath that they bear against any man or woman take away the clothes of the altar, and clothe the altar with doleful clothing, or beset the altar or the cross about with thorns, and withdraw light out of the church, or . . . do sing mass of requiem for them that be alive, in hope that they should fare the worse and the sooner die.

The clear implication was that the clergy themselves were sometimes involved in these perversions.

A plethora of sub-superstitions thus accumulated around the sacrament of the altar. The clergy's anxiety that none of the consecrated elements should be wasted or accidentally dropped on the floor encouraged the idea that the Host was an object of supernatural potency. The officiating priest was required to swallow the remaining contents of the chalice, flies and all if need be, and to ensure that not a crumb of the consecrated wafer was left behind. The communicant who did not swallow the bread, but carried it away from the church in his mouth, was widely believed to be in possession of an impressive source of magical power. He could use it to cure the blind or the feverish; he could carry it around with him as a general protection against ill fortune, or he could beat it up into a powder and sprinkle it over his garden as a charm against caterpillars. Medieval stories relate how the Host was profanely employed to put out fires, to cure swine fever, to fertilise the fields and to encourage bees to make honey. The thief could also convert it into a love-charm or use it for some maleficent purpose. Some believed that a criminal who swallowed the Host would be immune from discovery; others held that by simultaneously communicating with a woman one could gain her affections. In the sixteenth century John Bale complained that the Mass had become a remedy for the diseases of man and beast. It was employed by "witches . . . sorcerers, charmers, enchanters, dreamers, soothsayers, necromancers, conjurers, cross-diggers, devil-raisers, miracle-doers, dog-leeches and bawds." The first Edwardian Prayer Book accordingly insisted that the bread should be placed by the officiating minister direct in the communicant's mouth, because in past times people had often carried the sacrament away and "kept it with them and diversly abused it, to superstition and wickedness."

It was because of this magical power thought to reside in consecrated objects that ecclesiastical authorities had long found it necessary to take elaborate precautions against theft. The Lateran Council of 1215 had ruled that the eucharist and the holy oil should be kept under lock and key, and the later medieval English Church showed a keen interest in enforcing this stipulation. As late as 1557, for example, Cardinal Pole, in his *Injunctions* for Cambridge University, insisted that the font should be locked up, so as to prevent the theft of holy water. Thefts of the Host are known to have occurred periodically—three were reported in London in 1532—and communion bread continued to be employed illegitimately for magical purposes in the post-Reformation era: James Device, one of the Lancashire witches of 1612, was told by his grandmother, Old Demdike, to present himself for communion and bring home the bread.

Many of these superstitions, however, did not require anything so dramatic as the theft of the Host from the altar. Mere attendance at Mass might secure temporal benefits. In his *Instructions for Parish Priests* John Myrc, the fourteenth-century Austin Canon of Lilleshall, claimed the authority of St Augustine for the view that anyone who saw a priest bearing the Host would not lack meat or drink for the rest of that day, nor be in any danger of sudden death or blindness. "Thousands," wrote William Tyndale in the early sixteenth century, believed that, if they crossed themselves when the priest was reading St John's Gospel, no mischance would happen to them that day. The Mass could also be a means of prognosticating the future or of gaining success in some projected venture. The clergy disseminated stories of the miraculous benefits which had been known to spring from communicating, and of the disastrous consequences which participation in the ceremony might have for the unworthy communicant. In the Communion Service in the Prayer Book of 1549 the curate was required to warn the congregation that anyone who received unworthily did so to his own damnation, both spiritual and temporal, for in this way "we kindle God's wrath over us; we provoke him to plague us with divers diseases and sundry kinds of death." In the seventeenth century the Catholic Church was noted by an intelligent observer to teach that the Mass might still be efficacious for "safe-journeying by sea or land, on horseback or on foot; for women that are barren, big, or bringing forth; for fevers and toothaches; for hogs and hens; for recovery of lost goods and the like."

Like the Mass, the other Christian sacraments all generated a corpus of parasitic beliefs, which attributed to each ceremony a material significance which the leaders of the Church had never claimed. By the eve of the Reformation most of these rituals had become crucial "rites of passage," designed to ease an individual's transition from one social state to another, to emphasise his new status and to secure divine blessing for it. Baptism, which signified the entry of the new-born child into membership of the Church, was necessary to turn the infant into a full human being, and by the thirteenth century was expected to take place within the first week of birth. The Church taught that the ceremony was absolutely necessary for salvation and that children who died unbaptised were usually consigned to limbo, where they would be perpetually denied sight of the vision of God and even, according to some theologians, subjected to the torments of the damned. At the baptismal ceremony the child was, therefore, exorcised (with the obvious implication that it had previously been possessed by the Devil), anointed with chrism (consecrated oil and balsam) and signed with the cross in holy water. Around its head was bound a white cloth (chrisom), in which it would be buried if it should die in infancy.

The social significance of the baptismal ceremony as the formal reception of the child into the community is obvious enough, and it is not surprising that greater meaning should have been attached to the ceremony than the Church allowed. Even in the early twentieth century it was believed in some rural communities that children "came on better" after being christened. In the later Middle Ages it was common to regard baptism as an essential rite if the child were physically to survive at all, and there were stories about blind children whose sight had been restored by baptism. Sundry superstitions related to the day on which the ceremony should take place, the sort of water which should be used, and the qualifications of the godparents. There were also attempts to apply the rite in inappropriate contexts, for example, by baptising the caul in which the infant was born, or by exorcising the mother when she was in labour. Particularly common was the idea that animals might benefit from the ceremony. It is possible that some of the numerous cases recorded in the sixteenth and seventeenth centuries of attempts to baptise dogs, cats, sheep and horses may not have arisen from drunkenness or Puritan mockery of Anglican ceremonies, but have reflected the old superstition that the ritual had about it a physical efficacy which could be directed to any living creature.

Very similar ideas surrounded the ceremony of confirmation. This rite had originally been combined with that of baptism as one integrated ceremony of Christian initiation. But by the early Middle Ages the two rituals had drawn apart, though confirmation was still expected to take place when the child was very young. Various maximum ages, ranging from one year to seven, were prescribed by English bishops in the thirteenth century; and, although a minimum age of seven came to be thought appropriate, the custom was slow to establish itself: Elizabeth, daughter of Henry VIII, was baptised and confirmed at the age of three days. Only in the mid-sixteenth century did the Council of Trent require the child to be approaching years of discretion and capable of rehearsing the elements of his belief. At the confirmation ceremony the bishop would lay his hands on the child and tie around its forehead a linen band which he was required to wear for three days afterwards. This was believed to strengthen him against the assaults of the fiend, and the notion became current that it was extremely bad luck to untie the band under any circumstances. Here too physical effects were vulgarly attributed to the ceremony: a belief which survived until the nineteenth century, as evidenced by the case of the old Norfolk woman who claimed to have been "bishopped" seven times, because she found it helped her rheumatism.

Another ecclesiastical ritual with a strong social significance was the churching, or purification, of women after childbirth, representing as it did society's recognition of the woman's new role as mother, and her resumption of sexual relations with her husband after a period of ritual seclusion and avoidance. Extreme Protestant reformers were later to regard it as one of the most obnoxious Popish survivals in the Anglican Church, but medieval churchmen had also devoted a good deal of energy to refuting such popular superstitions as the belief that it was improper for the mother to emerge from her house, or to look at the sky or the earth before she had been purified. The Church chose to treat the ceremony as one of thanksgiving for a safe deliverance, and was reluctant to countenance any prescribed interval after birth before it could take place. Nor did it accept that the woman should stay indoors until she had been churched. Like the *Sarum Manual, Dives and Pauper* stressed that unpurified women might enter church whenever they wished, and that "they that call them heathen women for the time that they lie in be fools and sin . . . full grievously." But for people at large churching was indubitably a ritual of purification closely linked to its Jewish predecessor.

Radical Protestants were later to blame the ceremony itself, which "breedeth and nourisheth many superstitious opinions in the simple people's hearts; as that the woman which hath born a child is unclean and unholy." But a fairer view would have been to regard the ritual as the result of such opinions, rather than the cause. Virginity, or at least abstinence from sexual intercourse, was still a generally accepted condition of holiness; and there were many medieval precedents for the attitude of the Laudian Vicar of Great Totham, Essex, who refused communion to menstruating women and those who had had sexual intercourse on the previous night. Such prejudices may have been reinforced by the all-male character of the Church and its insistence on celibacy, but they are too universal in primitive societies to be regarded as the mere creation of medieval religion. The ceremony of the churching of women took on a semi-magical significance in popular estimation; hence the belief, which the Church vainly attempted to scotch, that a woman who died in child-bed before being churched should be refused Christian burial. The idea of purification survived the Reformation; even at the end of the seventeenth century it was reported from parts of Wales that "the ordinary women are hardly brought to look upon churching otherwise than as a charm to prevent witchcraft, and think that grass will hardly ever grow where they tread before they are churched."

It is hardly necessary to detail the allied superstitions which attached themselves to the ceremony of marriage. Most of them taught that the fate of the alliance could be adversely affected by the breach of a large number of ritual requirements relating to the time and place of the ceremony, the dress of the bride, and so forth. Typical was the notion that the wedding ring would constitute an effective recipe against unkindness and discord, so long as the bride continued to wear it. Such notions provide a further demonstration of how every sacrament of the Church tended to generate its attendant sub-superstitions which endowed the spiritual formulae of the theologians with a crudely material efficacy.

This tendency was perhaps less apparent in the various rituals accompanying the burial of the dead, such as the convention that the corpse should face East or that the funeral should be accompanied by doles to the poor. Important though such observances were in popular estimation, they related primarily to the spiritual welfare of the soul of the deceased, and were seldom credited with any direct impact upon the welfare of the living, save in so far as a ghost who could not rest quietly might return to trouble the dead man's survivors. Funeral customs are worth studying for the manner in which they helped to ease the social adjustments necessary to accommodate the fact of death, but by their very nature they do not testify in the same way as the other rites of passage to the extent of popular belief in the material effects of ecclesiastical ritual. Before a man died, however, he was extended the last of the seven sacraments, extreme unction, whereby the recipient was anointed with holy oil and tendered the viaticum. In the eyes of everyone this was a dreadful ritual, and from Anglo-Saxon times there had been a deep conviction that to receive the viaticum was a virtual death sentence which would make subsequent recovery impossible. The medieval Church found it necessary to denounce the superstition that recipients of extreme unction who subsequently got better should refrain from eating meat, going barefoot, or having intercourse with their wives. It may have been in an attempt to counter this fear that the leaders of the Church chose to stress the possibility that extreme unction might positively assist the patient's recovery, provided he had sufficient faith. The Council of Trent emphasised that the ceremony could boost the recipient's will to live, and Bishop Bonner wrote in 1555 that:

> Although in our wicked time small is the number of them that do escape death, having received this sacrament . . . yet that is not to be ascribed unto the lack or fault of this sacrament, but rather unto the want and lack of steadfast and constant faith, which ought to be in those that shall have this sacrament ministered unto them; by which strong faith the power of almighty God in the primitive church did work mightily and effectually in sick persons anointed.

This was to link unction to the Church's other rites of blessing and anointing the sick to which it was closely related, and in which the intention had been curative rather than merely symbolic. As such it represents a final manifestation of the physical significance which the sacraments of the Church were so widely believed to possess.

Next to the sacraments as a means of access to divine assistance came the prayers of the faithful. Such prayer took many forms, but the kind most directly related to temporal problems was that of intercession, whereby God was called upon to provide both guidance along the path to salvation, and help with more material difficulties. In times of disaster it was appropriate for the clergy and people to invoke supernatural assistance. Private men made their solitary appeals to God, while communities offered a corporate supplication, most characteristically in large processions arranged by the Church.

Such processions were common in medieval England as a response to plague, bad harvests and foul weather; and it was confidently believed that they could induce God to show his mercy by diverting the course of nature in response to the community's repentance. In 1289 the Bishop of Chichester ruled that it was the duty of every priest to order processions and prayers when he saw a storm was imminent, without waiting for orders from above.

This belief that earthly events could be influenced by supernatural intervention was not in itself a magical one. For the essential difference between the prayers of a churchman and the spells of a magician was that only the latter claimed to work automatically; a prayer had no certainty of success and would not be granted if God chose not to concede it. A spell, on the other hand, need never go wrong, unless some detail of ritual observance had been omitted or a rival magician had been practising stronger counter-magic. A prayer, in other words, was a form of supplication: a spell was a mechanical means of manipulation. Magic postulated occult forces of nature which the magician learned to control, whereas religion assumed the direction of the world by a conscious agent who could only be deflected from his purpose by prayer and supplication. This distinction was popular with nineteenth-century anthropologists, but has been rejected by their modern successors, on the ground that it fails to consider the role which the appeal to spirits can play in a magician's ritual and which magic has occupied in some forms of primitive religion. But it is useful in so far as it emphasises the non-coercive character of Christian prayers. The Church's teaching was usually unambiguous on this point: prayers might bring practical results, but they could not be guaranteed to do so.

In practice, however, this distinction was repeatedly blurred in the popular mind. The Church itself recommended the use of prayers when healing the sick or gathering medicinal herbs. Confessors required penitents to repeat a stated number of Paternosters, Aves and Creeds, thereby fostering the notion that the recitation of prayers in a foreign tongue had a mechanical efficacy. The chantries of the later Middle Ages were built upon the belief that the regular offering of prayers would have a beneficial effect upon the founder's soul: they presupposed the quantitative value of masses, and gave, as their most recent historian puts it, "almost a magical value to mere repetition of formulae." Salvation itself could be attained, it seemed, by mechanical means, and the more numerous the prayers the more likely their success. It therefore became worthwhile to secure other people to offer up prayers on one's own behalf. In the reign of Henry VIII the Marchioness of Exeter paid twenty shillings to Elizabeth Barton, the Nun of Kent, to pray that she would not lose her next child in childbirth, and that her husband would come home safely from the wars. Sir Thomas More told of a friar in Coventry who declared that anyone who said his rosary once a day would be saved. The *Enchiridion of Salisbury Cathedral* contained a formula with the rubric: "Whosoever sayeth this prayer following in the worship of God and St Rock shall not die of the pestilence by the grace of God." The Catholics, said Jeremy Taylor, taught "that prayers themselves *ex opere operato* . . . do prevail," and "like the words of a charmer they prevail even when they are not understood."

The medieval Church thus did a great deal to weaken the fundamental distinction between a prayer and a charm, and to encourage the idea that there was virtue in the mere repetition of holy words. It was the legacy of Catholic teaching, thought two Elizabethan pamphleteers, that "the ignorant sort, beholding a man affected but only with melancholy, are so strongly conceited that it is no physical means, but only the good words and prayers of learned men that must restore them again to their perfect health." Because medieval theologians encouraged the use of prayers as an accompaniment to the gathering of herbs, the notion survived that these plants were useless unless plucked in a highly ritual manner. The distinguishing feature of the village wizards of the sixteenth and seventeenth centuries was their assumption that the ritual and unaccompanied pronunciation of special prayers could secure the patient's recovery. This had not been the teaching of the medieval Church, for prayers, though necessary, were not intended to be effective without medical treatment. But the clergy had claimed that the recitation of prayers could afford protection against vermin or fiends and without the Church's encouragement of the formal repetition of set forms of prayer the magical faith in the healing power of Aves and Paternosters could never have arisen. The rural magicians of Tudor England did not invent their own charms; they inherited them from the medieval Church, and their formulae and rituals were largely derivative products of centuries of Catholic teaching. For, in addition to the prayers officially countenanced, there was a large undergrowth of semi-Christian charms which drew heavily on ecclesiastical formulae. The following extract from the commonplace-book of Robert Reynys, a fifteenth-century church reeve at Ade, Norfolk, is typical:

> Pope Innocent hath granted to any man that beareth the length of the three nails of Our Lord Jesus Christ upon him and worship them daily with five Paternosters and five Aves and a psalter, he shall have seven gifts granted to him. The first, he shall not be slain with sword nor knife. The second, he shall not die no sudden death. The third, his enemies shall not overcome him. The fourth, he shall have sufficient good and honest living. The fifth, that poisons

nor fever nor false witness shall grieve him. The sixth, he shall not die without the sacraments of the Church. The seventh, he shall be defended from all wicked spirits, from pestilence and all evil things.

The medieval Church thus appeared as a vast reservoir of magical power, capable of being deployed for a variety of secular purposes. Indeed it is difficult to think of any human aspiration for which it could not cater. Almost any object associated with ecclesiastical ritual could assume a special aura in the eyes of the people. Any prayer or piece of the Scriptures might have a mystical power waiting to be tapped. The Bible could be an instrument of divination, which opened at random would reveal one's fate. The gospels could be read aloud to women in childbed to guarantee them a safe delivery. A Bible could be laid on a restless child's head so as to send it to sleep. *Dives and Pauper* declared that it was not wrong to try to charm snakes or birds by reciting holy words, provided the operation was done with reverence.

CHAPTER TWENTY-ONE

~

Women in the
Late Medieval English Parish*

Katherine L. French

Although this section treats late medieval Christianity as a whole, we have already made some necessary and commonplace distinctions according to region (Moeller on Germany, Duffy and Thomas on England) and class (elite vs. popular, learned vs. unlearned). In spite of the long and deep historiography concerning late medieval religious culture one important distinction, gender, has been largely overlooked. Moeller and Duffy have encouraged us to examine how late medieval Christians experienced and participated in their religious culture. This begs the question: did women experience and participate in medieval religious culture differently than men? Katherine French says yes. French sees the parish and lay fraternities as the locus of late medieval religion. French examines how women participated in and contributed to parish life, including what kind of lay fraternities women created. She concludes that women played an important role in the late medieval religious life, although their participation was shaped and limited by societal norms. What were some of the limitations on female participation in parish life? What are some of the limitations to studying women's roles in medieval religious culture? Based on participation in parish and fraternal activities, how is female piety different from male?

In medieval and early modern England, the basic unit of public worship was the parish. Although women comprised half of the membership, their activities, religious or secular, have not received much attention in the historical

* © 2003 Cornell University Press. Katherine L. French, "Women in the Late Medieval English Parish," in *Gendering the Master Narrative: Women and Power in the Middle Ages*, eds. Mary C. Erler & Maryanne Kowaleski, Ithaca: Cornell University Press, 2003, pp. 156–173. Used by permission of the publisher, Cornell University Press.

literature. Scholars have focused on what they consider to be the more visible activities of men and have thereby gendered the collective behavior of parishioners male or mostly male. By adhering to this position, scholars have overlooked the importance of the parish as an institution that assisted female visibility. This visibility came to include collective action taken in all-women's groups. Indeed the parish became a major forum for women's group activities that provided them with opportunities unavailable outside the parish. Thus the expected limits of gender-related behavior expanded with respect to the parish. What was the significance of women's greater visibility and activity within the parish, and what did these expanded opportunities mean to women and their communities?

Although scholars have largely ignored the issue of women's parochial involvement, it did not go unnoticed by contemporaries, who were often disturbed by it. Women's parish involvement and their increasing visibility created a tension in parish life that the clergy and the laity tried to relieve by using this participation to affirm expected female behavior. Women themselves, however, were also a part of the process; their interests, while different from men's, were not always distinct from the patriarchal norms that governed them. Although women's visibility made their voices louder and their concerns more apparent to the parish, it did not turn the late medieval English parish into a female utopia. The maintenance of approved models of behavior was not without its subversive component, and women's participation in the parish both reinforced traditional gender roles and challenged women's secondary status. In this chapter, I will survey the range of women's participation in the parish, looking at how it drew on expected behavior for women and also created new opportunities for action and self-expression.

Canon law made the laity responsible for their parish churches, particularly the maintenance of the nave. To meet these needs, the laity appointed churchwardens to oversee the process. This obligation to maintain the nave provided women of all classes with a variety of ways to support their parishes. Women attended mass, provided labor and money for maintaining and furnishing the nave, and contributed their organizational skills and pious interests in support of the veneration of the saints. A woman's social status and stage of life also shaped her parish involvement. Wealthy women typically contributed more than less well-off women, and married women's participation differed from single women's. We must also understand women's parish participation as taking place under the legal and economic systems of late medieval England because the parish owned property and hired workers.

The work women performed for the parish was similar to the work they did for their households or in the larger community. The connection between domestic and familial concerns was a theme that ran through women's parish participation. Outside the parish, a married woman usually worked part time at many different jobs; in addition to helping her husband with his work, whether it was agriculture, manufacturing, or lordship, she also provisioned the house, arranged the meals, oversaw the kitchen garden, and attended to children and servants if there were any. Some women also ran their own businesses, although these tended to be small and temporary. Although there are examples of women artisans supplying parishes with goods and services, women generally played a subordinate role in maintaining the parish. Laundry and mending were predominantly women's jobs. John Mirk tried to valorize this work in his *Instructions for Parish Priests* by explaining that the altar cloths and the surplices must be clean for mass, but it was nevertheless still low paying and menial. When a parish brought in artisans to work on the church, women tended to look after them. When the parish of All Saints, Tilney in Norfolk needed to repair the church windows, Robert Nobile's wife lodged and fed the workers. Although women did most of the mending without overt male supervision, far fewer oversaw new sewing for copes, chasubles, altar clothes, and hangings that required embroidery or expensive, color cloth. As with other occupations involving women, they worked under supervision of men. In 1524, the small market town of Stogursey in Somerset employed a vestment maker and his wife to make new vestments for the church. The parish fed both of them in partial payment for their work.

Like the rest of the medieval economy, the church did not place the same value on women's work as men's, considering it to be less important and valuable. In the thirteenth-century diocesan statutes for Worcester, the bishop identified four saints' days—the feasts of Agnes, Margaret, Lucy and Agatha—when men were to work but women were not. In an anonymous fifteenth-century collection of sermons called the *Speculum Sacerdotale*, the author states that for three days after Easter, no one was to work. "But in the iiij daye it is lawefull to men for to tyle and use werky the erpe, but wymmen owep for to cese fro here werkys. And why? Rurale workis ben more nedeful þen other." Although the assumption that men were rural workers is anachronistic by the fifteenth century, this sermon articulated a commonly held belief about the relative worth of men and women's economic contributions. These values would have translated to women's work for the parish, and the jobs that parishes hired women to do reflected their larger socioeconomic roles. Even though women's level of involvement inside the parish was the same as outside the parish, it incorporated their concerns for the maintenance of the nave and provided the parish with needed labor.

Parishes depended on a variety of fund-raising strategies to hire artisans and to furnish the nave. Urban parishes tended to rely on rents from parish-owned property, whereas rural parishes hosted a variety of ales, festivals, and revels to raise money. All parishes relied on bequests and gifts. In these circumstances women's specific contributions are difficult to identify and assess. We know women attended ales and festivals and occasionally even organized them. For example, in 1537, Elizabeth Whochyng was one of the ale wardens for the midsummer ale in the parish of Trull in Bath and Wells. Women also frequently rented property from the parish, but overall their financial support was less than that of men because they typically earned less.

Gifts and testamentary bequests constituted the most common means of supporting the parish. Although wealth and personal interest could affect the level of parish support, there were also differences between men's and women's giving practices that reveal how legal and economic constraints further defined women's involvement. When we consider the material goods testators left to parishes in their wills, we can also see how both men and women demonstrated their pious concerns. The differences between men's and women's giving practices suggest that women used their notions of home economy and domesticity to act out their piety. Women's gifts to the parish reflected the relationships they had to their material goods and household possessions. For much of their lives, they could not count on being able to liquidate their material assets, and, consequently, their identification with objects—both as signs of their domestic skills and their gender—seems stronger than men's.

Because of the law of coverture, a married woman could not make a will without her husband's permission. As a result the majority of women's wills were written by widows. Some of the differences in the items left as bequests by men and women can be explained by the fact that widows were usually breaking up households, whereas men often had a family that still needed provisioning, which meant leaving the household intact. Women also gave what they controlled, usually items from their dowry, which often included household items. Despite these circumstances surrounding will making, we find that both women and men gave those items that had the most meaning to them and reflected a lifetime of interaction with their beneficiaries, such as the parish. In a survey of wills from Bath and Wells and Lincoln, the most common categories of gifts to parishes in men's wills were vestments; liturgical items, such as chalices, paxes, and candlesticks; and household items, such as tools and furniture. The three most common types of gifts that women gave to the parish were household items, such as sheets, table clothes, and dishes; clothing, such as dresses or kerchiefs; and jewelry, usually wedding rings, but also beaded necklaces. Men also gave more books than women. The differences between men's and women's bequests reflect some of the different concerns that they had for the parish. In particular, women were more likely to specify exactly how the parish should use their gifts, whereas men generally left this to the discretion of the churchwardens; they could use the bequests for the church or sell them and use the money as they saw fit. For example, when Henry Stephyns of Castle Cary in Bath and Wells made out his will, he left everything to his parish and made the churchwardens his executors. His will states that his goods were to be "fully spent about such necessary building as shall be thought most convenient by the most honest men of the parish for the maintenance of the church." Women, however, were less likely to leave this decision in the hands of parish administrators. The work in the household or the economy often required them to piece together limited resources, and their wills often explained how the goods should be adapted for parish needs. Avice de Crosseby of St. Cuthbert's parish in Lincoln left a wooden board to the parish clerk "suitable for making wax tapers," "j carpet . . . to cover the bodies of the dead," and "j very little leaden vessel to mend the eaves or gutter of the church." Lifelong habits of frugality and adaptability became expressions of piety and a means of influencing in small ways local religious observances.

Although adapting household goods to parish use was a pious act, it could also be construed as bossy and controlling. Women may have had less to give, but their directions as to how the parish should use their gifts required churchwardens to address their concerns. By offering suggestions, women became posthumously involved in parish administrative decision making— from which they had generally been excluded during their lives. Some women could be quite inventive in how they expected the parish to use their goods. Agnes Bruton, a well-to-do woman in Taunton in the diocese of Bath and Wells, left her "red damaske mantell and [her] mantell lyned with silk" to become costumes for the parish's Mary Magdalene play. Agnes Cakson of Addlethorpe in the same diocese asked that "a basyn, a laver, and a towell" be given to the font "to weshe folkes handes with when they crysten chylder." Denise Marlere, a brewster in Bridgwater in Bath and Wells, gave vats from her brewing business to the vicar, the parish chaplain, the parish, the chapel of St. Katherine, and the local hospital and Franciscan friary. She explained that they would be useful for wax making. More common, however, were women's instructions for how to turn their clothing and housewares into items of liturgical significance. Sheets became altar cloths, gowns and dresses became copes and vestments, and kerchiefs became corporaxes to cover the host. Agnes Sygrave of Stowe in Lincoln left to "the high altare of

Stowe my best shete to be an altare clothe, and my best kyrchyff to be a corporax." Dame Margaret Chocke of Ashton, in Bath and Wells went so far as to specify that when her "gown of blew feluett, [her] kyrtll of blew damaske, . . . and a coverlet of tapstry werek with eglis [eagles]," which were to "ley before the hyght auter in principal festes and other tymes," were not in use they were to "be occupied on a bedde in the chauntry house to kepe it from mothes." Even towels of diaper cloth, plain white linen without any embroidery or other identifying marks, were able to be close to the host. The donor's name might be forgotten, but this type of gift still elevated or sacralized the mundane items of her everyday life. Other women in the congregation would see the possibility that their own goods could be put in touch with God. Adapting household items to the liturgy connected women's work to the worship of God, but their instructions showed that they were attempting to hold onto what little economic power they had and not relinquish it completely to the men who ran the parish.

Another feature of women's bequests was that they left goods to individual saints much more frequently than men did. Wedding rings and kerchiefs were the most common items, but veils and girdles were also popular. Joan Mudford of Glastonbury, Somerset, left to the image of St. Mary one gold ring and a kerchief and to the statue of St. Katherine a gold ring. The saints received items that had physically marked the donor as a woman and were intended to adorn these female saints in similar ways: kerchiefs on the head, decorative girdles around the waist, and necklaces around the neck.

Parish fund-raising gave women further access to the liturgy and an opportunity to express their concerns through the sale of seats. With the introduction of pews in the fifteenth century, some parish administrations began to sell seats. Financing the parish by selling seats had the side effect of sanctioning the relationships and priorities that grew out of the seating arrangements. Women and men were expected to attend three services on Sundays, and they could also attend the daily mass and other canonical hours said by the parish and stipendiary priests. During services, men and women did not sit together. Women generally sat on the north side of the nave and men on the south, although some churches placed women in the back (or west) and men in the front (or east) of the nave. Once the laity began to install permanent seats, seating arrangements began to play a role in the social dynamics of the community because they visibly identified the sex and status of the occupant. Seating men and women separately gave women greater visibility. They became an identifiable group in a specific part of the nave, not intermingled with men.

Purchasing a seat appears to have been predominantly a women's concern. For example, between 1460 and 1530 in the parish of St. Margaret's, Westminster, 737 women bought seats compared to only 275 men. Women in this parish also changed their seats more often then men; 22 percent of women changed their seats compared to only 13 percent of men. This suggests a range of concerns regarding seat location that interested men less. A new seat might move one closer to the front to a better position for seeing the priest elevate the host, or it might put one closer to an image or chapel of special significance. Seating arrangements also marked rites of passage. In many parishes, such as St. Mary's in Dover, there was a pew for women to sit in while they were churched. Not only did the service mark a woman's successful childbirth, but her special place in the nave emphasized this accomplishment as well. Some parishes had separate seats for married and unmarried women. Similar arrangements occur in other town parishes such as St. Edmund's in Salisbury or Ashton-Under-Lyne in Cheshire, although the records are less detailed.

~

CHAPTER TWENTY-TWO

The Magnificent Ride: The First Reformation in Hussite Bohemia*

Thomas A. Fudge

By the fifteenth century, most of the heretical movements of the previous centuries had been wiped out (Cathars) or marginalized (Waldensians). From the end of the Great Schism at the Council of Constance in 1415 to the Protestant Reformation one hundred years later, the only significant challenge to Latin Christianity in Europe occurred in Bohemia. In the early fifteenth century a Czech scholar and preacher named Jan Hus became the center of a group of Prague intellectuals who began espousing theories for which they would be condemned. Among the most controversial were worship and Bible translations into local vernacular languages, the offering of both the bread and wine to the laity during Communion, and the denial of the authority of priests to discipline lay people. After Hus was executed as a heretic at the Council of Constance, these religious ideas combined with Czech resentment of German imperialism to foment a general rebellion in Bohemia. After a series of military engagements, Bohemian Hussites were allowed to enact their religious ideas without interference from the papacy or German bishops and nobles. Viewed from the top down, the Hussite rebellion seems to indicate a general failure of Latin Christianity. Viewed from the bottom up, however, the event highlights the fundamental role of Christianity in European society. In this selection, Thomas A. Fudge explains how popular songs and slogans help us discover the beliefs of everyday people on both sides of the conflicts. Why does Fudge choose songs and slogans for his sources? What do they reveal that other sources do not?

* © Thomas A. Fudge, 1998. Thomas A. Fudge, *The Magnificent Ride: The First Reformation in Hussite Bohemia*, Brookfield: Ashgate Publishing Company, 1998, pp. 186–194.

A recent book, provocatively titled *Music as Propaganda*, argues that "folk music, popular music, is the direct expression of a people in every epoch and culture." To put it another way, in a significant sense popular songs express the Zeitgeist of a particular society. When a single Hussite sneers defiantly that the false eucharist made by a Roman priest is good only for wiping one's backside (since it is *ipso facto* not the true eucharist) such an opinion can in no sense be regarded as a pervasive attitude. But when the same opinion is embodied in the lyrics of a ditty or song and sung by the masses, as for example in the popular song "Antichrist is now marching . . . already producing an arrogant clergy," then it may reasonably be considered a direct popular expression. Indeed, the social function of music should be underscored. Sociologists and anthropologists have demonstrated that no society exists without music. From time immemorial the ritual expression of popular songs has provided a window into the collective consciousness of the historical particularity of peoples and societies. In the context and milieu of Hussite Bohemia this is especially true. Popular songs emerged from the Bohemian vortex of social discontent and religious dissent as a medium of communication and expression of the collective Czech consciousness. Though the Czech historical context is rich in music and song the concern is not with Hussite hymnody. The songs analysed here are, for the most part, of a popular nature, ditties, ballads, or street-songs. What I have attempted to avoid are those songs which were probably sung mainly in services of divine worship. This requires subjective judgment. Some of these songs may well have been expressions of worship. It is also instructive to point out that the Czech language does not make a distinction between the *pisnijka* (little song or ditty) and the formal anthems, or between what might be considered hymns and folk-songs. Lines of demarcation between songs and sayings is fairly arbitrary. Singing a ditty and chanting a proverbial saying has more in common as an oral mode of expression than not. It is for this reason I have chosen to deal with popular songs and proverbial sayings as a common form of oral propaganda, albeit in separate categories.

In the Hussite milieu of fifteenth-century Bohemia it is reasonable to regard popular songs as a means of communication as well as a main vehicle for mass propaganda. Even in sixteenth-century Germany the primary mode of communication remained oral. Popular songs provide us with a means for understanding how ideas were spread especially in a volatile revolutionary context such as Hussite Bohemia. The Czech mobs in Prague and throughout Bohemia were not sufficiently literate in the conventional sense to write pamphlets, give speeches or compose treatises. But they could sing. Like the polemical theological treatises and startling broadsheets of the sixteenth century so likewise the rough cadences and shrill sounds of the popular songs in the fifteenth century provided a medium for ideas, communication, and propaganda.

Peter Burke has helpfully pointed out that singers in late medieval and early modern Europe fulfilled a very important function in society. Singing in the streets or in the marketplaces, these *Gassensanger* or *Marktsanger* drew attention to the message of the ballads they both sang and sold. The *Avisensanger* (news-singer) were those specializing in songs concerning current events. In the specific Bohemian context the equivalent might be the *kramdfskd pisen* (hawker's song). While not wishing to deny the existence or function of these street singers in Bohemia during the age of the Hussites, it is more important to understand the popular songs of the time as arising out of the popular movement directly and functioning as a vehicle of communication. While music may be regarded as an expression of a societal ethos, the function of popular songs as propagandist may indicate a deeper level of active commitment to a cause, idea, or particular attitude. Not all music is propaganda, but the music that is propaganda is a powerful medium for the advancement and communication of ideas.

Early Hussite hymns were basically folk-songs and it was these popular songs which preserved the folk tradition of the Czechs. The Hussite wars and the accompanying oral propaganda in terms of the popular songs in the fifteenth century gave a significant stimulus to vernacular Czech songs. For example, the Hussite revolutionary songs *Ktoz jsti bozi bojovnici* (Ye warriors of God), *Povstan, povstan, velike mesto Praiske* (Arise, arise, great city of Prague), and "Children, let us meet together" are among the earliest examples of such types of songs in any European country. The impact of the Hussite heritage of popular songs with their intensity and vigour left a profound influence upon Bohemia and neighbouring lands. While radical Hussites and Taborites considered most forms of art sinful, music was an exception. The impact and proliferation of popular songs historically helped shape Bohemia. Recent research in Czech archives uncovered more than 45,000 folk songs and these dating from only the last century and a half without consideration of the pre-modern era.

From the outset Hussite oral propaganda drew upon the familiar, signs of the times to both capture attention and thus secure an audience to make a propagandist statement. Through the medium of the song the message could take flight from the proverbial pages of the book to reach those conventionally illiterate. The songs could not fail to exploit the German/Czech conflict. After the German exodus from Prague following the *Decree of Kutna Hora* popular songs ridiculing the Germans and calling for Czech domination was like adding salt to an open wound. The Hussite song *Povstan, povstan, velike mesto Praiske* (Arise, arise, great city of Prague) both draws upon an historical and theological concept of the city of Jerusalem. Matăj of Janov had earlier written in his *Narracio de Milicio* that the Jerusalem experiment founded by Jan Milíč of Kroměříč was the beginning of a divine action through Christ to create from Prague, formerly a city of Babylon full of filth and shame, a city of light upon a hill—Jerusalem. The Jerusalem experiment formerly encompassing only 29 houses in Prague now expanded to include all of Prague as the city of the Lord. Not only had Prague been raised to a pinnacle of prominence, the Germans must give way to the Czechs.

> Arise, arise, great city of Prague
> Arise, arise, great city of Prague,
> all the empire faithfully toward the Bohemian
> land and all knights and all powers of the land,
> against that king of Babylon who threatens the
> city of
> Jerusalem, Prague, and all faithful people.
> Do not be afraid of the Hungarian king because
> his honour and virtue are very
> low, he will be defeated by humble people.

Throughout the full gamut of Hussite propaganda lies this Czech–German animosity. By drawing on the familiar theme of social grievance the Hussite propagandists created a galvanizing effect upon popular culture. Arbitrary lines were drawn and correlations imposed. The formula German equals Catholic and Catholic equals Antichrist soon found its way into the oral propaganda of the Hussite movement. By focusing attention on the anti-clerical mood the radical Hussites legitimated their own peculiar cause against the familiar complaint of the excesses of the Church.

During the first decade of the fifteenth century a popular song circulated wherein truth was portrayed as no longer having a place to dwell on earth:

> Song About Truth
>
> As I travelled around the whole world
> Inquiring among young and old
> I found no one willing to accept me
> So I have taken up my bed in heaven
> And have finally found my home . . .
> Hear, O God, our voices
> And in eternity give us a place to dwell near you
> That we may lie down and together
> With the angels praise you.

The chiliast hymn *Slýchal-Li kto od počátka* (If anyone has heard from the first) combined the complaints of Czech subordination and ecclesiastical excesses.

> The wretched are in anguish
> in every land, especially the Czechs, on
> account of the conceited priesthood.

The Hussites inveighed against the wealth of the Church which sets it in opposition to the divine law. Instead of authentic ministry, the conceited priesthood have become learned in the art of simony. This Judas clergy who forbid the proclamation of the gospel through song and word are set in diametrical opposition to the Hussite clergy who by implication are the true priesthood of Christ. The practice of Utraquism, a commonplace in Hussitism, also appears in juxtaposition to the traditional practice:

> You became masters with false learning
> Have you studied so that you could get wealthy by flattery?
> You dress in silk, laugh at the law of God and wallow in pleasure
> The learning with which you deceive people is woeful blindness.
> If you had studied in order to spread the truth
> of the heavenly father
> You would abandon pride
> and care for nothing but God alone.
> But this one has studied how to buy a church or get prebends;
> That one attends to the craftiness that is called
> Worldly wisdom, seeking benefices.
> They all praise the pope
> Because they look for simoniacal wealth with him
> They oppose God
> Although many of them confess that God's law
> commands all to drink God's blood and eat his body
> but this is not commanded by the pope.
> They do not let the gospel be preached
> read or sung to the simple people
> They do not wish to talk about God
> but only to run after wealth
> O Judas clergy.

This song illustrates the combining of social sentiment and doctrine in a single propagandist thrust: the Roman paradigm is subverted, the Hussites are offered as an alternative, and the cause of the common people is held out in the Hussite premise. Following the deaths of Jan Hus and Jerome of Prague at

Constance and the conciliar ruling against communion, Hussite propaganda became filled with invectives against the council and popular songs ridiculed the conciliar fathers and condemned their sinfulness with regard to their treatment of Hus.

> Concerning the Council of Constance
> O you Council of Constance
> Who call yourself holy,
> How could you with such neglect and great lack of mercy
> destroy a holy man.
> Has it been his guilt
> To show many their sin
> Moved to do so by God's grace
> so they would do penance
> without some cleverly contrived trick?
> Your pride and fornication Avarice and greed
> He sought to remove
> and to direct you on the way to truthful dignity.

Anticlerical satire, which may appear to be merely social comment, is often a special type of political satire. In this case popular opinion shapes the propagandist message. This is apparent because propaganda cannot create *ex nihilo*. It is confined to utilizing data which already exists, it does not create material in a vacuum.

The long daily sermons and the proliferation of popular songs characteristic among the radical Hussites may suggest the dominant form of communication. The incessant hammering away at the enemies of God as well as the Germans left no question in the popular mind that there was no essential difference between a German, an enemy of God, and an enemy of Bohemia. German dislike of the Hussite movement was equally widespread and as deeply rooted. This gave rise to an anti-Czech, anti-Hussite wave of propaganda in the form of popular songs. In 1417 the Hussite Jan Čapek composed the song, *Ve Jméno Božie Počněme* (Let us begin in the name of the Lord). This song was an effort to articulate Hussite doctrine in terms accessible to the popular movement. The doctrine of the Church was outlined in terms of the community of the predestined which was for all intents and purposes a repetition of Hus's teaching in *De ecclesia*. This treatise was read aloud to a group of people in the Bethlehem Chapel in the spring of 1413. The doctrinal outline in the song is radical in its denial of saints and images and represents a sectarian strain. The spread of Hussite doctrine reached epidemic proportions in Bohemia and the onslaught of anti-Hussite propaganda aimed directly at ridiculing and undermining the Hussite agenda.

> Hear oh Czechs!
> Mark it well, all faithful Czechs, they speak evil of you throughout
> all of Christendom . . .

When this attempt to influence popular opinion on the basis of mass consensual agreement from abroad failed, the anti-Hussites suggested snidely that the Hussite agenda was based on ignorance.

> A song about Rokycana and his sectarians:
> They sing Czech at Mass, perhaps they don't know Latin

In this song the anti-Hussite propaganda bemoaned the grievious harm that the Roman Church was suffering on account of those "rascal Husses and Heretics."

> You Czechs of the true faith,
> grieve for the injustice
> which is happening now to
> the holy Roman Church.

When this plea for pity fell on deaf Hussite ears, the songs thereafter began to manifest a degenerate quality of ridicule and abuse. The next logical step was to associate the Hussites with the devil and with heresy of generations past.

> On the capture of Sigismund Korybutovič:
> The evil one made *Engliš* a present for
> us, who goes around Prague softly,
> giving out a law from England
> which is not good for Bohemia.

Here *Engliš* is the Oxford Wyclifite Peter Payne who was called Master Engliš in Bohemia. Apart from Sir John Oldcastle, Payne was likely the most famous disciple of Wyclif in the fifteenth century. After his escape from England in 1414, Payne spent the remainder of his life until 1456 in Bohemia becoming a major spokesperson for the radical Hussite cause. Held in high esteem by a number of Hussite leaders he functioned in important Hussite diplomatic affairs. According to this popular song Payne (Engliš) was a gift from the devil. His stealthy movements about Prague suggest deceit and the unhealthy law is the Lollard code of Wyclif. As the archheretic of the later Middle Ages and condemned by the Church, Wyclifism made Hussitism that much more suspect as noted earlier, particularly in terms of Charles University and Jan Hus.

The anti-Hussite songs were no worse than their Hussite counterparts in terms of ridicule, satire, blasphemy, and obscenity. Yet it must be admitted that the propaganda of the anti-Hussites knew no bounds in agitating the popular imagination. To accomplish this the anti-Hussite propaganda framed its message in the familiar format of the liturgy. The best example is the so-called Wiklefitskou mši (Wyclifite Mass):

The creed

I believe in Wyclif, the lord of hell and patron of Bohemia, and in Hus, his only begotten son, our nothing, who was conceived by the spirit of Lucifer, born of his mother, and made incarnate and equal to Wyclif according to the evil will . . . ruling at the time of the desolation of the University of Prague at the time when Bohemia apostatized from the faith. Who for us heretics descended into hell and will not rise again from the dead nor have everlasting life. Amen.

The most oft-repeated part was the *Liber generacionis* which attempted to account for all the evil sons of heresy by tracing them back genealogically to Wyclif, the son of the devil.

The book of the generations

The book of the generations of all the accursed sons of the heretic: Wyclif, the son of the devil . . . Stanislav of Znojmo begat Jan Hus, Hus begat Marek of Hradec, Marek begat Zdeněk of Labouň, Zdeněk begat Šimon of Tišnov, Šimon begat Peter of Koněprusy

Knin begat Jerome, the athlete of Antichrist, Jerome begat Jan of Jesenice before the migration of the three nations and after the migration Jesenice begat Zdislav the Leper . . .

Index

About the Editor

James L. Halverson is professor of history at Judson University. He is the author of *Peter Aureol on Predestination: A Challenge to Late Medieval Thought* (1998) and coeditor of *Sources of World Civilization* with Oliver Johnson (2003).

~

About the Contributors

Rudolf Bell is professor of history at Rutgers University. His many publications include *The Voices of Gemma Galgani: The Life and Afterlife of a Modern Saint* with Cristina Mazzoni (2003), *How to Do It: Guides to Good Living for Renaissance Italians* (1999), *Holy Anorexia* (1985), and *Saints and Society: The Two Worlds of Western Christendom, 1000–1700* (1982) with Donald Weinstein.

Constance Brittain Bouchard is Distinguished Professor of Medieval History at the University of Akron. A Fellow of the Medieval Academy of America, some of her most prominent books are *Sword, Miter, and Cloister: Nobility and the Church in Burgundy, 980–1198* (1987), *"Strong of Body, Brave and Noble": Chivalry and Society in Medieval France* (1998), and *"Those of My Blood": Constructing Noble Families in Medieval France* (2001).

Peter Brown is Philip and Beulah Rollins Professor of History at Princeton University. He is the author of a dozen books including *Augustine of Hippo* (1967, 2000), *The World of Late Antiquity* (1971), *The Cult of the Saints* (1982), *The Body and Society* (1988), *Power and Persuasion in Late Antiquity: Towards a Christian Empire* (1992), *Authority and the Sacred: Aspects of the Christianization of the Roman World* (1995), *The Rise of Western Christendom* (1996, 2003), and *Poverty and Leadership in the Later Roman Empire* (2002). He has been the recipient of a MacArthur Fellowship (1982), a Guggenheim Fellowship (1989), and the Mellon Foundation's Distinguished Achievement Award (2001).

Marcus Bull is senior lecturer in medieval history at the University of Bristol. He is the author of numerous books and articles including *Knightly Piety and the Lay Response to the First Crusade: The Limousin and Gascony c. 970–c. 1130* (1993). He recently published *Thinking Medieval: An Introduction to the Study of the Middle Ages* (2005).

Caroline Walker Bynum is professor of Western European Middle Ages at the Institute for Advanced Study at Princeton University. A MacArthur Fellow from 1986–1991, she has served as president of both the American Historical Association and the Medieval Academy of America. Her book *Holy Feast and Holy Fast* received the Philip Schaff Prize of the American Society of Church History. Her book *Fragmentation and Redemption* received the Award for Excellence in the Study of Religion: Analytical-Descriptive Category from the American Academy of Religion. Her book *The Resurrection of the Body* received the Ralph Waldo Emerson Prize of Phi Beta Kappa and the Jacques Barzun Prize of the American Philosophical Society.

Mark R. Cohen is professor of Near Eastern studies at Princeton University. He won the National Jewish Book Award for *Jewish Self-Government in Medieval Egypt* (1980). *Under Crescent and Cross: The Jews in the Middle Ages* (1994) has been translated into Hebrew, Turkish, German, Arabic, and French. His most recent books are *Poverty and Charity in the Jewish Community of Medieval Egypt* (2005) and *The Voice of the Poor in the Middle Ages: An Anthology of Documents from the Cairo Geniza* (2005).

Georges Duby, late Chair of Medieval Societies at the Collége de France and a member of the Académie française, was one of the most prolific and influential medievalists of the twentieth century. Among his more prominent works are *The Sunday of Bouvines* (1973), translated in English as *The Legend of Bouvines* (1990), *The Year 1000* (1974), *The Age of the Cathedrals* (1976), *The Three Orders: Feudal Society Imagined* (1978), *The Knight, The Lady, and the Priest* (1981), *William Marshal: The Flower of Chivalry* (1984), and *L'histoire continue* (1991).

Eamon Duffy is professor of the history of Christianity, and Fellow and Director of Studies at Magdalene College, Cambridge. A leading voice on late medieval and Reformation England, his most important contributions include *The Stripping of the Altars: Traditional Religion in England, c. 1400 to c. 1580* (1994), *Saints & Sinners: A History of the Popes* (1997), *The Voices of Morebath: Reformation and Rebellion in an English Village* (2001), *Marking the Hours: English People and Their Prayers, 1240–1570* (2006).

Joan M. Ferrante is professor of English at Columbia University. A past president of the Medieval Academy of America, she has published many articles and several books, including *To the Glory of Her Sex: Women's Roles in the Composition of Medieval Texts* (1997), *The Political Vision of the Divine Comedy* (1984), and *The Lais of Marie de France*, a translation and commentary written with Robert Hanning (1978).

Richard Fletcher, late professor of history at the University of York, won the *Los Angeles Times* History Book Award and the Wolfson Literary Award for History for *The Quest for El Cid* (1989). He has authored a number of other books, including *The Cross and the Crescent* (2004), *Bloodfeud* (2002), *The Conversion of Europe: From Paganism to Christianity, 371–1386 AD* (1999), and *Moorish Spain* (1992).

Katherine L. French is associate professor of history at SUNY New Paltz. In addition to numerous articles, she is the author of *People of the Parish: Community Life in a Late Medieval English Diocese* (2001).

Thomas A. Fudge serves as Director of the Hewitt Research Foundation. He is the author of two books about the Hussite movement: *The Magnificent Ride: The First Reformation in Hussite Bohemia* (1998) and *The Crusade against Heretics in Bohemia* (2002).

Herbert Grundmann served as president of the Monumenta Germaniae Historica from 1959 until his death in 1970. His most important work, *Religiöse Bewegungen des Mittelalters* (1933), set the agenda for all subsequent scholarship on medieval religious culture. His other important works include *Ketzergeschichte des Mittelalters* (1963) and *im Mittelalter* (1965). His many articles are collected in the three volume *Awgewählte Afsätze* (1976–1978).

Karen Louise Jolly is associate professor of history at the University of Hawaii at Manoa. She is the author and editor of numerous studies on early medieval religion, including *Tradition and Diversity: European Christianity in a World Context to 1500: Edited Primary Sources* (1997) and *Popular Religion in Late Saxon England: Elf Charms in Context* (1996).

Lester K. Little is Dwight W. Morrow Professor Emeritus and a Senior Fellow of the Kahn Liberal Arts Institute at Smith College. His principal publications include *Religious Poverty and the Profit Economy in Medieval Europe* (1978), *Liberty, Charity, Fraternity: Lay Religious Confraternities at Bergamo in* the Age of the Commune (1988), *Benedictine Maledictions: Liturgical Cursing in Romanesque France* (1993), and with Barbara H. Rosenwein, *Debating the Middle Ages: Issues and Readings* (1998).

Rob Meens is professor of history at the Universiteit Utrecht. He has written dozens of articles on early medieval religious culture and the history of penance and is coeditor of *The Bobbio Missal: Liturgy and Religious Culture in Merovingian Gaul* (2004).

Bernd Moeller is Professor Emeritus of Church History at the Georg-August-Universität, Göttingen. Best known in the English-speaking world for his seminal book *Imperial Cities and the Reformation* (1972), he is a leading scholar of late medieval and Reformation Germany.

Andrew P. Roach is currently lecturer in history at the University of Glasgow. A former economic forecaster, he has contributed significantly in several fields, including late medieval French religious culture, the application of network theories to religious movements, and the teaching of history to undergraduates.

Jane Tibbets Schulenburg is professor of history in the departments of Liberal Studies and the Arts, Women's Studies, and Medieval Studies at the University of Wisconsin, Madison. As well as *Forgetful of Their Sex: Female Sanctity and Society ca. 500–1100* (1998), she has published several articles on medieval women, women in the medieval church, female sanctity and gender, and sacred space.

Keith Thomas is a Fellow of All Souls College, Oxford. His books include *Religion and the Decline of Magic* (1971), *Man and the Natural World* (1983), and *The Oxford Book of Work* (1999).

Ian Wood is professor of early medieval history at the University of Leeds. Recent publications include *The Merovingian Kingdoms 450–751* (1994), *Gregory of Tours* (1994), and *The Missionary Life* (2001).